BATTLESHIP SAILORS

BATTLESHIP SAILORS

The Fighting Career of HMS *Warspite* Recalled by her Men

Harry Plevy

CHATHAM PUBLISHING

LONDON

First published in Great Britain in 2001 by Chatham Publishing,
61 Frith Street, London W1D 3JL

Chatham Publishing is an imprint of Gerald Duckworth & Co Ltd

British Library Cataloguing in Publication Data
A catalogue record for this book is available from the
British Library

ISBN 1 86176 151 1

Typeset by Dorwyn Ltd, Rowlands Castle, Hants

Printed and bound in Great Britain by The Cromwell Press, Trowbridge, Wilts

Contents

List of Illustrations

Introduction

My interest in HMS *Warspite*, which has become almost an obsession, goes back a long time. She was my favourite ship as a schoolboy in the Second World War, when she always seemed to be in the news and in the thick of things – Narvik, Matapan, D-Day. I saw her, for the first and only time in my life, on 12 September 1951. With friends I was on holiday in the West Country and sat on the sea-wall at Penzance listening on a small portable radio to Randolph Turpin's return boxing match with Sugar Ray Robinson. One of the passers-by stopped to listen and in answer to my query told me that the hulk lying in the shallows off Marazion, with rusting ribs pointing to the sky like the skeletal ribcage of some dead animal, was the famous *Warspite*. I felt somehow ashamed for her. Then, in the 1970s, I was conducting a party of metallurgy students on an industrial visit to the Wolverhampton Metal Company. Our factory guide pointed out that the crane being used in the stockyard had come from HMS *Warspite*, and my interest was renewed. In the late 1980s I was again in the West Country, trying to come to terms with personal bereavement, and found myself on the muddy-bottomed path, with its steep grass-covered sides sprinkled with primroses, leading to Prussia Cove. It was 23 April 1987, St. George's Day, and exactly forty years to the day since the ship had gone aground there. That same trip I visited the nearby Devonport Dockyard and was shown the berth from where *Warspite* had been launched over seventy years before.

My interest and research continued sporadically until, encouraged by my family, and in retirement and freed from the everyday necessity of earning a living, I decided to write a book, to put it all down before time and tide took away all the men and the memories. The book attempts to focus on the human side of her story, using eye-witness accounts of the men who sailed on, with or against the *Warspite*. It thus has German, Italian and American as well as British naval and civilian input. I have only included sufficient contextual background – political, strategic and tactical – to allow the reader to understand the part that the ship played in the two World Wars and the intervening years of peace. What I have laboriously tried to achieve in the book was succinctly expressed by Sir Winston Churchill in a speech to the House of Commons on 12 November 1940:

> History with its flickering lamp stumbles along the trail of the past, trying to reconstruct its scenes, to revive its echoes, and kindle with pale gleams the passion of former days.

This then is the book, the story of a great battleship, dedicated to the Sons of the Old Lady: The Men of the *Warspite*.

Harry Plevy
Codsall, Staffordshire
14 August 2000

Acknowledgements

I am indebted to very many organisations and people, some of whom are sadly no longer with us, for their help in the research for, and preparation of, this book. In preparing my acknowledgements I have made every effort to trace and contact copyright holders or their next of kin. Given the passage of time since some of the events described in the book took place, the changes that have occurred over the years among publishing houses and organisations, and the resulting transfers of copyright ownership, I have inevitably been unable to trace some copyright holders. If therefore an acknowledgement has been omitted or misplaced, I apologise, and will make every effort to remedy the mistake or omission in any subsequent reprint or edition of the book.

The following persons have shared with me their memories of HMS *Warspite* or, as copyright owners, have allowed me to quote from the documents of relatives. Wherever known I have given the last title or rank of the contributor. I have chosen in my acknowledgements not to include honours and decorations, simply because I have been unable to guarantee the accuracy or comprehensiveness of such a listing. I hope that my contributors will understand and forgive this decision. I am indebted to: Captain G.J.M. Andrewes for Admiral Sir William Andrewes, Lady Clark for Commander A.H. Ashworth, Mrs S. Burton for Commander H.C. Burton, Mr D. Dandy for Mr F. Dandy, Brigadier G.L.D. Duckworth for Captain A.D. Duckworth, Mrs J. Ellis for Surgeon Captain G.E.D. Ellis, Mrs I.E. McNeile for Commander N.A. McNeile, Commander P.J. Mosse for Commander J.P. Mosse, Mrs W.M. Snelling for Chief Petty Officer F. Parker, Mr N.V. Roskill for Captain S.W. Roskill, Mrs Sewter for Chief Petty Officer J.W. Sewter, Mr R. Anderson, Mr and Mrs H. Barber, Mr E. Barth, Mrs

E. Bower, Mr D. Brugge, Mr S. Caretti, Mr C. Carter, Mr D. Chinn, Mr F.N. Davies, Mr G. Elfendahl, Mr B. Erickson, Mrs S. Erickson, Mr J. Fallis, Mr P.O. Hanson, Mr P. Harms, Mr W. Haskell, Mr W.T. Hatch, Commander P. Hoare, Captain M.H. Hutton, Lieutenant W. Huy, Mr J.L. Jordan, Mr G.R. Katzenberger, Mr R. Lamb, Mr R.W. Lush, Mr R. Matthews, Mrs H.M. Munoz, Mr G. Nelson, Captain R.L. Newbury, Mr R.J. Paquette, Mrs S. Pelton, Mrs M. Penland, Ms S. Reitan, Lieutenant-Commander F.C. Rice, Mrs L. Riddle, Mr T. Robinson, Mr A. Rogers, Mr A.K. Schick, Mrs H. Smith, Mrs J. Stockler, Mrs L.V. Stone, Mr C. Taylor, Mrs V. Trammell.

I wish to acknowledge and thank the following publishers, authorities and agencies for kindly giving permission to reproduce extracts from books, newspapers, periodicals and letters: Curtis Brown Ltd. on behalf of the Estate of Sir Winston Churchill for *The World Crisis*, Copyright W.S. Churchill 1923, David Higham Associates Ltd. for *It Might Happen Again: The Autobiography of Admiral of the Fleet Lord Chatfield* and *Mutiny at Invergordon*, by Divine, D., Mrs Hillie McKendrick for *A Sailor's Odyssey: The Autobiography of Admiral of the Fleet Viscount Cunningham of Hyndhope*, Mr N.V. Roskill for *HMS Warspite* by Roskill, S.W., Sheil Land Associates Ltd. and the publishers Macmillan for *Deep as the Sea*, Copyright © Joy Packer 1975, J. Hodder and Stoughton Ltd. for *The True Glory: The Royal Navy 1914 -1939* by Arthur, M., and *The Fringes of Power: Downing Street Diaries 1939-1955* by Colville, J., Sutton Publishing for *Invergordon Scapegoat: The Betrayal of Admiral Tomkinson* by Coles, A., Cypher for *The Hunters and the Hunted* by Brennecke, J., Lionel Leventhal Ltd. for *Memoirs: Ten Years and Twenty Days* by Doenitz, K., The Masters and Fellows of Pembroke College, Cambridge, for *Meredith Dewey: Diaries, Letters and Writings*, John Murray for *Cunningham* by Winton, J., Andre Deutsch Ltd. for *Crete 1941; The Battle at Sea* by Thomas, D.A., Cassell and Co. for *Battleship Warspite* by Tarrant, V.E., Perry Publishing, U.S.A, for *Victory Gardens and Barrage Balloons* by Wetzel, F., Ian Allen Publishing for *Battleship at War,* by Coward, B.R., The Pentland Press Ltd. for *Knock on Any Door* by Finnigan, P., Harper Collins Publishers for *Fighting Admiral* by Macintyre, D., and *Under Cunningham's Command, 1940-1943* by Stitt, G., Ms

M Connell for *Fighting Destroyer: The Story of* HMS *Petard* by Connell, M.M., Naval Institute Press, Annapolis, U.S.A. for *The Italian Navy in World War II* by Bragadin, M., Oxford University Press for *From Dreadnought to Scapa Flow* by Marder A.J., The University of Birmingham for extracts from the Austen Chamberlain Papers, The Oratory, Birmingham for extracts from their records, Her Majesty's Stationery Office for permission to reproduce Crown Copyright/Ministry of Defence material, News International Syndication for extracts from *The Times*, Atlantic Syndication Partners for extracts from *The Daily Mail*, *The Bremerton Sun*, *The Seattle Times*, *The Cornishman*, the Commonwealth War Graves Commission and the Royal National Lifeboat Institution.

In addition to the aforementioned books I found the following to be particularly useful and informative on naval affairs and events during the first half of the twentieth century, and wish to acknowledge their contribution: *A Sailor's War* by Lombard-Hobson, S., *The Battlecruisers* by Bassett, R., *The Lower Deck of the Royal Navy, 1900-1939*, by Carew, A., *The British Navy: A Concise History* by Warner, O., *Battlecruiser Invincible* by Tarrant, V.E., *Fleet to Fleet Encounters* by Grove, E., *The Great War at Sea; 1914-1918* by Hough, R., *British Battleships: 1892-1957* by Pears, R., *Just an Old Navy Custom* by Hampshire, A.C., *The Second World War: The Gathering Storm* by Churchill, W.S., *Narvik* by Macintyre, D.

People and organisations who have given me help and advice, or made their facilities and services available to me over the years include: The Trustees and staff of the Imperial War Museum, and in particular Mr R.W.A. Suddaby, Keeper, The Department of Documents and Mrs H. Roberts of the Photography Archive, The Brotherton Library, University of Leeds and Mr R. Davies of Special Collections, Ms J. Ruhrmund of Morrab Library, Penzance, Mrs S. Gosling of Purfleet Heritage and Museum Centre, Mrs D. Manning of Puget Sound Naval Shipyard, Bremerton, U.S.A, Staff of Churchill Archives Centre, Churchill College, Cambridge, Dudley and South Staffordshire public libraries, Commander C.W. Crichton and Mr P. Ridolfo of Plymouth Naval Base Museum, Captain Alessandro Valentine of Stato Maggiore della Marina, Rome, Bundesarchiv: Militararchiv, Freiburg, Germany, Mr C.B.

Tye of the North Russia Club, and Mr P. Finnigan of the HMS *Warspite* Association.

Advice and technical assistance has been given to me by Mr J.E.G. White and Mr J. Archibald with translations, David Cave Photography, Dudley, and Mr R Spear with photography, and Mr M. Hallett of the University of Wolverhampton with the preparation of maps.

My grateful thanks go to my family who have given me unfailing and unstinting help and support over the years. To my late first wife Ella, who encouraged me to take up the project and greatly helped with the research, abstracting and typing of early drafts; to my wife Pauline who encouraged me to take up the project again after a gap of many years and who has been a tremendous supporter, and a patient listener, and has worked extremely hard and uncomplainingly with the word-processing of a number of drafts and the preparation of the finalised book; to my son Neil who has always shown a very keen interest in the book, and has helped enormously with the research and proof reading as well as turning up a number of unexpected research leads and references to the ship and its crew members, and finally, to my daughter Julia whose teenage scepticism has kept me constantly aware of the need to keep the reader interested and entertained. I hope that I have succeeded.

CHAPTER 1

The Advent of the Battleship Era

HMS *Warspite* and her four sister ships *Queen Elizabeth*, *Barham*, *Malaya* and *Valiant* were arguably the greatest-ever British battleships. *Warspite* was certainly the most enduring, with a service life of some thirty years and an unsurpassed record of involvement in action in two World Wars. In her lifetime she gave heavy blows and survived hard knocks which, as her story will show, were not always given and taken in action with her enemies. Her crew and sister-ships were subject to her whims and never quite knew what to expect from *Warspite*. Until her end in the 1950s she was a capricious lady with a lineage that dated back to Elizabethan times.

She was the seventh British warship to bear the name *Warspite*. The first, built in 1596, took part in the siege and sacking of Cadiz in the June of that year under the command of Sir Walter Raleigh. Although wounded in the thigh during the action, he led his squadron with considerable dash with *Warspite*, or *Warspight*, in the lead position. It was a precedent that the seventh *Warspite*, her captains and crews, were to emulate over three centuries later.[1] [2]

Warspite's parentage was rooted in the Victorian and Edwardian eras. This was a period of great evolution for the Royal Navy. There had been the shift from sail to steam; the transition from wooden to iron to steel hulls, and then the armour-plated protection of these hulls and the upper works of ships; the change in armament from smooth to rifled-barrels, from muzzle to breech loading, and from solid shot to armour-piercing shells; and the repositioning of this armament from inside the hull, with the guns firing from broadside gunports, to rotating turrets on the upper deck. All these developments in turn brought about changes in naval strategy and tactics. Since these changes were all taking place at more or less the same time, and because each affected the others, this period of transition led to much experimentation in naval architecture and construction. Thus the Admiralty, despite general progress towards modernisation, found itself towards the end of the nineteenth century with a mixed collection of ships differing markedly in endurance, speed, armament and operating capabilities. This made their efficient operation, in any co-ordinated sense, very difficult. At the same time the growth and dispersed nature of the British Empire and the general movement towards similar colonisation by competing powers required an efficient navy. The years of trials and testing had led the naval architects to concentrate on the development of standard types or classes of warship, each designed for a specific role, to meet the country's needs in the early years of the twentieth century.

Pride of place at this time was held by the battleship, descendant of the earlier ships-of-the-line. Of massive construction, heavily armed and armoured, and as a consequence somewhat slow and ponderous, the battleship was designed to slog it out with its rivals and endure. In later years, of course, the advent of underwater weapons and the introduction and rapid development of airpower render the battleship obsolete, but at the time, and indeed for the next half century until the Second World War, the battleship was to reign supreme. The awesome power of a squadron of battleships in line ahead was an open expression of a country's pride and power, and Britain was determined to be at the front of international and naval affairs. While the British taxpayers might skimp on their Army they were generally indulgent with the Navy, but the taxpayers' money was generally spent on the provision of ships rather than on the welfare of the crews, with a vast gulf existing between the status and well-being of the officers and that of the men. For the lower deck life and conditions were hard, rewards were poor, and by present day standards discipline and punishments harsh. Nevertheless the Royal Navy was a popular calling for the young men of the nation and service compared favourably with more humdrum life in cities and the country. The poor pay and conditions were to continue well into the twentieth century; indeed upwards of 1200 men of the Atlantic fleet were to mutiny at Invergordon in 1931 in protest over a proposed drastic reduction in their pay.

The early years of the twentieth century saw a series of political events and realignments that were considerably to influence the whole question of national defence and naval strategy. They also heralded the start of a naval arms race that was to lead to the First World War. The alliance in 1902 between Britain and Japan was intended to preserve the status quo in the Far East and maintain Britain's trading interest with China. It also allowed Great Britain to concentrate on events nearer home, particularly after the power and influence of Russia in the Far East was severely damaged when its Baltic fleet, having sailed around the world to do battle with Japan, was annihilated by that country's navy under Admiral Togo at Tsushima in 1905. The threat from Russia, who with France had long been regarded as a likely adversary, was further diminished as a consequence of the Anglo-Russian Convention of 1907, and the growing Entente Cordiale with France rendered any threat from that traditional enemy increasingly unlikely. The new European threat was from Germany, whose Kaiser Wilhelm, a grandson of Queen Victoria, had great ambitions for Germany which included an overseas empire and a navy to match that of the British.

Fortunately for the British nation and its Navy they had in that period Admiral of the Fleet Lord Fisher* as First Sea Lord. He was to be a major influence on naval policy and warship construction for a further two decades. Winston Churchill, who was the First Lord of the Admiralty from October 1911 to May 1915, credits Fisher with the all-important and far-reaching steps taken to enlarge, improve and modernise the British Navy in the early years of the twentieth century:

> I first met Lord Fisher at Biarritz in 1907. We stayed for a fortnight as the guests of a common friend. He was then First Sea Lord and in the height of his reign. We talked all day long and far into the nights. He told me wonderful stories of the Navy and of his plans – all about Dreadnoughts, all about submarines, all about the new education scheme for every branch of the Navy, all about big guns and splendid Admirals and foolish miserable ones, and Nelson and the Bible, and finally the island of

* John 'Jacky' Arbuthnot Fisher was First Sea Lord from 1904 to 1910 and from October 1914 to May 1915.

> Borkum*. I remembered it all. I reflected on it often. I even remembered the island of Borkum when my teacher had ceased to think so much of it. At any rate, when I returned to my duties at the Colonial Office I could have passed an examination on the policy of the then Board of the Admiralty.(3)

To counter German ambitions Fisher was responsible for the concentration of British fleets in home waters, the scrapping of great quantities of miscellaneous ships of obsolete fighting power, and the great naval construction programmes of 1908 and 1909. This period also saw the introduction of technical innovations such as the submarine and the water tube boiler, advances in the size of naval ordnance, and social changes such as a common naval education scheme and a system for the crewing of ships in reserve.

There was also the introduction of the 'all big gun' ship. Britain's position as a paramount naval power took a gigantic leap forward in 1906 with the introduction of HMS *Dreadnought*, the aptly-named first 'all big gun' turbine-driven battleship. *Dreadnought* was very much Fisher's child. Even in an age when technological systems were infinitely less complex than they are today she was a landmark in naval development. Equally remarkable, and a testament to the drive and determination of Fisher and his watchwords of 'Ruthless, relentless, and remorseless' was the speed of her construction. *Dreadnought*'s keelplate was laid on 2 October 1905, she was launched by King Edward VII on 10 February 1906, ran her sea trials on 3 October and was commissioned in December in the same year.

So startling were her innovations and the power of her 20,000-ton displacement, 21-knot speed and armament of ten 12in guns instead of the more usual four, that *Dreadnought* immediately rendered obsolete all other battleships in the world. This included of course those in the British Navy. Her introduction heralded the start of a great naval arms race and increasingly expensive construction programmes among the competing world powers. Yet so rapid had technological development become that *Dreadnought*

---

* Borkum, one of a chain of small islands off the Dutch-German coast, was presumably thought, at a time of a growing naval challenge from Germany, to be of strategic importance in relation to the German naval bases at Bremerhaven and Wilhelmshaven.

herself was to pay the price of being the pioneer and be obsolescent by, and take no part in, the great Battle of Jutland only ten years later.

Not all of Fisher's innovations in this Edwardian era were to prove so successful. In juggling with the three ever-present interrelated constraints of warship design – speed, hitting power and the ability to absorb punishment in return – Fisher came up with the hybrid battlecruiser class. They were to be faster, but less well armed and decidedly less well armoured than the battleship class. Thus HMS *Invincible* introduced two years after the *Dreadnought* had a speed of 25 knots and eight 12in guns. However she only had a 6-inch thick belt of armour plate compared with the 11-inch belt of *Dreadnought*. The decks and upper works were equally less well-protected. This inherent design weakness, this inability to absorb heavy punishment particularly from heavy-calibre plunging shell-fire from ranges of 15,000 to 20,000 yards, was ultimately to prove to be an Achilles heel. Plunging fire was to make a funeral pyre of the British battlecruisers; *Invincible*, *Indefatigable* and *Queen Mary* at the Battle of Jutland on 31 May 1916, and the *Hood* when tackling the German battleship *Bismarck* almost exactly twenty-five years later on 24 May 1941, were all sunk suddenly and catastrophically at the height of their battles and with a combined loss of 4722 lives. They were major naval disasters and a demonstration of the adage that only a battleship could confidently take on a battleship and hope to survive.

The embodiment of that belief, and arguably the classic battleship design of the era, was the *Queen Elizabeth* class which included HMS *Warspite*. Others in the five-ship class, built as part of the 1912 construction programme for a total cost of some £15 million, were *Queen Elizabeth*, *Barham*, *Malaya* and *Valiant*. As the 5th Battle Squadron they formed a fast and formidable group intended, in keeping with naval strategy of the era, to pursue and get behind an enemy fleet, presumed to be German, and cut off its escape. All five ships served in both World Wars and were to undergo numerous refits and modifications during their lifetimes. They fought in many battles and received numerous grievous wounds; and all, apart from *Barham*, survived enemy action and the rigours of the sea for thirty years.

The class were the first battleships in the world to be completely oil-fired and have a design speed of 25 knots. This gave enormous advantage over the conventional coal-fired battleships of the time in terms of greater speed and longer range, which, coupled with the ability to refuel at sea in all but the worst weather conditions, increased time at sea by eliminating the dirty, laborious and time-consuming coaling operation. The changeover from coal to oil, a revolutionary naval concept, was not accomplished without difficulty. According to Churchill's account:

> During the whole of 1913 I was subjected to an ever-growing difficulty about the oil supply. We were now fully committed to oil as the sole motive power for a large proportion of the Fleet, including all the newest and most vital units. There was great anxiety on the Board of the Admiralty and in the War Staff about our oil fuel reserves. ... The war consumption itself had been estimated on the most liberal scale by the Naval Staff. The expense of creating the oil reserve was however enormous. Not only had the oil to be bought in a monopoly ridden market, but large installations of oil tanks had to be erected and land purchased for the purpose. Although this oil-fuel reserve when created was clearly, whether for peace or war, as much an asset of the State as the gold reserve of the Bank of England, we were not allowed to treat it as capital expenditure; all must be found out of the current Estimates. At the same time, the Treasury and my colleagues in the Cabinet were becoming increasingly indignant at the Naval expense, which it might be contended was largely due to my precipitancy in embarking on oil burning battleships and also wantonly increasing the size of the guns and the speed and armour of these vessels. On the one hand, therefore, I was subjected to this ever-growing naval pressure, and on the other to a solid wall of resistance to expense.[3]

The battles with the Treasury and Parliament were hard fought. Churchill, seeking to secure the long-term supply of oil for the Navy, pushed through Parliament what he termed the Anglo-Persian Oil Convention. It was progressed against considerable opposition:

> ... from economists depreciating naval expenditure; members from mining constituencies who were especially sensible of the danger of departing from the sound basis of British coal; oil

> magnates who objected to a national inroad into their monopolies; Conservatives who disapproved of State trading; partisan opponents who denounced the project as an unwarrantable gamble with public money and did not hesitate to impute actual corruption.(3)

Eventually, in February 1914, some six months before the outbreak of the First World War, the Naval Estimates were passed. A week later the Government agreed that a contract should be entered into with the Anglo-Persian Oil Company, whereby the Government would acquire for about £2 million a controlling interest in the undertaking. In 1987, when the British Government sold off its remaining interests in British Petroleum (BP), the company was valued at approximately £20,000 million.

One other major advantage that the class had over other battleships of their era was the size and power of their 15in guns. The *Queen Elizabeth*s were the first battleships to mount guns of this size. Their eight 15in guns could each fire a shell weighing nearly a ton some twenty miles, at a rate of six rounds every five minutes. Compared with the 13.5in guns of their contemporaries, the 15in gun gave 30 per cent more hitting power and an increase of 50 per cent in the explosive effect produced by a shell penetrating the armour of the enemy. This gun was produced straight from the drawing board and remained in service in British and other nations' battleships until the 1950s.

As with the introduction of oil firing, the introduction of the 15in gun, under the joint patronage of Churchill and Fisher, was not accomplished without considerable misgivings:

> Until I got to the Admiralty (1911) I had never properly appreciated the service which Mr McKenna and Lord Fisher had rendered to the Fleet in 1909 by their leap forward from the 12 inch to the 13.5 inch. ... The increase of 1.5 inch in the calibre of the gun was enough to raise the British shell from 850 pounds to 1400 pounds. No fewer than twelve ships were actually building on the slips for the Royal Navy armed with these splendid weapons, quite unsurpassed at that time in the world, and firing a projectile nearly half as heavy again as the biggest fired by the German Fleet.
>
> I immediately sought to go one size better. I mentioned this to Lord Fisher at Reigate, and he hurled himself into its advocacy with tremendous passion. Nothing less than the 15 inch gun

> could be looked at for all the battleships and battlecruisers of the new programme. To achieve the supply of this gun was the equivalent of a great victory at sea; to shrink from the endeavour was treason to the Empire. What was it that enabled Jack Johnson to knock out his opponents? It was the big punch.(3)

The introduction of an untried gun of such revolutionary size was a tremendously risky undertaking:

> We knew the 13.5 inch well. All sorts of new stresses might develop in the 15 inch model. If only we could make a trial gun and test it thoroughly before giving orders for the whole of the guns of all the five ships, there would be no risk; but then we should lose an entire year, and five great vessels would go into the line of battle carrying an inferior weapon to that which we had it in our power to give them. Several there were of the responsible authorities consulted who thought it would be more prudent to lose the year. For, after all, if the guns had failed, the ships would have been fearfully marred. I hardly remember to have had more anxiety about any administrative decision than this.
>
> I went back to Lord Fisher. He was steadfast and even violent. So I hardened my heart and took the plunge. The whole outfit of guns was ordered forthwith. ... From that moment we were irrevocably committed to the whole armament, and every detail of these vessels, extending to thousands of parts, was redesigned to fit them. Fancy if they failed. What a disaster. What an exposure. No excuse would be accepted. It would all be brought home to me – 'rash, inexperienced', 'before he had been there a month', 'altering all the plans of his predecessors' and producing 'this ghastly fiasco', 'the mutilation of all the ships of the year'. What could I have said? Moreover, although the decision, once taken, was irrevocable, a long period of suspense – fourteen or fifteen months at least – was unavoidable.
>
> However, I dissembled all my misgivings. I wrote to the First Sea Lord (Fisher) that 'Risks have to be run in peace as well as in war, and courage in design, now may win a battle later on'.(3)

Everything turned out all right; the gun was a brilliant success.* It fired a 1920lb pound shell 35,000 yards, and achieved remarkable accuracy at all ranges.

Bigger, faster, more heavily armed and armoured battleships than the *Queen Elizabeth*s were yet to come, but by then battleships were no longer undisputed masters of the sea. In many ways the class represented the high point of the battleship concept and power, and HMS *Warspite* the epitome of the battleship spirit. This spirit is captured in a passage, slightly modified, which could have been written with *Warspite* in mind:

> The launch of a ship is to all who witness it a stirring and inspiring moment. As she slides gracefully down the slipway, one feels she is leaving her birthplace never to return. Into her body the riveters have hammered her character, and as she lies alongside the wharf 'completing', the character will be further moulded. She will put on her armour and with pride will receive her many weapons; she will receive the great engines that are to give her mobility, and will be endowed with the scientific achievements of her age. Finally, beautified by the friendly hands of skilled workmen, she will await her crew, the comrades that are to find in her an ever friendly home, as she will be their willing servant. One day they will board her, the tramp of their feet will resound on her decks and they will take her unto themselves, masters of her destiny, and will lead her far from her home to the great waters. She will possess the spirit of her predecessors, a spirit that will be constantly developed and strengthened, by her experiences in the service of her country. To the true sailor she will be no inanimate mass of metal but a living thing, the reincarnation of others that have borne her name. Her life, assuredly, will be a hard one but she will never falter; the demands on her will be severe, even cruel, yet she will always respond. She will be battered by heavy seas, shell may crash through her coat of armour and violent explosions may rend her hull but she will never complain – she will, rather, glory in her life, remembering the deeds of her forebears, and she will give back to those who guide her and had

* Testimony to the enduring qualities of the British 15in gun was borne out when four spare 15in mountings, originally manufactured in the First World War for HMS *Courageous* and *Glorious* (converted to early aircraft carriers), were fitted to HMS *Vanguard*, the last British battleship to be built, some twenty-seven years later in the Second World War. Two specimens of these great guns and their one-ton shells, from the monitor HMS *Roberts* and the battleship HMS *Ramillies*, now guard the entrance to the Imperial War Museum in London. These are the only surviving examples of the 15in naval gun on public display in the UK. They each weigh 100 tons. The left-hand gun is from *Ramillies*, and the right-hand gun was originally fitted to her sister-ship *Resolution* in 1915. It was removed in 1938, stored until 1944, and then fitted to *Roberts*, a shallow draft bombardment 'monitor'. The 15in guns of *Warspite*, *Ramillies* and *Roberts* were still being used some thirty years after they were first introduced, adding their weight to the naval bombardment of the D-Day beaches on 6 June 1944.

trained her, all that they had given to her. In time she will grow old, tired, and even no longer admired, but she will still retain her self respect. Safe in some friendly haven she will dream away the hours; until one day, her old friends who created her will take her home and will dismantle her hull, so that only her honoured name will remain in the seaman's mind. But her spirit will not die; it will hover in the rafters of the shipyard, ready and eager to inspire another of her name.(4)

This then is the story of HMS *Warspite* and of the men who sailed and fought with her.

CHAPTER 2

The Early Years and the First World War

HMS *Warspite* and her four sister ships of the *Queen Elizabeth* class were the most formidable warships of their day. Her extensive and versatile range of armaments comprised:

- A main armament of eight 15in guns, mounted in four twin turrets on the main deck. They could fire, at maximum elevation of 20 degrees and with a standard charge, a 1920lb shell 23,400 yards, or over 13 miles.
- A secondary armament of fourteen 6in guns, two in open mountings on the foredeck and the remainder in casements, six on either side.
- An anti-aircraft armament of two 3in guns in open mountings on the foredeck;
- Two submerged torpedo rooms, one aft of 'A' and the other aft of 'Y' magazines, each with two 21in torpedo tubes.

The ships, which each carried a crew of 950, had a designed displacement of 31,500 tons. By launch *Warspite*'s displacement had risen to 33,410 tons. She was driven by engines designed to produce a speed of 25 knots at 75,000hp. The extra weight meant that the ships never quite achieved this. During contractor trials *Warspite* achieved 24.65 knots at an overload power of 75,510hp.

The keelplate of *Warspite* was laid down at No. 3 slipway, Devonport Naval Dockyard, on 31 October 1912 by Mrs Stokes, wife of the Admiral Superintendent of the Dockyard. She was launched on 26 November 1913, the ceremony being carried out by Mrs Ivy Chamberlain, wife of Austen Chamberlain, in company with Winston Churchill, then First Lord of the Admiralty, exactly on time at a quarter past three, before an enormous crowd of the general public. The weather was kind, a beautiful day for

November, and it was a happy, almost family, occasion. Austen Chamberlain's step-mother Mary, writing to her own mother, recorded that:

> Last week Ivy launched a great battleship at Plymouth – the *Warspite* – and they had a most delightful time. They took little Joe* ... [who] ... helped bluejackets to coil ropes and clean brasses.(1)

The *Warspite* was the largest ship ever built at Devonport and, after fitting-out at the North Yard of the Dockyard, she was officially commissioned on 8 March 1915 by her first commanding officer, Captain Edward M. Philpotts. The occasion was commemorated by Mrs Chamberlain's gift of a White Ensign. In thanking her for the gift Captain Philpotts recorded how busy they had been in commissioning the ship. In his memoirs one of her crew, John Chessman, at that time a young sailor, confirms the amount of work that was necessary to turn *Warspite* into a fighting warship.

> The filthy *Warspite*, that is the thought that first crossed my mind when we boarded her, pitch and filth and dirty grease marks 'tween decks and more so on the upper decks. Shortly afterwards came a pep talk from Captain Philpotts our future C.O. A very likeable sort of bloke he seemed, but only the future would decide that. After appealing to us all to work together to make the *Warspite* a happy ship he concluded 'I'm afraid the ship herself looks far from a happy one at the moment, but I am sure when we put to sea tomorrow, everyone will endeavour as one to bring her back to the spick and span condition any and all of HM ships not only deserve but simply must attain to hold our proud heritage ever in the forefront of all nations with eyes on the oceans of the world'.(2)

After commissioning and fitting out, *Warspite* left Devonport and the West Country on her way to join the Fleet, already six months into war with Germany.

> So it was early in March 1915 on a grey overcast sort of morning HMS *Warspite* slid away from the basin wall which had witnessed her completion and was towed through the open end by a couple of busy little tugboats, and stern first too. A little stress is placed on this in view of *Warspite*'s sometimes remarkable gyrations on

* Young son of Austen Chamberlain.

> future dates. Through the Sound where the accompanying tugs screeched a discordant farewell and so to the open sea and the rugged West Country coast on our starboard beam.(2)

As was to be expected with a new ship, especially one with so many innovative features, *Warspite* was not yet free of dockyard attention and adjustments. Although these occasions presented an opportunity for some shore leave they had their drawbacks, as Midshipman A.H. Ashworth was to find out. His diary for 6 April reads:

> Discovered the loss of my 'oilskin' at lunch. Some damned dockyard matey. Bye Jove! I hope my curses on his head come true'.(3)

Warspite arrived at Scapa Flow on Tuesday 13 April to join the 5th Battle Squadron but found the base empty of her sister ships – they were away at sea exercising. Their return gave *Warspite*'s crew the opportunity to show off their new ship; Sub-Lieutenant Packer in a letter home wrote:

> We are looking awfully smart now and today with Mrs Austen Chamberlain's gift, a sixteen foot silk white ensign flying at the ensign staff, we were the envy of all eyes ... I dined with the Captain, E.M. Philpotts, last Friday and very nice too. He really is the best skipper in the Navy, and Commander H.T. Walwyn too. We are undoubtedly very lucky and have a very happy ship.(4)

Warspite, which in her later years was affectionately known throughout the Navy as 'The Old Lady', was to prove a skittish maiden; her captain and crew never quite knew how she was going to perform, she was temperamental and had a tendency to go off on a course of her own choosing.* *Warspite* had a number of 'mishaps' in her early years, before becoming arguably the best-known and best-loved of all the battleships of the Royal Navy.

Thus it was that on 16 September 1915 the brand new ship grounded at a speed of 14 knots on Dunfermline Reef in the Firth of Forth while on passage from Scapa Flow, and had to put into Rosyth for a week of temporary repairs before moving to Jarrow shipyard for more permanent repairs. Midshipman Lycett Gardner records in his diary entry for 20 September:

* In his memoirs John Chessman suggests that 'she really should have been called '*Forspite*', if only on account of her vagaries when in the company of other ships.'(2)

The enquiry started on board today. I do hope the Skipper and Navigator will get on all right. The damage appears to be more serious than first supposed. We may get some leave.[5]

The repairs took until 20 November 1915. The findings of the Court of Enquiry absolved the ship's officers of negligence but considered that 'the temporary disablement of this important vessel was due to a grave error of judgement'[6] and reprimanded the Captain and Navigator.

Barely two weeks later, on 3 December 1915, she was in collision with her sister-ship HMS *Barham*. As witnessed by John Chessman there was an element of farce in the collision. He recorded that:

We were steaming in line ahead at a speed of sixteen knots, HMS *Barham* as flagship was head of the column. We ... were astern of her at the regulation distance of two and a half cables. Now any alteration of speed is signalled with flags flying at the yard-arm by the leader of the column, ... At that time flag G headed the one or two numeral flags indicating the change of speed. Only when that signal was acknowledged by the other ships in company with an answering pennant ... which meant that the signal had been seen and understood, only then was the signal hauled down at the senior officer's discretion. However, immediately that did occur the change in engine revolutions were to be telegraphed to the engine room. If this was carried out correctly the change in speed was smooth and controlled to the extent of there appearing to be no change in bearing or distance. Now the instance I am presenting was if nothing else calamitous. The *Barham* hoisted the signal G8 which would indicate a reduction of speed equivalent to eight knots. In view of the fact that we were then doing sixteen I could not believe I was seeing aright. I had never, nor do I believe anyone else there had either, seen indicated a change of speed of this nature. Of course I was only small fry, a Signalboy, and accordingly not expected to make the smallest of noises. I heard the Signalman report to the Chief Yeoman who in turn reported to the Captain according to the regulations as 'Eighteen knots, Sir'. Quickly I jabbed the Signalman in the back 'You've made a mistake' I almost shouted, 'The signal is eight knots not eighteen; tell him or we'll be in a right bloody mess'. The signal came down, the officer of the watch spoke down the engine-room tube giving instructions for the revs to be raised to the appropriate level for

> eighteen knots. In a matter of seconds we closed on the *Barham*'s stern, which was not surprising considering she had decreased speed to eight knots at the moment that we had increased to eighteen. One cannot explain such a predicament ... what I can see even today is the spotlessly white quarter deck of the *Barham* way down below, so far below, weaving this way and that like a scared cat trying to avoid a dog. Thirty thousand tons of man-o-war in the slough of despair and hope in a prayer ...(2)

Although the *Warspite* was put full astern in a last desperate attempt to avoid the collision, her port bow crashed into the starboard quarter of the *Barham* and, as she broke away, she lost her port anchor and cable and started to take water forward.

Below decks, the crew felt the full impact. Sub-Lieutenant Packer, then a junior gunnery officer on the ship, wrote to his father:

> We gave our sister quite a nudge. It was very rough and I was between decks talking to Commander (G) when suddenly there was a shock. The ship bent and jumped like an india-rubber thing, engines full steam astern and our cable going out with a run and a rattle. I thought we'd caught a mine. Commander (G), who'd been blown up once, didn't seem a bit worried but merely said 'Ah -' and told a bugler to sound off Collision Stations. I ran forward to my station for Close Watertight Doors and found the whole place thick with steam and water swishing in for'd so I got the cell prisoners who are down for'd up out of it. Our bow was split like a pea-pod and we could only make about ten knots home against a bad head sea. Not too nice in a possible submarine area ... We worked day and night shoring up etc., and got in all right.(4)

Both *Barham* and *Warspite* carried out emergency repairs and were ordered back to Scapa Flow for inspection and further work, after which *Warspite* sailed to her home port, Devonport, for refit and more permanent repairs. These took until 21 December 1915. It was an opportunity for some shore leave. Midshipman Gardner's diary entry for Saturday 18 December tells us:

> Hands painting ship. Put in for weekend leave. Only got it into Plymouth. Better than nothing. Got off at 12.30 and took Griffiths to lunch at the Grand with mother. Went to hear the marine band at the Guildhall. Very good music. Tea at Goodbody's afterwards and then back to the Grand Hotel. Turned in at 10.30. (5)

A subsequent Court of Enquiry confirmed that the collision had occurred because of a misreading of signals, and blame was apportioned to several officers on both ships. In John Chessman's words:

> I had been right but ignored. The result cost the taxpayer thousands of pounds and might so easily have cost the lives of the men in both ships. And I wasn't even called in to give evidence at the ensuing enquiry. The fault lay with the Signalman alone and yet he received not so much as a reprimand.[(2)]

On *Warspite* there was considerable sympathy for the Captain, particularly in view of the earlier grounding mishap. Gardner's entry for 7 December in his Midshipman's Diary records that:

> The opinion in the higher circles in the wardroom is that if the Skipper hadn't done what he did do, when he did it, the B would now be at the bottom.[(5)]

Those first months were not an auspicious start to an illustrious career, and *Warspite* was already being talked of as 'an unlucky ship'. The events of mid-summer 1916 were to change all that – at least for a time.

The early months of the year had seen both the British Grand Fleet and the German High Seas Fleet engaged in a cat and mouse game of trying to draw out the other from its base and then to wrong-foot it in a decisive main fleet action. There had been a number of North Sea skirmishes which could have led to a major action – an attempted attack by the Harwich Force on what was believed to be a Zeppelin base at Hoyer had provoked retaliatory shelling of Lowestoft by elements of the German High Seas Fleet. There were other planned or executed provocations as 1916 wore on. Then, in late May, British Naval Intelligence determined that the German High Seas Fleet had left its bases at Wilhelmshaven and was out in the North Sea. This was the opportunity for the long-awaited big match.

> On the morning of 30 May 1916 I had the feeling, that [*sic*] was it. We had again been ordered to raise steam for full speed and prepare for sea. In mid-afternoon the heat-haze playing around the funnels indicated a readiness to move out. This proved to be one of the times we were to ...[(2)]

All the British Grand Fleet set sail from its northern bases: the Battle Fleet, under the Commander-in-Chief Admiral Jellicoe, made up of battleships from Scapa Flow in the Orkneys and Invergordon in the Moray Firth; and the Battlecruiser Fleet, under Admiral Beatty, reinforced by the 5th Battle Squadron of *Queen Elizabeth* class battleships, from Rosyth in the Firth of Forth.

The long-awaited encounter, at Jutland Bank off the west coast of Denmark in the North Sea, was to prove to be a confused and inconclusive contest, with both sides subsequently claiming that they had the best of it, and to some extent the welter of official reports, newspaper articles and eye-witness accounts only added to the confusion and subsequent controversy.

The opening hours of the battle were orderly enough:

> On past Burnt Island at a steady sixteen knots, the battlecruisers and following in line the 5th Battle Squadron consisting of *Barham*, *Warspite*, *Valiant* and *Malaya*. The hum of powerful engines filled the air and smoke-stacks belched direction. Beyond Burnt Island the escorting destroyers waited to join us and taking [*sic*] up stations port and starboard, two to each capital ship. A mighty array steaming into a glorious early summer evening. War just a crazy dream in all that loveliness.(2)

Beatty was flying his flag in HMS *Lion*, a 26,270-ton battlecruiser laid down at Devonport in 1910 and completed some two years later. *Lion*, armed with eight 13.5in guns, was capable of 27 knots, but, like all the battlecruisers of her era, she was lightly armoured on her upper decks and hence vulnerable to penetration and damage from heavy shells of 12in and heavier calibre. *Lion* was accompanied by *Princess Royal*, *Queen Mary* and *Tiger*, making up the 1st Battlecruiser Squadron, and *New Zealand* and *Indefatigable* of the 2nd Battlecruiser Squadron. *Indefatigable* was on temporary detachment to the 2nd Battlecruiser Squadron in place of HMS *Australia*, sister ship of the *New Zealand*. *Australia* and *New Zealand* had been in collision some time previously and *Australia* was still in dry dock undergoing repairs.

The 5th Battle Squadron of fast battleships, *Barham*, *Valiant*, *Warspite* and *Malaya*, were also on temporary attachment to Beatty's fleet of battlecruisers. The fifth ship of the class, *Queen*

Elizabeth, was in dock at Rosyth and not ready for sea at the time of departure. The battleships were replacing the 'other Invincibles' – *Invincible*, *Inflexible* and *Indomitable*, which together with *Indefatigable* made up the 3rd Battlecruiser Squadron. These three ships were away at sea on gunnery practice under the command of Rear-Admiral Hood when the news broke that the German High Seas Fleet was at sea. Admiral Beatty was thus leading his fleet of ten capital ships and an array of scouting cruisers and escorting destroyers to do battle on that fateful day. They were all to take a fearful battering from their German counterparts in the next few hours.

Daybreak on 31 May 1916 found *Warspite* and her companion ships steaming almost due East at 20-21 knots. The battlecruisers were ahead. Surgeon-Captain G.E.D. Ellis remembers that 'the weather was exceptionally fine, with a cloudless sky and a calm blue sea.'(7) At 14.30 Beatty's battlecruisers were about 200 miles north of the German coast. His 5th Battle Squadron was five miles astern, and his whole fleet was about 60 miles south of Jellicoe's main battlefleet. This latter force of twenty-four battleships plus supporting forces was also steering south at speed, in a six column line abreast formation. Rear-Admiral Hood and his 3rd Battlecruiser Squadron, having been urgently recalled from their gunnery exercises the previous evening, was engaged in a scouting role some twenty-five miles ahead of Jellicoe's main fleet, preparing to rejoin Beatty's battlecruiser fleet some forty miles to the south.

Then contact was made. Unexpectedly one of Beatty's light cruisers, scouting ahead, spotted enemy ships and the six battlecruisers turned to intercept, opening fire at 15.45, at a range of some 14,000 yards. Beatty's intention was to cut off the enemy fleet from its base. His enemy, Vice-Admiral Von Hipper, turned his five battlecruisers to meet the threat and for the next fifty minutes a bloody fight ensued with the two fleets running south-east on parallel courses.

On *Warspite* entry into the battle had been controlled, if impatient; routine, preparation and exercises had filled the day. Then at 15.40 Commander Walwyn, the ship's Executive Officer, received a message from the Captain 'to get the hands up at once'. Walwyn, in a contemporary account, records that:

> I at once sounded off 'action', and passed the word round to everybody to get cleared away as fast as possible. Message from the Captain to ask why I had sounded 'action' and that he wanted me. Went up to the bridge and got rather 'bitten', as apparently he only meant get the hands shaken up and get some tea, etc. early. Anyway I explained that they were well on the way clearing away and should like to get everything ready and get tea after if there was time. I remained on the forebridge and it was pretty plain that there was something serious doing: we were now steering S.S.E. Captain decided to go to action stations right away, and we went on clearing everything for action.(8)

Thus it was, at 16.00 hours, that Chessman, having just finished his afternoon watch,

> was just going below to have my tea when at the top of the last gang-way I was stopped in my tracks by the shrilling of the boson's pipes 'All hands to action stations' and the bugler sounding 'The Charge'. I turned about, hunger unsatisfied and made for the Signal Distribution Office situated under the Flag Deck.(2)

His post was a small exposed steel platform surrounded by a low handrail. His job was to note and record the changes of speed as indicated by the flags flown by the neighbouring ship. The seventeen year-old was to note and record other, more terrible things on that momentous day.

'The Charge' had been sounded and charge they did. In his desire to get to grips with the German Fleet and cut it off from its base, so that it could be brought to action against Jellicoe's main Battle Fleet, Beatty had allowed his battlecruisers to get ahead of the more powerful, but slower, battleships of his 5th Battle Squadron. The battleships were now striving to catch up and get every knot of speed from pounding engines. Surgeon Ellis, whose skills were not yet needed, observed that:

> From our own wash along the ship's side and the noise of the propellers, noticeable aft, we were also going at a pretty good speed. No records of course were taken, but Nelson told me afterwards that he thinks we did 26 possibly – 'and a bit'. Our best previous, coming north from Plymouth the first time, was 24.8 and we developed 78,000 horsepower on that occasion. Our designed h.p. is 50,000.(7)

Things were not going well with Beatty's battlecruisers. At 16.02 two 11in shells from the *Von der Tann* hit *Indefatigable* at a range of 16,000 yards. Two more shells struck in the next salvo. Almost immediately there was a huge explosion; *Indefatigable* rolled over to port and was gone, taking 1017 officers and men with her. At 16.26 the third British ship in line, *Queen Mary*, was struck by two 12in shells from *Derfflinger* at a range of 15,000 yards and blew up in a great mushroom cloud of smoke rising 600 to 800 feet high: 1266 officers and men went down with her. At this, Admiral Beatty reportedly turned to his Flag Captain in HMS *Lion* and observed 'There seems to be something wrong with our bloody ships today', a remark which the Flag Captain observed 'needed neither comment nor answer.'(9) But Beatty's agonies were not yet over. He was later to lose another battlecruiser at 18.34 when the *Invincible* blew up and sank in less than a minute with the loss of 1019 officers and men, including Admiral Hood, when struck by the 12in shells of the German battlecruisers *Lützow* and *Derfflinger*. There were only six survivors. All three battlecruisers had been rent asunder by heavy calibre shells plunging through thinly armoured decks and setting off colossal internal magazine explosions.

On *Warspite*, Walwyn, continuing to oversee preparations and to 'action things', went into 'B' turret. Morale was high:

> Bartlett, provided with morphine syringe etc., was very pleased with himself. Walker, as usual, very cheeky and always there. Hoisted battle ensigns and Union Jack at after struts and masthead. Found everything all right and Curtess asked whether he should load, but I told him to wait for the usual routine orders ... Wished we had a bit more time to prepare but felt quite happy about things; it was now about 4 o'clock. Got orders to 'load and train Red 20'. Could not see anything at all; hazy and a lot of smoke about. We were now steaming very hard ... Everybody in the turret in very good spirits, and I asked Grenfell if he had any cotton wool. He said he hadn't and passed me a lump of cotton waste, enough to stop the ears of a donkey, which I chucked back at him and almost at once got the order to 'stand by'.(8)

The 5th Battle Squadron came into action at approximately 16.08 when *Barham* fired on and hit the *Von der Tann*. *Barham* and

Valiant then shifted fire to the *Moltke*, while *Warspite* and *Malaya* concentrated upon the *Von der Tann*.

> I made out five columns of smoke in the mist and that was all I could see, no masts or anything else. Opened fire on cruisers, range about 21,000 yards. *Barham* and *Valiant* were firing too.(8)

At 16.45 the British battlecruisers turned to the North when Scheer's battlefleet came into sight, Beatty ordering reversal of course to starboard in an attempt to draw the German forces towards Jellicoe's closing main battlefleet. Five minutes later the four surviving British battlecruisers were all steering north-westwards while the 5th Battle Squadron and the German battlecruisers were hotly engaging each other, but going in the opposite direction.

> I suddenly saw our battle cruisers coming close by about four cables in the opposite direction and I realised they had turned back. I saw *Queen Mary* and *Indefatigable* were adrift but never for a moment realised they had gone. Before this we had passed through a mass of black water with an 'M' class (destroyer) picking up people. I heard afterwards that this was the *Queen Mary*.(8)

Beatty was flying a signal to Admiral Evan-Thomas, in command of the 5th Battle Squadron, for him to turn, in succession, 180 degrees to starboard. Either because the signal was late in execution, or because *Barham*'s receipt and reaction were slow, or because of the limitations of communications in that era, particularly in the heat and confusion of battle, the battleships did not begin to turn until 16.54.

> I had not seen any speedflags on the *Barham* ahead for ages it seemed. Small wonder! Huge columns of black smoke from her stacks blotted out completely such aids and most everything else.(3)

Barham turned first, followed at minute intervals by *Valiant* and *Warspite*. As they turned, in a very congested patch of the North Sea, the battleships came under heavy fire from the converging German main fleet battleships about 20,000 yards away. The action was so fierce that *Malaya*, the last ship in the line, turned early, cutting across *Warspite*'s stern before taking up her station again. Hipper and his battlecruisers also turned northwards at almost exactly the same time.

> Found we were turning fast to starboard following our line and as we came round ... I saw five enemy battlecruisers on the port bow. They were steaming the same way we were going and going very hard. A mass of black smoke, and I could see only their masts and the tops of their funnels ... and stern wave showing up white and very high.[8]

It was about this time that *Warspite* opened fire with her 15in guns.

> Opened fire on [their] number 5. I could not have laid them myself, spotting frightfully hard, and we were all short the first few salvos. Range, I think, 23,000 yards. They straddled us once or twice but we had not been hit so far. Blast from A [turret] was awfully bad and blew salt water and dust into my eyes which watered like blazes. I distinctly saw one salvo hit [their] Number 5 and she turned away about six points to port and went away in a cloud of black and white smoke. We turned our attention to Number 4 as 5 by this time was out of range and the guns on the stops at 23,000. Guns were constantly bumping stops, and layers reported they could not follow. It was a wonderful and rather horrible sight to see the constant orange flicker of flame along the line when they fired. I remember timing their salvos, and when my boy [sailor] called 'stop' they fell about four minutes later a bit short.[8]

The firing of the 5th Battle Squadron was proving highly effective and in order to combat it the German battlecruisers were having to periodically withdraw out of range. This tactic was confirmed by the First Gunnery Officer of the *Derfflinger*:

> ... we saw that the enemy were being reinforced. Behind the battlecruiser line approached four big ships. We soon identified them as the *Queen Elizabeth* class. There had been much talk in our fleet of these ships ... their speed was scarcely inferior to ours (twenty six knots), but they fired a shell more than twice as heavy as ours. They engaged at portentous range ... they soon came within the range of our Third Squadron* and were engaged by the ships at the head of the line, particularly the flagship, the *König*. In this way the four English battleships came under the fire of at least nine German ships, five battlecruisers and from four or five

* Comprising German battleships armed with 12in guns.

> battleships. At these great ranges I fired armour piercing shell ... In a sense this part of the action, fought against a numerically inferior but more powerfully armed enemy, was depressing, nerve racking and exasperating. Our only means of defence was to leave the line for a short time when we saw that the enemy had our range. As this manoeuvre was imperceptible to the enemy, we extricated ourselves at regular intervals from the hail of fire.(10)

In this battle of the big ships, smaller vessels had to be vigilant or lucky if they too were to survive to fight another day. Midshipman Fairthorne, 'lucky to be appointed to HMS *Warspite* some fourteen days before she came into action off the coast of Jutland.'(11) was able to observe and admire the way the British destroyers tried to avoid the heavy salvos:

> It was a most thrilling sight watching our destroyers. As soon as a shot fell nearby, they would steam right into the splash, knowing that it would be extremely unlikely for a second to fall in the same place.(11)

Other smaller ships were less fortunate, or perhaps scorned the dictum of discretion being the better part of valour. Sir Robert Arbuthnot's 1st Cruiser Squadron of ageing, almost obsolete, armoured cruisers built in the early 1900s had been scouting ahead of Jellicoe's main battlefleet. Arriving on the scene at around this time, *Defence* and *Warrior* dashed in, perhaps recklessly, to engage the opposing German scouting cruisers and the already badly damaged *Weisbaden.* In the heat and dash of battle they cut across the bows of Beatty's battlecruisers, narrowly avoiding collision, and suddenly found themselves under the 12in guns of the German battlefleet as it came out of the early evening mist some 18,000 yards away. Outranged and outgunned, the two ships were annihilated. *Defence* blew up and disintegrated, sinking with all hands at 18.20. *Warrior* was hit by over twenty shells and reeled away. The dying moments of *Defence* were clearly observed by the deck officers and men of *Warspite*, herself under heavy fire. Captain Poland of *Warspite* later wrote to his brother, in a mixture of professional admiration and private emotion:

> Then I saw the *Defence* coming down our starboard bow [engaged side] heading straight at the enemy, with a cloud of

> black smoke amidships and aft. She was banging away and going full speed, masthead colours and all the rest of it, and made a very gallant show. I saw three salvoes fall across her in quick succession, beauties. A flicker of flame ran aft along her forecastle head and up her fore-turret, which seemed to melt. Then - whoof, up she went, a single huge sheet of flame, 500 feet high, mixed up with smoke and fragments. As it died down I saw her crumpled bow, red hot, at an angle of sixty degrees, and then she sank. I nearly vomited – God it was an awful sight. I couldn't get to sleep that night for thinking of it. The whole thing, from the moment I saw her couldn't have taken twenty seconds[12]

Boy Sailor Chessman's memories of the event, were perhaps more confused, though no less vivid and emotional:

> Those poor buggers down there. I was actually finding time to pity someone else. White ensigns flying at every available point, ... the two four funnelled and not so new cruisers sailed on our starboard beam not more than thirty yards distant. So near I could have read their names if I hadn't recognised them ... What the hell were they doing there? ... they hadn't a chance of making it count at this range. They both looked brave, so brave. But not for long ... horror of horrors ... I watched over six hundred officers and men shrivelled up in no more that ten seconds flat. The Union Jack on the stern of the *Defence* lit up like a huge match and ... from that single flame ran a holocaust of fire, dead centre and the length of the vessel. In under ten seconds a gallant ship completely disintegrated without trace, not a lifebelt or even a cap on the surface she so recently covered. Strange, I wasn't shocked, not yet ...[2]

Perched on his exposed platform young Chessman was having to put his shock to one side and focus his concerns on his own predicament, for by now *Warspite* was herself in serious trouble and starting to take hits.

> The flashes and explosions were now organised and full of purpose. Six or more huge splashes rose mast high and no more that ten yards away on our starboard side. ... The third lot of splashing soaked me from head to toe. I stared into the mist fascinated. ... I was seventeen, this was my baptism of fire, the big stuff I mean. I watched the flames stab the mist, heard the exploding charges and watched and waited. It seemed a long wait, long

> enough to conjecture if the last flames had despatched something with your name on it that time. A whistle overhead, like the introduction to a tornado and crump! More fountains, rising this time on the other side. I started doing mental sums. Seeing how they had straddled us well and truly, how long before they slide-ruled us out of existence?(2)

He was not alone with his fears; older more experienced men were sharing them, even the Ship's Executive Officer, who admitted that:

> One salvo came very close, just short, smothering us with spray, and I am afraid I ducked and talked to Grenfell a minute. We then turned 16 points in succession and trained around full speed to the other beam.
>
> Very soon after the turn I suddenly saw on the starboard quarter the whole of the [German] High Seas Fleet; at least I saw masts, funnels, and an endless ripple of orange flashes all down the line, how many I didn't try to count, as we were getting well strafed at this time, but I remember counting up to eight. The noise of their shell over and short was deafening ... that frightful crack, crack, crack going on the whole time. Felt one or two very heavy shakes but didn't think much of it at the time and it never occurred to me that we were being hit.(8)

But they were being hit, and to some effect. Commander Walwyn, the ship's Executive Officer, received a message from the Captain to go aft and see what was the matter as the ship had been badly hit.

> Told everybody in the turret ['B'] that we were doing alright and to keep her going. Machinery working like a clockwork mouse and no hangup of any sort whatsoever. I told Curtess to take over ... Walker to go down below and join me when he could on the mess deck. Ran down port superstructure ladder and tried to get into port superstructure; all clips* were on, so I climbed up over No. 2 cutter. Just as I got up, one came through the aft tunnel with an awful screech and spattered about everywhere. I put up my collar and ran like a stag, feeling in a hell of a funk.(8)

After meeting up below with Walker 'grinning all over',(8) he sent him to inform the Captain that there was nothing wrong so far as he

* Hatch locking clips.

could see. But the Captain's concern was understandable, and he was not the only crew member thinking that the ship had been badly damaged. Down below, confined and unable to see the enemy ships, members of the crew could only hear and feel, and for some of them suffer, the effects of the German shells. Surgeon Ellis recorded in his War Diary:

> A little later we got our first hit. It seemed to be on the armour abreast of our station, on the waterline, from the closeness of the sound, but actually it was some way further aft I believe. One could hear the distinct sound of metal striking against metal, and it was quite different to any of the subsequent hits we received, as if it had struck broadways on without exploding* ... Wherever it hit, the whole ship 'jumped' sideways from it.(7)

The moment of that first hit was also to remain with Bill Fell, a young midshipman. He was, with others, in the Transmitting Station, secured beneath heavy locked hatches in the bowels of the ship, five decks down:

> Then all of a sudden there was a monumental crump which sounded as if all the tea trays in the world, full of crockery, had been dropped on our heads; the whole ship rattled and shook. We realised we'd been hit by something pretty big. We were only just recovering from that when there was an even worse crash which knocked us off our stools. I was dazed and when I sat up I was in water. Apart from one stuttering light in the corner it was pitch dark. Worst of all was the complete silence. No sound of the engines, no sound of the action, no sound except for swishing water.
>
> After a moment, I noticed that down all the voice pipes was spurting a good old sluice of water – so we were slowly flooding. I think we all began to come to about the same time and two young midshipmen, who had only been on the ship a couple of weeks, began to whimper a bit. The senior midshipman went across and banged their two heads together and dropped them back into the water. Well, that solved that problem.
>
> We then went back to trying to do our job, but of course no information was coming down. Then reassuringly, the engines started and we found a few lamps and got them going. But we

* It was probably an armour-piercing shell which failed to explode.

were still anxious about our situation. The senior midshipman found his way to the voice pipe and called up 'Foretop? Foretop?'. He then paused. 'What another one gone up? Splendid.' He was in fact speaking to a mythical Foretop through a wrecked voice pipe. Of course we didn't realise that, and so our morale shot up. After that we waited and waited for about an hour and a half. Then we heard banging on the hatches and someone let us out.(13)

Warspite was now being continuously straddled and hit as the Executive Officer continued his damage assessment tour of the ship. His duties over the next few hours arguably gave him, of all the crew, the most comprehensive view of the damage *Warspite* was to receive, and of the way the crew coped with her time of trial. He was to find bravery and bravado, calm and confusion, humour and horror:

> Went through Forecastle Mess Deck and was just going forward when a 12 inch came through the side armour on boys' mess deck. Terrific sheet of golden flame, stink, an impenetrable dust and everything seemed to fall everywhere with appalling noise. Called for No. 2 Fire Brigade... and we got the hoses out and put out a lot of burning refuse. Several of the Fire Brigade were sick due to the sweet sickly stench, but there was no sign of poison gas ... Smoke was pouring up from holes in deck, and it occurred to me that high angle magazine was very near. Told Pring to disconnect ... [and] ... stand by to flood from middle deck position. Water from cut fire mains was pouring below and smoke soon stopped. Everybody busy 'souvenir' hunting and had to put hose on them to make them take cover below again.(8)

A further souvenir-hunting episode was to exasperate the Executive Officer when he came across a 12in shell which had finished up, unexploded, above the engineers' workshop:

> The filling was sticking out like a chock of wood and a couple of stokers were trying to chip the fuse out. I luckily stopped this little effort. It is extraordinary the amount of damage this one shell did if it did not explode ...(8)

Although Walwyn was not to know it at the time, the shell had done considerable damage to one person in the boys' mess deck which was receiving more than its share of enemy attention:

> Went below again and found that a second shell had come into the boys' mess deck ... Smoke was pouring out of the wet provision room and seeing Pring leaning against bulkhead told him to flood it. He seemed dazed and silly and I 'bit' him for not getting on quicker. I didn't know at the time that he was very badly hit; anyway he did the job before he was too far gone.(8)

Pring had indeed been badly hit. Surgeon Ellis records that after the battle, during the night, he made rounds of all the casualties. He visited Pring who had been put into one of the cabins:

> A shell had come in further aft, knocking down a W/T* door on top of a Chief Stoker called Pring, wrecked the Band master's cabin and finally come to rest on top of a ladder leading down to the engineers' workshop. Only the tip of the shell had gone, the rest was intact† ... Pring, whom we had discovered to have a very large haematoma – the biggest I have seen – of the abdominal wall, and now that it was all over [he] was suffering from a good deal of shock ... as well as being struck by a small fragment of the shell which had caused a wound to the front, had extricated himself [from under the door] and continued to do strenuous work all through the action. He was awarded the D.S.M.‡ for his conduct.(7)

Other men were equally brave and resilient. The Executive Officer found that:

> Men everywhere were simply splendid, and all so cheery and although I confess it was mighty unpleasant and unnerving I myself had plenty to do, but for those who had to merely wait it must have been a thousand times worse. The noise was so perfectly appalling, and you couldn't hear at all between decks, and the worst of it was knowing nothing.(8)

Surgeon Ellis found that:

> For a time we were left in quietness, but we learnt over the phone that Williamson was being kept busy aft, several shells having come in there apparently ... our casualties were comparatively very slight

---

* Watertight.

† This was the shell that the two stokers were attempting to dismantle.

‡ Distinguished Service Medal.

> ... The worst cases we had sent down to us forward were of burns, due to cordite fire breaking out in the starboard battery. Eleven cases, including Father Pollen, the R.C. Chaplain, were brought down suffering from very severe and extensive burns of the face, body and limbs. They were so badly burned that one could do very little to relieve them of the pain and shock. Injections of morphine seemed to have little, if any, effect upon them.
>
> As regards dressings, the specially prepared picric acid lint was at first applied, but they could not be kept on owing to the pain causing the patients to tear their bandages off, and they were accordingly dressed afterwards with either boracic ointment or oil. This proved more successful, but the restlessness of the patients all the time they were on board made it a very difficult matter to keep them protected by dressings ... the Bandmaster, one of the cooks (I forget his name) worked indefatigably the whole time in looking after the patients, as did all the Doctors' party stationed down with us. It was no easy job either, as they required constant attention and watching to guard against them hurting themselves through moving about (one could not keep them still even with repeated injections of morphia).(7)

The cause of the burns was witnessed by Walwyn:

> Heard a lot of groaning on battery deck. Went forward to get up fore end when I was told I was wanted at once as there was a bad fire on superstructure. A fragment from the shell bursting by starboard 6 inch gun had come through the roof of the battery deck and actually hit the after 6 inch cordite case containing four full charges. As bad luck would have it they had just given the order to 6 inch to load and the cartridge number had a charge half out of the case in his arms. This box and four others went up, cases actually melted and so fired. Whole of No 6 six inch starboard were frightfully burned and several more on No 5 gun ... Pollen, RC Padre, did very well with wounded being badly burned himself.(8)

One of the badly-burned seamen died on board and two others in hospital subsequently. Surgeon Ellis pays particular tribute to Father Pollen who:

> ... sustained his burns (face, hands and legs), through helping to rescue the men of the gun's crew who were on fire from the

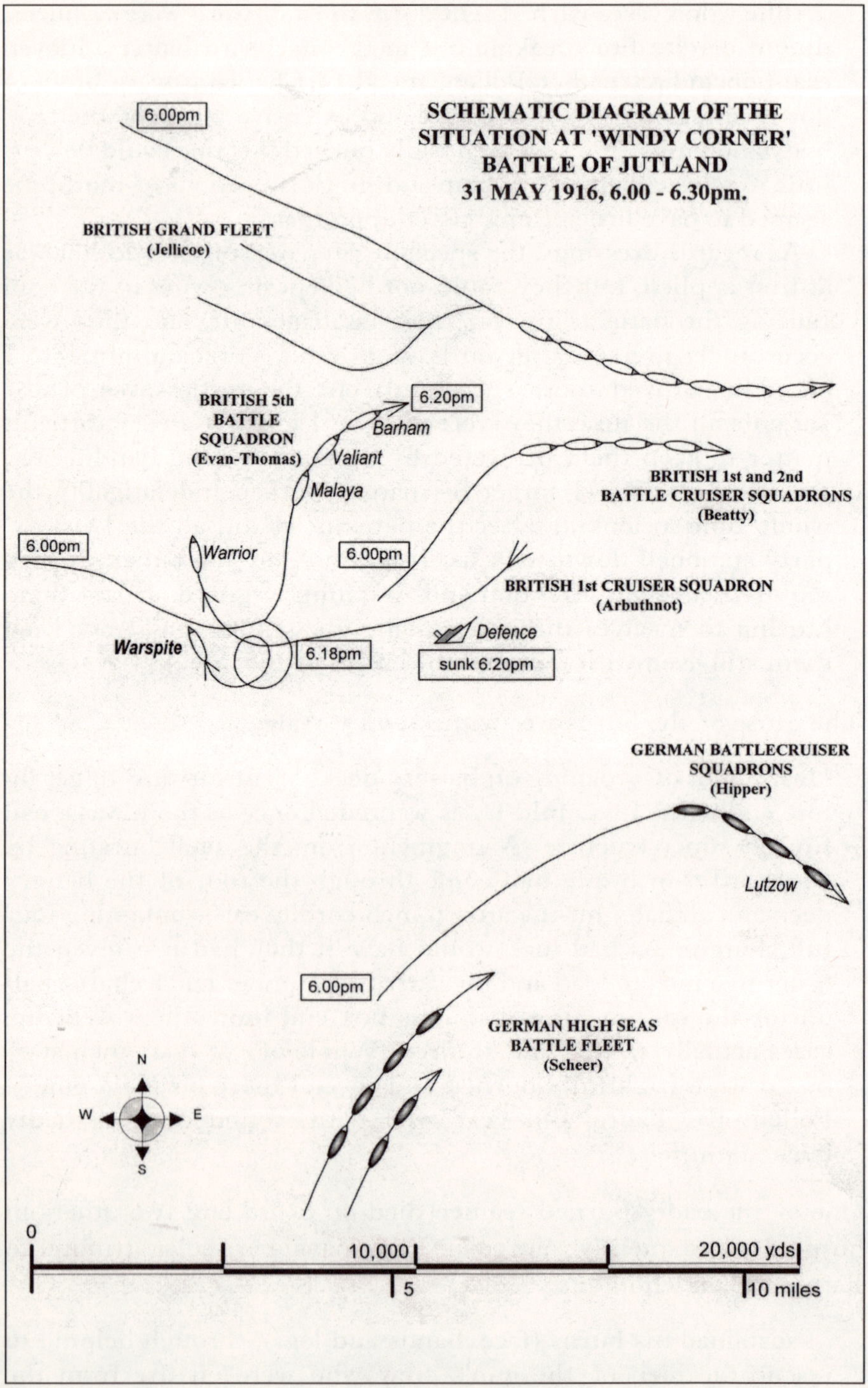
SCHEMATIC DIAGRAM OF THE
SITUATION AT 'WINDY CORNER'
BATTLE OF JUTLAND
31 MAY 1916, 6.00 - 6.30pm.
6.00pm
BRITISH GRAND FLEET
(Jellicoe)
BRITISH 5th
BATTLE
SQUADRON
(Evan-Thomas)
6.20pm
Barham
Valiant
Malaya
BRITISH 1st and 2nd
BATTLE CRUISER SQUADRONS
(Beatty)
6.00pm
Warrior
6.00pm
BRITISH 1st CRUISER SQUADRON
(Arbuthnot)
Defence
Warspite
6.18pm
sunk 6.20pm
GERMAN BATTLECRUISER
SQUADRONS
(Hipper)
Lutzow
6.00pm
GERMAN HIGH SEAS
BATTLE FLEET
(Scheer)
N
W
E
S
0
10,000
20,000 yds
5
10 miles

> cordite. He is 56 years old, but stood the shock well, and at no time whilst he remained a patient on board uttered any complaint that he was suffering. He received the D.S.C.* for his action.(7)

Father Anthony Pollen was a much-respected member of the ship's company and a man of great ability and experience. Although self-effacing and retiring by nature he could and did stand his ground. On first reporting to Captain Philpotts on *Warspite* he had been met with: 'I hope that we shall get on, but I think it fair to tell you that I don't like Catholics'. To which Father Anthony replied: 'I am sure, Sir, that we shall get on, as to be candid, I detest Protestants'. (14) Apparently they did get on and played golf together during the short intervals of shore leave at Scapa.

In contrast to the catastrophe that had befallen the starboard 6in battery, Midshipman Fairthorne, writing later for the magazine of his old school on experiences from the opposite side of the ship, reported that:

> My station during the action was the port six inch battery. These guns, which form the secondary armament of the ship, were not fired at all, the range being too great for their effective use ... I had nothing to do at all the whole time, except help with the hoses whenever a fire broke out.(11)

Perhaps in deference to the youth of his readers, Midshipman Fairthorne, who had been a fellow schoolboy himself only three or four years earlier, spared them the horrors of what had occurred on the starboard side of the ship. He did however have one sad note to impart on the fate of another old boy:

> We were extremely sorry to lose one of our best [Sub-Lieutenant F.A. Single]. He was at Grange with me and always did his best to give any help with my work on board. I was talking to him as 'Action' sounded, and he was in the best of spirits. He was buried with the rest who fell with him on our arrival at the home port with all honour and respect.(11)

Surgeon Ellis, with no young readers to consider, was more specific and records in relation to Sub-Lieutenant. Single's death:

* Distinguished Service Cross.

> Another large shell burst in about the same place (as the one which badly injured Chief Stoker Pring), striking Single in the abdomen and killing him instantly, and blowing another man to pieces.(7)

In this hour of horror there were to be moments of humour. One man in particular, the Fleet Paymaster, without action station duties and roaming the ship, was to be both the focus of some hilarity and a steadying influence. Commander Walwyn noted:

> Had a cigarette the port side of cooks lobby or rather started one to steady my feelings. Had a yarn with the Pay who was wandering about in a 'kapok' waistcoat using appalling language as to when the Grand Fleet were going to turn up. Had a laugh together anyway.(8)

The Fleet Paymaster had also acquired a reputation for luck:

> He wandered about all over the ship during the action, and everytime he moved on somewhere else for a change it appeared that a shell came in just where he had left. He was up in the wardroom lobby during part of the time when we were being badly 'strafed' later on, and some marines who were there also called out to him to come into the gunroom where, they said, 'you can see them splashing fine, Sir!' They had lifted up one of the deadlights apparently. The Paymaster's reply was 'No blooming fear, I don't want to see the damn things. I'm going down below whatever!' Before doing so however he told the half-deck sentry who was, though a trifle scared at his exposed position, still solemnly perambulating up and down the lobby, the Major having forgotten to relieve him, to come down out of it also. He came!(8)

The Marine contingent, part of the make-up of the crew of all capital ships of the time, do seem to have been a pretty phlegmatic lot. Walwyn found in one part of the ship:

> everybody was very cheery and anxious for news which I couldn't give as I hadn't the faintest idea what was happening, marines of port six inch supply were playing cards on the deck quite happily.(8)

The Executive Officer must have found the crew's steadfastness and the moments of levity a blessed brief relief from the continuing personal horrors he met when undertaking his damage assessment and control duties. His account of that day is littered with fragments of horror and fear. He found:

> Three stokers were dead in voice pipe flat, one having his head blown off and another badly smashed to pieces, rather a horrible sight but the burnt ones were far worse.(8)

When surveying the damage caused by a hit above the waterline on the port side he found that:

> Looked very bad as a large triangular piece had been blown out ... about a foot above water. The fresh water and oil fuel tanks had been blown to pieces and everything in an awful state of dust, oil, fuel and filth ... Men trying to plug the hole but tons of water was coming in and washing them back all the time. As it was all oil fuel they looked like a lot of goldfish, swimming about. A marine passed the remark 'This will mean a drop of leave'. Tried for a bit to plug and shore up with hammocks, but it was hopeless, as the force of the seas was tremendous. Decided to fill the whole compartment with hammocks and started a strong party filling the whole show chock full of them. It eventually took nearly six hundred hammocks to fill it up which effectively stopped it but not till late that night.(8)

Although they were not to know it, *Warspite* and her crew were now reaching their time of supreme danger. Once again fickle fate was to intervene and favour 'lucky' *Warspite*. Throughout the engagement *Warspite* and her sister-ships had been continuously manoeuvring, seeking to gain positional advantage and bring their collective broadsides to bear whilst avoiding colliding with each other. Beatty was also endeavouring to draw the now joined-up enemy fleets towards Jellicoe's rapidly approaching force. It was during such a manoeuvre, and almost at the time of HMS *Defence*'s ordeal, that fortune was to frown, and just as quickly smile, on *Warspite*. Captain Phillpotts' personal account simply records:

> At 6.18pm course was altered to the northwards, following the motions of *Barham* and *Valiant*; but as we were apparently closing *Malaya* I ordered 'Port 20', and then the steering engine started to give trouble.(6)

Midshipman Fairthorne's account succinctly puts the context and consequences of the trouble:

> It was during a manoeuvre that we were troubled with the steering gear. Instead of following the next ship ahead to port, our helm jammed, causing the ship to swing to starboard and turn a complete circle. This caused us to close the enemy and for twenty minutes the *Warspite* stood up to the concentrated fire of the five enemy battlecruisers. When they had eventually steamed out of range, our engines were stopped and the damage made good temporarily. But we were out of action, and had a heavy list to port.(11)

The Executive Officer's account gives more detail. After again checking on the continuing damage – and particularly that near to the waterline on the port side – Walwyn received a message that the Captain wanted to see him at once.

> Captain asked me how things were and I started to tell him. He said 'I don't care a damn about the damage, can we join the line? I hadn't the faintest idea what the situation was or what had happened and must have seemed a bit queer. Anyway I said 'If she gets another hit [on] the port side I don't think she will stand it' I was thinking of the wing engine room hit! I did not know anything about the steering gear having jammed ...(8)

The Executive Officer was later able to piece together 'cause and effect' of the jamming, as he explains:

> The Steering Gear episode was rather extraordinary. The hit by the port wing engine room had buckled the after bulkhead of the centre engine room on which the steering engine is secured. This gave it a hot bearing and it was labouring heavily. When turning to port to deploy astern of Grand Fleet we were very close to and inside *Valiant*. Captain did not think we could turn safely and gave the order 'Port 20' to swing under *Valiant*'s stern. Quartermaster got a bit 'rattled' and forced the wheel too quick which overrode telemotor gear due to the engine lagging with hot bearing. Having got a swing out, order was given 'Starboard 20' and they could not get more than 5 degrees starboard on, ship had therefore 10 degrees port helm on and completed the circle twice, turning through 32 points towards the enemy's fleet. She was checked at the end of second circle by going astern port and

> brought out [of the circling] by screws. The whole [German] leading division concentrated on us and we got very heavily hit and everybody thought we had gone. Huns thought so too, and ceased firing, luckily for us, but they no doubt could not see us for splashes, spray and smoke.(8)

It was fortunate for *Warspite*'s crew that the enemy, moving out of range and being distracted by the attentions of the other 5th Battle Squadron ships and the timely arrival of Jellicoe and his Grand Fleet, curtailed the onslaught. The plight of *Warspite* was indeed dire; according to the Executive Officer's itemised survey she had received thirty-one damaging hits, of which at least thirteen were from heavy calibre 11- and 12in shells. It was later estimated that about half of the heavy hits were received at what was to become known as 'Windy Corner' during her circulations. It was not only the enemy who thought *Warspite* was done for; Lieutenant-Commander Tovey*, on the destroyer *Onslow*, herself badly damaged in the action involving *Defence* and *Warrior*, and seeking to make her own way home, was heartened by the sight of:

> *Warspite*, apparently stopped in a forest of water spouts, doomed as it seemed to destruction, but replying to the enemy's fire with all her guns – an inspiring sight for the lonely destroyer.(6)

On *Warspite*:

> Down below all we knew about it at the time was that the ship suddenly took a list to port, and instead of righting herself as she would have done had it been an ordinary turn, kept keeling over indefinitely ... as it persisted we concluded that she had been hit heavily somewhere ... and it was the beginning of her going right over. The PMO† and I, I remember, looked at one another, for we were both, I think, certain that she was going, but after an appreciable length if time the list stopped, and she gradually got back on an even keel again.(8)

Captain Poland, Royal Marines, in command of 'X' 15in turret, also thought that his ship might be finished:

---

* Later to become Admiral of the Fleet Lord Tovey of Langton Matravers, and Commander-in-Chief of the Home Fleet.

† Principal Medical Officer.

> Just then our troubles started. The hit aft appeared to have upset our steering gear and we careered out of line heading towards the enemy ... The others of course went on and we had to take all that at least a couple of divisions of the High Seas Fleet could give us. I gave up hope of seeing Rosyth again then. They hit us and hit us damned hard. Beautiful salvos, fired in ripples, and three out of five guns hitting ... (12)

Because of her gyrations, co-ordinated director-controlled firing from *Warspite*'s guns was not possible, and the four 15in turrets were put under local control. This put extra responsibility on the gunnery officers. Poland later wrote:

> I couldn't get anything from X turret so went into local control. Then I couldn't find the enemy – I could see his splashes and feel them all over us but I couldn't see him. I started training around but apparently the ship was turning the other way. My second officer was howling for permission to fire at something, but I refused to do so until there was something visible to fire at especially as just about this time I was under the impression I only had a round or two left as I thought my magazine was flooded. Altogether it was a most unhappy period. I got a report that my magazine was shot through, so I ordered the crew out and told them if there was any danger of fire - to flood. Then I went down and found that it was only the compartment above that was full of water, so we got the crew down and went on, keeping the cordite dry with tarpaulins over the hopper. The N.C.O.s were very good indeed. They stood fast with one or two men until I came down although they had a lot of smoke down from above. ... We had about a quarter of an hour of this hammering and then the Grand Fleet arrived. I've never been so thankful for anything in my life.(12)

Warspite's gyrations were to prove a fortuitous godsend for the armoured cruiser *Warrior**. Heavily damaged when her sister-ship *Defence* had been literally obliterated, she received much needed respite from enemy fire when the *Warspite*, a much more attractive target for the German gunners, circled helplessly around her. Some observers interpreted this, in a legend that persists to this day, as an

* With the enemy fire concentrated upon *Warspite*, the seaplane carrier HMS *Engadine* was able to take *Warrior* in tow. However she was too badly damaged, and sank the following day when still some 160 miles east of Aberdeen.

extremely gallant attempt on the part of *Warspite* to deliberately draw the enemy fire away from the stricken *Warrior*. In fact it was an involuntary consequence of the jammed steering. Surgeon Ellis confirms this:

> It was at this time that the '*Warrior* incident' occurred. Our circling brought us into a position close to the cruiser, between her and the enemy, ... they had been having a rather unpleasantly hot time of it, and thought apparently that our circling was done purposely in a chivalrous attempt to take the fire away from them on to ourselves. It is a pity to have to say this but our movements just then were entirely unpremeditated.(7)

Warspite was now stopped, not making way.

> I remember noticing that we were stopped and then he [the Captain] gave the order 'Half speed ahead both' ... Went below and was at the port side hits again when I got a message asking could we go sixteen knots and I said 'Yes' or it may have been 'What speed can we go' and I said 'sixteen.'(8)

Captain Philpotts reported to Admiral Evan-Thomas, on *Barham*, on *Warspite*'s damage, defective steering and reduced speed capability, requesting the present position of the battlefleet which he obviously wished to rejoin. His Admiral however clearly decided that her damage and defective steering would make *Warspite* more of a handicap than a help in any further co-ordinated fleet actions, particularly should these actions continue into the night. It was now early evening and Evan-Thomas ordered her back to Rosyth. For *Warspite* the battle, but not the danger, was over.

For her crew the fortunes of fate had smiled unequally. While the majority were to emerge unscathed, at least physically, some had died instantly and some slowly and in great pain. Some had suffered severe wounds and others slight knocks. Included among the latter was the young Chessman, who years later wrote in his account of how, although he couldn't remember it happening:

> ... my hands were covered in blood and I was also bleeding freely from a gash on the right side of my neck ... Incidentally these were not afterwards classified as wounds. They continued to be dressed for a whole week and were clinically termed 'abrasive weals'. I couldn't have cared less.(2)

He was young and had survived his first battle.*

Others perhaps would have welcomed a slight knock as a clear manifestation of their involvement in the great battle of Jutland:

> Jack Ingle fell down a hole in main deck and cut himself which raised a good laugh. The joke afterwards was that he called himself 'wounded' and wore a gold (wound) stripe till it was forcibly removed by Gun Room.(8)

As the battle moved away from them, the crew took stock of their plight:

> We were moving through the water slowly, at about six knots, heading back towards Rosyth, and there was no ship in sight, or noise of firing, anywhere. There was still a dull red glow from the sun left in the sky, low down, but it was very hazy, and impossible to see any distance. The sea was still calm ...(7)

The ship was a shambles but still seaworthy:

> As regards the ship it is difficult to say what one's feelings were on looking at her. Only a few hours before she had been one of the cleanest and smartest looking ships in the fleet, her decks spotlessly white, and her light grey paint, freshly put on only recently, gleaming everywhere in the sunshine.
>
> Now her decks were filthy, littered with debris and in places torn up by shells, one of the quarter deck ladders had been blown away, her funnels had ragged holes in them, the small iron ladder on X turret had been bent and twisted ... whilst the side of the turret was covered with marks from glancing hits, and the general appearance was in about as absolute a contrast to what it had been before as well could be ...The damage fortunately, was on the whole more spectacular than real. She was afloat, and barring bad weather perfectly seaworthy.(7)

'X' turret, where Captain Poland, R.M., had found such difficulty in trying to engage the enemy during *Warspite*'s desperate gyrations, had taken something of a pasting:

---

* Fortune was soon to frown on John Chessman. Shortly after Armistice Day, November 1918, arguably as a consequence of his Jutland experiences, he developed neurasthenia, a form of nervous debility, and left the service in 1919. He suffered ill health for a number of years. In 1955 he had three operations for laryngotomy which thereafter rendered speech very difficult. Nevertheless he lived, showing great courage and resolution, for a further eighteen years. He died in January 1974.(15)

> 'X turret had a direct hit, looked like an 8 inch, right hand side ... but no damage whatever inside, in fact they did not know they had been hit.(8)

Below decks the damage was extensive and serious. *Warspite* was badly holed, many compartments were flooded and fires were still being brought under control, but, provided the weather held over the next few hours, the consensus was that she would make it back to Rosyth.

By now it was approaching nightfall, the crew were tired and hungry, and reaction to the events of the day was starting to set in:

> Tried to 'darken ship' as best we could, but the holes everywhere made this rather hopeless; plugged with canvas and deckcloths ... Had a talk with Guns. Leeke and Simmonds and we arranged to start big parties trying to get water out of the various compartments, but everyone was feeling the reaction a bit and decided to leave things until daylight. Kept 6 inch section and two [15in] turrets manned and lay down for a few hours.
>
> By this time one felt one wanted something inside, so repaired to the wardroom, found they had got some food of some sorts going, sardines and a tinned tongue. Had a brandy and soda, biscuits and cheese; everybody very cheery.(8)

Boy Sailor Chessman had dined earlier. During the height of the battle fellow signalman George Sault, a Canadian, had occasion to come up to the exposed platform to greet Chessman with:

> I thought it was warm down below but jeez, it's bloody hot up here. They did ask me to come up to give you a bloody medal but I thought you'd sooner have this corned beef sandwich instead.(2)

He was right; Chessman had not eaten since first coming on watch hours earlier.

Throughout the night watches the crew worked to shore up bulkheads, try to stem the flooding and generally tidy up the ship. Gradually things were got more shipshape and, with daylight, confidence grew that they would make it home.

> One could feel she was sluggish, owing to her flooded compartments ... and any sea was bound to put the strength of her structure to a severe test. Still she was a Devonport ship, and the

> Eng. Commander after a thorough investigation of every part of her had been able to report that she was absolutely alright, and capable of maintaining any speed that was required of her up to the full power of her engines. We had increased to sixteen knots during the night ...(7)

Life on board had started to return to normality:

> In the morning the wardroom servants came and laid the tables for breakfast as usual, there being no longer any reason why the ordinary amenities of civilisation should not be observed, but the sight of white tablecloths amidst the somewhat dishevelled surroundings* and individuals did look a little incongruous.(7)

The long journey home was not to be without incident, and daylight found *Warspite* steaming at 18 knots on a zigzag course for Rosyth. In anticipation of the British ships leaving their ports to do battle, the Germans had placed a line of submarines across their path. Although one of the U-boats made an abortive attack on a screening cruiser, they had failed to intercept the main body of British ships. They had however remained on station, hoping to ambush the returning ships when they would be perhaps less vigilant after their long hours of battle. Warned by the Admiralty, the British ships were aware of the danger. Thus:

> About 7.00am, Captain sent for me and said he was certain we should be attacked by submarines, and to do all I could to get everything as ready as possible. Got upper deck 6' crews closed up and went on getting rafts, etc. built ... About 9.00am two torpedoes were fired at us, one missed across the bow, the other followed up astern alongside the starboard side. We increased [speed] to 21 and zigzagged all the time. Decided to get all the wounded out of after medical station and close all doors on the ship.(8)

While this decision to shut all the doors in order to prevent further flooding and their probable sinking in the event of them being struck by a torpedo was the correct one, particularly in view of the state of the seriously damaged and already part-flooded ship, it must

* A 6in shell had come in through the ceiling of the wardroom and out through the side, demolishing the wardroom table and wrecking the stove, armchairs and piano.(8) The piano was subsequently sold for £6 in Dunfermline as a souvenir of the battle.(7)

have been a shock to the crew, reminding them, especially those stationed below decks, of the danger that they were still in. Those below would be only too aware – and some had seen with their own eyes only hours before – how quickly a ship could sink or even explode when hit hard enough in a vulnerable spot. Their chances of escape from a closed-up ship would be minimal should such a catastrophe happen to them. For Surgeon Ellis, therefore, the news of the near miss of the torpedoes and the resulting order to evacuate the wounded and shut all watertight doors:

> ... was a new complication and had the effect of making me feel I wanted to go up on deck at once – for what reason I don't know – but the P.M.O. went on writing with his usual imperturbability so that for sheer shame I felt bound to stay also.(7)

The torpedo attack had been a close run thing, submarine *U 51* had only narrowly missed her target. Further submarine attacks were attempted as the morning wore on:

> About ten opened fire on a submarine on port quarter, range about 600 [yards]. Port 6' fired about eight rounds at periscope. McDonald swore he saw conning tower and so did the gun layer ... About 11.45, submarine came up about 50 yards on port bow; if we had not been steering from the engine room we might have got her, but it took a certain interval to get through*. The foremost 3 pounder could not get sufficient depression to fire as she passed.(8)

The strain of the present predicament and the stress of the last twenty-four hours were now taking their toll of the crews' nerves. Walwyn again:

> This forenoon was I think, about the worst part of the whole show as everybody was very much on edge. Even Peter and Bill had a barging match and everybody was irritable.(8)

Such was the danger from submarine attack that Captain Philpotts had requested a screening escort to meet them, but it was not until 13.30 that six torpedo boats came out from Rosyth and joined them. Once in position, they had the greatest difficulty in carrying out

* i.e. to communicate from the bridge to the engine room.

their escorting task since *Warspite*, despite the damage to her hull and innards, and still on a zigzagging course, had by now worked up to a speed of some 23-24 knots.

Without further incident *Warspite* and her crew passed under the Forth Bridge at about 15.30, some forty-eight hours after leaving, and went immediately into the dry dock vacated by the *Queen Elizabeth*. She was so flooded that she was drawing 35 feet 6 inches aft at the time instead of her usual 31 feet. But *Warspite* was home with her crew, who shared a feeling of relief:

> ... and we came safely in. I am bound to say I heaved a sigh of relief as we passed the bridge, and the cheers from the troops made one feel quite gulpy.(8)

For others the memory of the homecoming was that it had been less than welcoming. Midshipman Fell remembers that:

> I don't think we gave any thought to how we would be received at home. But as we passed up the Firth of Forth and under the bridge, all the railway people were lined along it. To our dismay they shouted 'Cowards! Cowards, you ran away' and chucked lumps of coal at us. We were received at Rosyth with very, very great disapproval by the local people. They were all in mourning black hats and black arm bands. They all felt that the Great Fleet had suffered a complete defeat and that some ships, like the *Warspite*, had run away. That was the news that had reached Scotland and it was twenty four hours before things got better, when the other ships returned and more facts were known.(14)

Because *Warspite* was uninhabitable the crew were put up in barracks and other ships, in particular the *Queen Elizabeth* and *Dreadnought*, both of which had been completing a refit and thus missed the battle. Surgeon Ellis was found a cabin on the *Queen Elizabeth*:

> ... and I went to bed that night surrounded by every conceivable luxury, even to a large box of his own chocolates which Middleton brought up and put alongside my bunk for me to help myself to in case I shouldn't sleep. I did though, although I felt so wide awake until I got between the sheets that Middleton had to force me to go and turn in.(7)

The crew had all shared in an unforgettable forty-eight hours. Young Chessman had watched the wounded being evacuated to waiting ambulances and then the dead carried from the ship:

> Each litter covered with the Union Jack and borne down the gangway by sorrow stricken comrades. After the last had departed a huge slice seemed to have been cut out of all our lives.(2)*

For Surgeon Ellis, older and more mature, the feelings were no less poignant:

> Next morning I went and had a look all round the ship as she lay in dock, and it may have been emotional, but I felt I just loved her. And I think now that there is no other ship like her.(7)†

By the time that *Warspite* was docked and the rest of the British Fleet was making its way home, the German Fleet was already back at its bases. It had been a complex and drawn-out battle that was to provoke great controversy for a good many years over its conduct and consequences. At its simplest level of interpretation, the Battle of Jutland can be divided into three phases. In the first, the contest – between Beatty's battlecruisers, supported by the four battleships of the 5th Battle Squadron, and Hipper's battlecruisers – had gone the Germans' way. The British had lost *Indefatigable* and *Queen Mary*, although on paper they should have overwhelmed their opposing forces. In the second phase of the battle, which began with the arrival on the scene of Scheer's High Seas Fleet and Beatty's run to the North in order to draw the German ships onto Jellicoe's Grand Fleet, *Warspite* had been disabled. She had been ordered home at about the time of Jellicoe's arrival and the opening clash of the main fleets at about 18.20 to 18.30. The situation was by then very confused; not only were the capital ships slugging it out, but the lesser ships, cruisers and destroyers, were also enjoying their

* They were all buried at Dulmeny and Queensferry Cemetery, West Lothian. The dead included two civilian Canteen Assistants, both from Devonport, employed by the Admiralty for work on board ships.

† Surgeon Ellis, following medical training, joined the Navy in 1912 and held sea-going appointments on a number of ships, including HMS *Warspite*, and ashore in R.N. Hospitals. He was mentioned in dispatches for his work on the Russian convoys in 1944-5, before retiring after thirty-four years service, with the rank of Surgeon Captain. He then took up general practice in the National Health Service in Leicester and Devon before finally retiring to Cornwall. He died in 1970.

own affrays, seeking the opportunity to finish off crippled opponents or launch torpedo attacks, or to fend off similar attempts from their opponents. As Jellicoe was later to report to the Admiralty:

> The whole situation was so difficult to grasp, as I had no real idea of what was going on and we could hardly see anything except the flashes of guns, shells falling, ships blowing up, and an occasional glimpse of an enemy vessel.(16)

Although fortunes fluctuated during the manoeuvring, cut and thrust, ebb and flow of this naval duel, collectively the German ships were now starting to feel the weight of the British superiority in ships and firepower. They were getting the worst of it and suffering heavy damage if relatively little loss of ships. In the final, night action, phase Scheer skilfully extricated his fleet from a deteriorating position, allowing their escape and leaving Jellicoe and his now combined fleets in command of the North Sea. The Germans had left the field early and thus forfeited the game, but it was an inconclusive and from a British point of view a disappointing outcome. It had not turned out to be another Glorious First of June for the British Navy; it was not a clear-cut victory in the manner of Trafalgar, but it was decisive in determining the future conduct of the war at sea.

Both sides had fought hard and fought well, had made mistakes and suffered heavy losses in ships and men. In material and human terms the British had come off worst but had the numerical superiority in ships and men better to withstand the losses. Just as the Germans had won the opening round of the sea battle, so they won the opening round of the propaganda campaign. The Admiralty had immediately imposed a blackout on news of the battle:

> ... censorship clamped down on one and all. We were allowed to send just one postcard with only two letters on each, these were O.K ...(2)

The *Times* of 2 June, reporting the initial official release under a column heading 'Great Naval Battle – Heavy Losses', reflected the scarcity of information and increased the nation's foreboding:

> The British ships on which the brunt of the fighting fell were the Battlecruiser Fleet and some cruisers and light cruisers supported

> by four fast battleships. Among these losses were heavy. The German battlefleet, aided by low visibility, avoided prolonged action with our main fleet, and soon after these appeared on the scene the enemy returned to port though not before receiving severe damage from our battleships.(17)

In contrast to the negative nature of early British releases, German communiqués, particularly to newspapers in neutral countries, were buoyant and positive. Thus the next day's *Times*, of Saturday 3 June, quoting from a Special Correspondent in the Hook of Holland, gave its readers the news that:

> The German papers are rejoicing over what they describe as the sea battle of the war. Germany is beflagged and jubilation is unbounded ... the [German] Fleet has inflicted a victorious blow on the mightiest fleet in the world.(18)

The correspondent went on to report the surprise expressed in the Dutch papers that, although the German communiqué had been issued some twenty hours earlier, no British communiqué had yet appeared, particularly as the German Fleet, if completely victorious as claimed, had been the one to retire from the battle. The Dutch papers also observed, rather mischievously, that

> It was expected that the result will make a great impression in England as it was always supposed there that the German Fleet had only to appear to be wiped out.(18)

The early German reports claimed that the *Warspite* had been sunk. Later reports conceded that some of their ships has been considerably damaged, while Copenhagen sources reported that the greater part of the German Fleet had returned, but dispersed and severely damaged.

Over the next few days the true position, and the veracity of the various reports, was to become clear. By Monday 6 June the Dutch view was that Germany had not gained much by her characteristic attempt to 'rush' neutral opinion by her claims of a crushing victory over the British Navy. The British may have received a nasty shock, but German losses were also severe and the results of the battle were far less serious for the British.

In the final tally the German side lost the pre-dreadnought battleship *Pommern*, the battlecruiser *Lützow*, four light cruisers and five destroyers. On the human side they lost some 2551 dead. The British lost the battlecruisers *Invincible*, *Indefatigable* and *Queen Mary*, the three armoured cruisers *Defence*, *Warrior* and *Black Prince*, one light cruiser and seven destroyers. 6097 British officers and men died, 5069 of these on the five large ships which blew up. Besides the actual losses many ships on both sides were badly damaged, but at the end of the battle Scheer had only ten undamaged dreadnoughts to Jellicoe's twenty-four. All the damaged British ships were back at sea within two months, but it took six months for all the German ships to be repaired and fit for service.

Warspite, although among the worst damaged of the British ships, having received some thirty-one hits, thirteen of which were from heavy-calibre shells, escaped relatively lightly in human terms, losing one officer and fifteen men killed, including the two civilians on board, and four officers and thirteen men wounded out of a crew of just over a thousand. She had fared better than many of her fellow ships in the battle; her sister-ship *Barham* lost twenty-six dead and thirty-seven wounded. Repaired and replenished, *Warspite* returned to the 5th Battle Squadron and was back at Scapa Flow on 23 July.

After the excitement of the battle, sober reflection took over. The country was becoming disillusioned with the conduct of the war and disappointed in the performance of its Navy. In France a slogging stalemate had set in, the Battle of Verdun had already lasted over three months and the horrors of the Somme were yet to come; on the Russian front things were not going at all well; and the attempt a year earlier by the Navy to force the Dardanelles, in order to put Turkey out of the war and relieve the Russian allies, had ended in bloody failure and the resignations of Churchill and Fisher. There was a mounting crisis over both the supply and quality of munitions – the shell crisis – and Government leadership was leaving room for criticism. On the very day of the Battle of Jutland the *Times* Parliamentary Correspondent had observed:

> On the eve of a Parliamentary recess of three weeks duration the P.M., Mr Asquith, was confronted today with a somewhat incongruous task. He had to ask all those in munitions areas – both munitions workers proper and others – to defer their Whitsun holiday until later in the year, ignoring the example Parliament its about to set.[19]

On the Home Front, the Zeppelin raids and shortages brought about by the increasing U-boat offensive against allied merchant ships were starting to cause concern.

The one perceived saving grace, the bulwark of the Nation, had been the Navy which now felt the post-Jutland disappointment and was in turn dismayed. Even within the Navy things were not well; there was to be much concern over the coming months, and indeed years, about the design and hence vulnerability of its battlecruisers, the quality of its gunnery and shells, its communications and the co-ordination between the Admiralty and the Fleet, and the collaboration between its senior commanders at sea. For the Navy it was a period of low ebb. There was a feeling, totally unjustified, of self-reproach among the sailors that they had let everyone down at Jutland, that they had not repaid the Nation's faith in them. Life on board ships of the Grand Fleet returned to something like wartime normality, even tedium, and boredom with the generally poor weather conditions and lack of leisure facilities at the northern bases.

Under such circumstances sailors have traditionally tried to overcome any boredom and to make the best of things, and on occasion of course have been known to overdo it. Such an occasion was that described by Midshipman Fairthorne, which shows how the *Warspite* dealt with such domestic matters:

> A man charged with drunkenness complained that someone had added alcohol to the fresh water tank. In commiserating with him, the Executive Officer ordered the ship's police to arm him for sentry duty during his leisure hours to prevent such a lamentable recurrence.(11)

Life on board *Warspite* was never boring for long; only a month after rejoining the Fleet she was again in trouble. On 24 August 1916 it was the turn of the *Valiant* to receive the embrace of her sister-ship. As described in the account of the recently qualified and promoted, at seventeen and a half, Signalman Chessman:

> A few weeks after our return we were detailed to carry out ... night target practice within the confines of Scapa Flow in a portion of the waters reserved for that purpose. Everything concerning the exercise itself was carried out without anything

> amiss occurring. Our return to the anchorage however once more summoned up the Jonah which seemed to permeate *Warspite*'s very bowels. ... I was on the upper deck and off watch as we returned to our anchorage when I saw the unbelievable. In the dark a huge object loomed up directly ahead on our course. It was just not possible. A few seconds later we hit the obstacle which proved to be our next at anchorage, HMS *Valiant*. We struck her practically amidships and immediately there was feverish activity on both vessels. The accepted drill on one ship colliding with another is for the colliding vessel to maintain as far as possible her position at the end of the contact. The reason for this is to minimise the inrush of water through the breaches of both [vessels] which may have taken place in both on contact. So there we were in the inglorious situation of resting in the guts of one of our sister ships and in harbour too! The *Valiant*'s fuel tanks appeared to have been fractured, while *Warspite*'s long suffering bows were once again stove in. Poor Captain Philpotts. Who by all that is Holy had pushed him overboard this time? He appeared to have aged another ten years, but no angry protestations, no adverse criticism either. Just apparently renunciation [*sic*] to being in command of the Jonah of all Jonahs.(2)

The consequences were to be serious. Both ships were considerably damaged and *Warspite* had to go back into Rosyth dockyard for two months of repairs, returning to the Fleet on 28 September. The subsequent Board of Enquiry blamed both ships equally and the Admiralty ordered both Captains to be tried by courts martial on charges of hazarding their ships. Both were found guilty and sentenced to be reprimanded. Although the sentence on Captain Philpotts was annulled on grounds of a technicality, it is the view of the naval historian Roskill(6) that the latest collision, coming on top of the earlier mishaps and misdemeanours of the ship, effectively ruined the future career prospects of *Warspite*'s first Captain. On 19 December 1916 Captain Philpotts was relieved of his command of *Warspite* and replaced by Captain C. M. de Bartoleme.

As always for the crew of *Warspite* it was a time of mixed fortunes. While the end of 1916 saw the effective ending of the career of her first Captain, the beginning of 1917 brought an upward step to the illustrious career of another *Warspite* stalwart. On 1 January 1917 her Executive Officer, Commander H.T. Walwyn, awarded the

D.S.O.* after Jutland, was promoted to the rank of Captain. He was eventually to gain a knighthood and attain the rank of Vice-Admiral.†

1917 was to be significant year both for the progress of the war and in the increasing disillusionment of its protagonists. On the Eastern Front the Russians were faring badly. A series of military setbacks, increasing civilian hardship and dissatisfaction with the conduct of the war led to rebellion, the collapse of its war with Germany, and the October Revolution. This easing of its Eastern Front commitment allowed the German High Command to concentrate upon its Western Front and the continuation of the bloody stalemate in Northern France. Although America had entered the war on the Allied side in April 1917, its ultimately decisive injection of fresh men and material was not to reach full flood until later in the year.

In contrast to the action and excitement of the previous year, 1917 was to be a period of continuing post-Jutland disillusionment for the Navy. The sailors, especially those of the Grand Fleet, perhaps felt that they had lost their premier position in the hearts of the Nation. Understandably the British people in 1917 were more concerned with the actions and sufferings of her soldiers in Northern France than the inactivity of her sailors in northern ports. Any disillusionment with the Navy was further fuelled by the ongoing, and at times quite acrimonious, debate in Government, naval circles and the press on the leadership and conduct of the war, continuing retrospective analysis and counter-argument on the lessons of Jutland, concern over the increasing U-boat menace and the somewhat belated introduction of the convoy system to protect the ships bringing supplies to Britain. The year culminated in the abrupt dismissal on Christmas Eve 1917 of Jellicoe, promoted to First Sea Lord after Jutland only eighteen months before.

For the Grand Fleet it was a year of tedium with the ships alternating between bases at Scapa Flow and Rosyth. There were some sweeps in the North Sea covering Scandinavian convoys, and there was a minor collision between *Warspite* and a destroyer on 11 June,

* Distinguished Service Order.

† Vice-Admiral Sir Humphrey Walwyn; Governor of Newfoundland from 1936 to 1946.

but this was not, by *Warspite* standards, anything to speak of. But there was no action, no rematch against the German High Seas Fleet also languishing in its home ports. It was now to be a supporting role for the British Navy, protecting the transportation of food, war supplies and troops across the High Seas and the English Channel, not set-piece fleet actions with her capital ships.

There was another factor inhibiting Beatty, now in Command of the Grand Fleet, from more aggressive efforts to tempt out the German High Seas Fleet for a rematch. For many months there was to be a critical shortage of heavy-calibre shells as civilian munitions factories worked long hours to meet the demands of the army in France, and to replace the stocks of suspect shells which had proved to be less effective than German ones at Jutland. Ironically, one of the causes of declining morale among British sailors was their poor pre-war rates of pay, and the consequent financial hardships of their young families at home in comparison with their civilian neighbours, enjoying the fruits of their much better pay and overtime opportunities in munitions factories. The general unrest about pay and conditions in the Navy did eventually result in the Autumn of 1917 in a number of improvements for the lower deck sailors, but pay was still abysmally low compared to civilian rates. There was, for example, a 2d a day increase for Able Seamen rising to 5d a day for Chief Petty Officers. At the lowest level, the pay of an Able Seaman was still only one shilling and ten pence (1s 10d) per day. It was the first real increase in basic rates since 1860.

The smouldering unrest in the Fleet of 1917 was to be replaced on *Warspite* in early 1918 by another form of smouldering – and another mishap. On 7 February the Vice-Admiral commanding the 5th Battle Squadron hoisted his flag on *Warspite* and took up residence. He was soon to be introduced to the foibles of his flagship. This time it was to be ordeal by fire. According to the 1 March diary entry of Midshipman H.C. Burton:

> This day, but for a very kindly Providence, might have been *Warspite*'s last. A fire broke out in the Port Wing Engine Room. I had to relieve decks and at 7.45 I saw both funnels smoking and I wondered if we were raising steam. I happened to look forward again about five minutes later and all the forecastle deck was obliterated with what was obviously oil fire smoke, thick and oily.

> I thought nothing of it for the moment until the Q.M.* said 'Fire, Sir, Fire' and I then realised that the smoke was pouring out amidships. Officer of the Watch went and reported to the Captain who asked 'How do you know there's a fire?' Fire stations were sounded off, and being Extra Midshipman of the Watch I went round to call officers. Carter refused to believe me and turned over to go back to sleep again. Smoke was now pouring out of the Port Wing Engine Room Exhaust and the heat below was so intense that the exhaust fumes which came out by the pinnace burnt and blistered the paint on that boat. Hoses were soon turned on, both on deck and in the W.E.R.[(20)]

Fortunately the fire was under control by 08.15 and the crew carried on to breakfast. Two men had to go to hospital with smoke inhalation and others received minor burns. It took a gang of twenty dockyard mateys and *Warspite*'s emergency repair party a month to repair the damage and clean up the mess. The repairs, together with a refit at Rosyth, kept *Warspite* out of action until 6 May. On 3 June Captain de Bartelome was relieved of his command and was replaced by Captain H. Lynes.

The war was to drag on until the Armistice of 11 November 1918. Then, on 21 November, the remnants of the German High Seas Fleet – nine battleships, five battlecruisers, seven cruisers and some fifty destroyers – arrived off Rosyth to formally surrender and be interned. The German Fleet, including *Warspite*'s Jutland opponents, emerged slowly from the early morning mist to be met by intimidating columns of British ships. Beatty had under his control at that time 370 ships and some 90,000 sailors. When abreast of the German ships the Grand Fleet turned, by squadron, through 180 degrees and formed up on either side of their recent enemies to escort them into captivity. It was intended as a show of strength and of humiliation. The comparison between the victor and the vanquished could not have been more striking. The victorious ships were at 'Immediate Readiness' with all ensigns flying and guns trained outboard. The vanquished fleet, disarmed with breech blocks left behind in Germany, the ships dirty and rusting, was in a sorry state. There had been mutinies throughout 1918 in the

* Quartermaster.

German ships and ports, and the crews were demoralised, unkempt and mutinous.

By noon the whole fleet was anchored in the Firth of Forth when Beatty made the signal 'The German flag will be hauled down at sunset today, Thursday, and will not be hoisted again without permission.'(6) It was a momentous day for the sailors of both fleets. As recounted by Boy Sailor Frank Dandy, born in 1902:

> I remember it well. We stood lined up on the deck of the *Barham* when the German Fleet sailed in. We were next in line to the *Warspite*. She was a good ship, the *Warspite*, but not as good as *Barham* mind.(21)

The surrendered fleet eventually moved into permanent captivity at bleak and wintry Scapa Flow. It was to be a short captivity. On 21 June 1919, in a well-organised conspiracy, the German High Seas Fleet was scuttled at its moorings under the noses of its captors.

CHAPTER 3

The Inter-War Years

The change from war to peace brought inevitable changes for the Nation and the Navy and for *Warspite* and her crew. On 7 April 1919 Beatty's Grand Fleet was decommissioned and the two principal fleets of the reorganised Royal Navy became the Home (or Atlantic) and the Mediterranean Fleets. *Warspite* served in the Home Fleet from 1919 to 1926, she and her *Queen Elizabeth* class sister-ships formed its 2nd Battle Squadron. The overall Commander-in-Chief was Admiral Sir Charles Madden who had commanded the 1st Battle Squadron at Jutland. Other Grand Fleet ships were dispersed to various overseas stations to resume their representation of British and Empire interests, and a disposal programme of older ships was begun. The crews were similarly dispersed or disposed of. Reservists and 'hostilities only' sailors returned to their civilian jobs or to unemployment, time-expired sailors were put on reserve, and many regular officers, without immediate prospects of a naval posting, resigned their commissions or went onto half pay. For those sailors who remained there was continuing lower deck unrest in the immediate post-war years over pay, which was still far below civilian rates. For those posted to *Warspite* it was a time to get acquainted with her foibles and her layout.

One stalwart who remained on *Warspite* for a number of years after the war was Father Pollen, now recovered from the burns suffered at Jutland. *Warspite*, designed with flagship duties in mind, had a suite of five 'luxury' cabins and a walkway over the stern of the ship for the use of the Admiral and his staff. After the war there was a period when she was not a flagship, and hence there was no requirement for the cabins. Out of deference to his age, Father Pollen – the oldest officer by far on the ship, and with his distinguished record and years of service on *Warspite* – was allocated use of the Admiral's suite. One day while sitting in one of the cabins, he heard steps along the corridor as one of the ship's company, a new Petty Officer who obviously did not know his way about this part of the ship, was clearly looking for someone or something. Two or three of the doors of the suite were tried without success, then the fourth one. When the P.O. found Father Pollen instead of the person or article he was seeking he apologised and withdrew, only to be heard by Father Pollen* muttering to himself as he walked away: 'Takes up half the ****** ship, he does'.(1)

After serving in home waters throughout 1919 *Warspite* sailed for Gibraltar with the rest of the Atlantic Fleet in January 1920 to take part in combined exercises with the Mediterranean Fleet. On her return in May, *Warspite* was ordered to the Irish coast in response to increasing Sinn Fein troubles, ready to provide off-shore support and landing parties in support of the authorities. Early in June she embarked a Royal Marine battalion at Plymouth and landed them at Queenstown. Then, when coal and railway strikes broke out on the UK mainland in 1921, *Warspite* was sent on a similar policing role on Clydeside. It was not an easy time for her sailors, many of whom had relatives involved in the civil unrest of the immediate post-war period.

Despite the civil troubles, however, naval routine continued, and the annual Spring exercises with the Mediterranean Fleet became a fixture. It also became a regular feature of the Spring cruise for Father Pollen to organise and conduct parties of Roman Catholic sailors to the shrine of St James the Apostle whenever the Atlantic Fleet visited the Spanish port of Vigo(1). It was during the Spring cruise of 1924 that *Warspite* paid her first visit to Malta. It was to be the forerunner of many such visits and stays over the next twenty

* Father Pollen was a boy at the Birmingham Oratory and, after studies in Germany, joined the Oratory as a priest in 1883 at the age of 23. He joined the Navy in his mid-fifties at the outbreak of the war, and served on *Warspite* for several years during and after the war before returning to Birmingham Oratory, where he served as a priest and member of that community for fifty-seven years. Awarded the D.S.C. for gallantry at Jutland, he was reputed to be a man of great personal ability, but self-effacing and retiring. He was also reputed to have become somewhat eccentric in his later years, insisting on keeping naval hours, and being noted for taking 'early to bed, early to rise' to an extreme, to the consternation of his fellows in the community. He died on 5 October 1940 at the age of 80.

years, as Malta, with its excellent harbour at Valetta and its first-class dockyard and facilities, became the main base and training area for the Mediterranean Fleet, which *Warspite* in the fullness of time was to join.

Returning to home waters in the summer of 1924, *Warspite*, with other ships of the Atlantic Fleet, went on a round of goodwill visits to seaside towns. While these allowed the ships' company local leave and an opportunity to enjoy the civic hospitality of the town, the reciprocal Open Days entailed extra work for the crews. Captain A.B. Cunningham, then in command of a Destroyer Flotilla of the Atlantic Fleet and later to fly his flag in *Warspite* as Commander-in-Chief of the Mediterranean Fleet during the Second World War, records that such 'Hurrah Visits':

> were regarded as part of the amenities for the attraction of visitors, rather like a fun fair. They came on board in their hundreds. We did our best to entertain them and show them round the ships. They left us with our decks dirty, littered with cigarette ends, empty ice-cream cartons and the grisly and gummy remains of shrimps and other edibles in paper bags or cast or crammed into odd holes and corners, even the working parts of the guns.[(2)]

On 26 July 1924 *Warspite* took part, with some 157 British warships plus representatives of other friendly navies, in the first post-war Royal Review at Spithead. Following the Review the *Queen Elizabeth* class of battleships was allocated to the Mediterranean Fleet, with HMS *Barham* as the flagship of the 1st Battle Squadron under Rear-Admiral William Fisher, apparently known in the fleet as 'The Great Grippa'. *Warspite* did not sail with them; after guard ship duties during Cowes Week she was paid off and entered Portsmouth Dockyard for her first major refit. It was to take two years, and was undertaken at a time of considerable uncertainty for the navies of the world largely due to the political manoeuvring of their governments.

For the British Navy there were two major issues, one internationally driven and the other nationally inflicted, that were to be major determinants for its future direction. The first of these was the question of naval rearmament. Following the cessation of hostilities the participating nations were faced with the costs of reconstruction and the return, so far as possible, to peacetime normality. Thus while no country really wanted, or could afford, to engage in another naval arms race such as that which had occurred between Germany and Great Britain in the years immediately prior to the war, equally none of them wanted to be left behind in the post-war pecking order of naval supremacy. The United States in particular was not willing for Great Britain to resume its pre-war position as undisputed master of the seas, with a navy that was superior to that of any other nation – and in any case Britain could no longer afford the costs of outbuilding the United States. Germany and Russia had been eliminated from any immediate naval building contest, but other countries were pressing their claims, notably Japan, who was seen by the United States as needing to have their ambitions in the Pacific contained. Former allies such as France and Italy , with overseas commitments and their own ambitions of empire, equally had to be accommodated in any post-war naval balance.

There was also a growing groundswell of debate as to the future role, and hence make-up, of the nations' navies. The battleship still reigned supreme as a manifestation of naval power, but recognition of the threat to this supremacy from the air and from underwater weapons was starting to gain momentum. There was also a recognition in some naval circles that the days of set-piece, once-and-for-all-battles between major fleets were probably past. No nation could dare risk everything on one naval battle modelled on Jutland. Nevertheless, battleships were still considered to be needed for insurance against aggression, as a deterrent, and as a recognisable signal of a nation's pride, virility and ambition.

An agreement or accommodation, accepted – however grudgingly – by all parties, on the respective sizes and make-up of the major navies of the world was eventually reached at the Washington Conference of 1921. The Agreement was to be a significant influence upon the future of battle ship development and provision. Its main features were: the abandonment of the Anglo-Japanese Alliance and, in effect, a moratorium on developments in naval bases and fortifications in the Pacific region, and an agreement on the distribution of capital ships. Britain, the United States and Japan agreed on a 5:5:3 ratio, with a maximum of fifteen ships each for Britain and the United States and nine for Japan. There was also an agreement to limit the maximum tonnage of all new warships to 35,000 tons and a maximum gun calibre of 16in, with a proviso that the displacement of existing capital ships could be increased by up to 3000 tons in order to accommodate additional defensive systems against submarine and air attack. There was no binding agreement on the prohibition or control over the development of submarines. Over the next twenty years most nations, notably Japan and Germany – who as a vanquished power was not a signatory to or participant in the Washington agreement – were to circumvent both the spirit and the letter of the accord. This was to have serious consequences for Britain and her navy. In hindsight this short-sighted treatment of Germany – neither effectively controlled, nor brought into the framework of international agreements – was a material contribution to her military re-emergence by 1939.

The immediate post-war years and early 1920s, reinforced with the consensus of the Washington Conference, saw the scrapping of some 1.5 million tons of Britain's warships, and the release of thousands of men – mostly into civilian unemployment – under the 'Geddes* Axe' At the end of 1923 the Royal Navy had been reduced to 100,000 officers and men. This was followed, also in 1923, by the introduction by the Government 'Ten Year Rule', as an instrument of policy for the Chancellor of the Exchequer. This laid down, for the spending guidance of Whitehall and the Services, that it was to be assumed that there would be no great war for the next ten years, and that the rule would be extended afresh each year until circumstances necessitated its revocation.

It was against this background of political and economic restraint that *Warspite* went for her first major refit. She had already undergone some minor modifications to her profile, equipment and armament, to meet the new threats of war at sea. There had been an experiment of fitting jagged or toothshaped baffle plates to her funnels and masts to break-up her clean vertical lines and hence to hinder the efficiency of enemy range finding. Her anti-aircraft guns were increased in calibre and number, and for a time she carried a light spotting and reconnaissance aircraft on her two superimposed

* Sir Eric Geddes. Conservative M.P. for Cambridge 1917-22. Among a wide range of public posts, he was First Lord of the Admiralty in 1917-18 and Minister without Portfolio in 1919.

'B' and 'X' turrets. By training the turrets into the wind the aircraft could take off without additional power assistance, from a platform extending to the gun muzzles. It was a contrived and seemingly hazardous enterprise, dreamt up by naval designers wrestling to secure the future of battleships. The spotter plane, once aloft, had the choice of either landing on the sea alongside the ship to be hoisted aboard by crane, or flying on to any nearby land base.

Warspite emerged from the dockyard in 1926 after a two-year refit costing some £1 million, with an unsightly bulge along the length of her hull, a modified bridge and her two funnels trunked into one. The effect of the bulges, intended to reduce hull damage from torpedoes by causing them to explode away from the main hull of the ship, was to increase her beam from 90 feet to 104 feet. The trunking of the original forefunnel into the after funnel was designed, taken together with the remodelled bridge structure, to keep the bridge clear from smoke in a following wind. Smoke interference had bedevilled gunnery observation at Jutland. *Warspite*'s defence against low flying torpedo-carrying aircraft was enhanced by provision for the fitting of the recently-developed eight-barrelled, 2pdr 'Pom-Pom' gun and 4in guns were installed to deal with higher-flying bombers. The sum effect of these changes was to increase both the beam and draft of *Warspite*, increasing her displacement to just over 31,000 tons and reducing her maximum speed by one or two knots.

Warspite was recommissioned at Portsmouth on 6 April 1926 with a complement of 925 officers and men, under the command of Captain G.K. Chetwode. After working-up trials, she was about to leave for the Mediterranean to join the 1st Battle Squadron when the General Strike broke out. The Government responded by, among other measures, dispatching ships to the larger ports and seaside towns in anticipation of breakdowns in law and order. *Warspite* was ordered to Greenock to help safeguard the Naval Dockyard. The crew found themselves in an unusual and difficult position. Lieutenant-Commander Packer, in his second spell on the ship, wrote to his wife:

> What a day we have had. At 7 o'clock this morning we arrived here and were met by a staff officer with orders to land seven parties of various strengths – 350 in all – to guard oil tanks and pipe

> lines and torpedo-factories about ten miles up river. So we crashed up the Clyde in a tug and arrived alongside a small cruiser, the *Comus*, lying in the middle of Glasgow at Prince's Docks. My own party of two platoons of sailors and two of marines have to guard the docks – a big place much bigger than Cape Town Docks. All the food ships are coming in here and being discharged by Volunteer Workers whom we protect. It's fairly peaceful really, an odd bottle or two over the rail and a few words of abuse ... The strikers surround every gate with Peaceful Pickets – they are allowed by law – and they are the most amazingly Peaceful Pickets. Just stand and spit. The Volunteer Workers all seem to be medical students or unemployed ...(3)

Warspite was relieved by HMS *Hood* on Monday 10 May. On 12 May the General Strike collapsed and *Warspite* sailed to the Mediterranean. She arrived at Malta on 20 May and next day became the flagship for the first time of the Mediterranean Fleet, flying the flag of Admiral Sir Roger Keyes*. Flagship duty, providing accommodation and a sea-going headquarters for the C-in-C, was to be one that *Warspite* was to perform on many future occasions.

Malta had been the principal base of the Mediterranean Fleet for well over a century, offering a strategic midpoint position between Gibraltar at the Western end and Suez at the Eastern end of that enclosed sea. It was a vital link in the chain of ports to India, Australia, New Zealand and Great Britain's eastern empire. As a naval base, Malta had deep-water berths and protected harbours that could accommodate the whole of the Mediterranean Fleet. It had a well-equipped dockyard, barracks, hospitals and medical facilities and sports grounds. It also offered the attractions of Valetta and Sliema. A popular destination for the off-duty lower deck was Strada Stretta, otherwise known as 'The Gut', in Valetta, the capital town of the islands. Although less than a quarter of a mile long, this Mecca of off-duty servicemen was notorious for its dance halls, bars and brothels. As alternative attractions for the less adventurous, or the financially straitened sailor, there were the White Ensign and the Vernon, two clubs close to the jetty in Grand Harbour

* Later to become Admiral of the Fleet Lord Keyes of Zeebrugge and Dover.

which provided cheap meals, tombola and overnight accommodation.

For the officers, Malta was a much sought-after posting; life in the Mediterranean Fleet could be most congenial in the 1920s and 1930s. Married officers, particularly those of higher rank or independent means, were usually able to have their wives join them. The cost of a sea passage from England was only £10 and hotel or rented accommodation was readily available, as were servants at low wages. Some of the richer officers lived and entertained on the grand scale. Socially, for the officers there was membership of the Union Club in Valetta, the Sliema Club and the racecourse at Marsa. When the fleet was in harbour during the winter months there was a constant round of tea dances, drink and dinner parties.

A typical evening for the off-duty unaccompanied officer of the period would be as described by Lieutenant-Commander W. Andrewes*, then the torpedo officer on *Warspite*:

> This evening I dined in the *Revenge*, very early, with the Carnes and then went on to their concert show, given by their ship's company at the Carradine Theatre. It was quite amusing and I only dozed off for a very few moments, but William Carne went completely to sleep and had constantly to be prodded by his wife.(4)

For all ranks, participating in sports of all kinds was almost a religion. For the lower deck there was much inter-ship competition in football, cricket, boxing, hockey, watersports and sailing. For the officers there was golf, tennis, horseracing and polo – especially polo when Admiral Keyes was Commander-in-Chief. He actively encouraged his younger officers to take up the sport; the cost of hiring a pony was only five shillings a chukka – half-a-crown for midshipmen. Many officers had their own mounts, since both the horses and their stabling and feed were cheap in Malta. The Commander-in-Chief brought out his own string of ponies from England – Fame, Lurcher and Warwick – all named after ships that he had commanded or served on in his early career. He also formed a four-man team called The Centurions, named after the battleship HMS *Centurion*, his last command as a captain before attaining flag

* Later Admiral Sir William Andrewes.

rank. Although the composition of the team varied with availability, a regular player was Lieutenant Victor Crutchley* who had gained the Victoria Cross on HMS *Vindictive* during the 1918 Zeebrugge raid led by Admiral Keyes. Lieutenant Crutchley was later to become a distinguished Captain of *Warspite*.

While sport was an important element in the Mediterranean Fleet's inter-war annual round of fleet manoeuvres, ships' exercises and diplomatic visits to foreign ports, it was not the only competitive occupation. All activities, both in port and on the seasonal cruises, were intended to ensure that the crews kept up their morale and efficiency. Every ship's crew was keen to be the smartest looking ship, first to hoist 'evolution completed' at the end of some particular fleet exercise or drill, 'cock ship' in the frequent regattas, and to have the best concert parties.

In early June 1928, Admiral Keyes ended his term as Commander-in-Chief. It was also time for changes on *Warspite*; she was replaced by *Queen Elizabeth* as flagship of the new Commander-in-Chief, Sir Admiral Frederick Field. *Warspite* became the flagship of the First Battle Squadron, flying the flag of Vice-Admiral Sir John Kelly. His Chief of Staff, and the new Captain of *Warspite*, was Captain J.F. Somerville†. Besides the Admiral and Captain there were other colourful characters among *Warspite*'s officers at this time, as a newly arrived cadet was to vividly remember:

> We boarded the battleship *Warspite* by the port after gangway. The starboard side was strictly the preserve of the Admiral. We 'fell-in' on the quarterdeck and Brian Goodenough being the senior cadet of the group reported 'six cadets come aboard to join, Sir.' We were taken to our chestflat where we unpacked our trunks and tin cases and stowed our gear in sea chests which were rather more battered than at Dartmouth.
>
> We were given rather less than the customary twenty-four hours in which to 'sling our hammocks', but finding myself free for a brief period in the afternoon, I innocently wandered on to the quarterdeck with my brand new telescope, steadied myself

* Later Admiral Sir Victor Crutchley, V.C.

† Later to become Admiral of the Fleet Sir James Somerville. Commander of 'H Force' based at Gibraltar, 1940-2, and Commander-in-Chief, Eastern Fleet, 1942-4.

> against an awning stanchion and started to scan the scenery. Suddenly there was an anguished rather high pitched bellow 'Mister bloody cadet, do you think that stanchion is put there to decorate your arse? F*** off'. The voice was that of Lieut.-Commander Patrick Archdale, our dreaded 'Snotties Nurse', who was responsible for the training, discipline and general behaviour of some twenty-four midshipmen and us six cadets. ... The Commander was 'Hooky' Walker, a colourful character who had lost an arm at the Battle of Jutland and wore a silver-plated hook which he waved to great effect to emphasise an order. He was held in great awe and affection by all and sundry.(5)

The one thing that did not change among all the comings and goings was *Warspite*'s nose for mishaps. Captain Somerville, popular, good humoured and with a buoyant forceful personality, liked to 'cut a dash'. Making an impression, or 'pulling a stunt', was all-important in the inter-ship rivalry of the Mediterranean Fleet, but there is a thin line between cutting a dash and courting disaster. The Fleet had been exercising out of a harbour on the island of Skiathos in the Aegean. There were two entrances, one wide and easy to navigate but involving a longer route to and from the anchorage, the other, though offering a shorter route, narrow and poorly-surveyed. The easy route was the one usually taken, but on 12 July 1928 Somerville, in pursuit of the spectacular, decided to take *Warspite* out by the narrow alternative. No obstructions were shown on the chart. Nevertheless *Warspite* struck a submerged rock and was badly damaged. Admiral Kelly's flag was transferred to *Barham* and, surprisingly, Captain Somerville took over command of the new flagship. In the ensuing enquiry the officers in command at the time of the mishap were acquitted of blame as the charts in use, based on a survey carried out forty years earlier in 1887, were deemed 'imperfect'. *Warspite* was forced to return to Portsmouth for repairs and most of her crew were paid off. She was recommissioned in late January 1929 but, because of turbine trouble, did not sail to rejoin the Mediterranean Fleet until 14 March 1929.

Among the new members of her crew were four young midshipmen, fresh out of Dartmouth on their first seagoing posting. One of them, Hubert Fox, lording his newly acquired naval know-how in a letter to his parents, describes a typical day:

On an ordinary day when neither On Watch, Pocket Boat or duty Cadet, one turns out at 06.15 or 06.30 and does rifle drill or P.T. (physical training). Then at about 06.50, the junior cadets (i.e. ME) start putting Bluebell on the brightwork in the gunroom. Actually, in my case, I am employed scraping paint off a scuttle (A scuttle is not the thing coal is kept in, but the nautical name for porthole or window). It has about six layers of paint with putty underneath which has been there since the beginning of time so it does not come off easily. We scrape it off so that there will be more brightwork for us and our successors to clean in the future.

At about 07.35, or when you think fit, you go and shift into uniform and if possible shower yourself down with a sponge. Breakfast at 08.00 and then at 09.00 divisions, or not sometimes. After that we all start work for the forenoon (nautical term for morning). Work is rather a general term: it includes all sorts of things, seamanship, navigation and nauticalities of all sorts, not necessarily sitting down in a gunroom. This lasts until about 12.00 when we have dinner (nautical term for lunch). But the ink in that pen has finished, so I have to continue in pencil.

At 1.15 (1315) we start again, working, which stops at 3.30 (1530) for tea. Then we go ashore until 7 or 7.15 when we clear up the gunroom. Then we dress for dinner and try to cold shower ourselves. Dinner at 7.45: then there is a signal exercise at 9. After which, turn in if you like; otherwise play cards or read. I am nearly always turned in by 10.30 or before.(6)

Light-hearted though the letters home were, they could not disguise the demanding nature of much of the training. Thus, early in February 1930:

Any moment this morning I will have to go away in my cutter, in sole command, to pick up torpedoes which we are about to fire. It is a fairly rough sea. The only objection to this performance is the fact that all the officers watching on board shout conflicting orders (That was my impression the last time I did it).(6)

A fortnight later Midshipman Fox found out, literally at first hand, how physically hard seagoing duties could be:

Being lowered in the sea-boat last Wednesday I caught my hand in the disengaging gear I think and smashed it to pulp. However

> I had to pick up two torpedoes from a destroyer and bring them back to the ship. When alongside the purchase bust and another one had to be rove so that altogether it was about an hour before we were hoisted in and I was treated. All that was very unpleasant.
>
> The miracle of it was that no bones were bust; it was bruised and cut about out of recognition. The end of one finger completely off (and nail) and another one much the same. I was told by the sick bay that I missed £2,000 and having to find another job by a fraction of an inch.(6)

One suspects that the young sailor was rather proud of his injury received in the line of duty. But there were pleasures as well as pain. *Warspite* had gone to Alexandria, Egypt, in early January and there was an opportunity for a little sightseeing:

> On Sunday I went up to Cairo by train. We went through the delta country which grows cotton with great success. Cairo was very interesting. I visited the Pyramids, the Sphinx, the Bazaars and the Museum. The Sphinx was disappointing, there were too many people about and too many advertisement hoardings.(6)

The Spring cruise of 1930, 'to show the flag', took *Warspite* to ports in the South of France. Proper behaviour at Ship's Dances, put on to entertain the more prominent citizens of the host towns, was part of the training curriculum of young officers. The young midshipmen obviously thought it necessary to add their own twist:

> We make certain that there aren't any wallflowers at Ship's Dances by having a competition , the prize a bottle of champagne for the midshipman who dances most often with the ugliest woman.(6)

In May *Warspite*, who had again become fleet flagship on 18 November replacing *Queen Elizabeth*, returned to Malta for a few days clean-up, prior to taking home the Commander-in-Chief, Admiral Sir Frederick Field, on his promotion to First Sea Lord. The flagship at this time was a particularly happy and efficient ship; as Lieutenant-Commander Andrews noted in his diary of 2 May:

> Things really run well in this ship and the ship's company are very happy. They behave very well and are great workers on the

whole. My torpedo division are the pick of the whole lot. Of course they should be so, as they are all carefully picked men with outstanding ability. I do everything I can to encourage a superiority complex amongst them, which I think is good for them, as if they believe they are smarter and cleaner and more efficient than any other part of the ship, they will become so and remain so.(4)

Perhaps the happiness of the ship's crew, and their imminent return to the United Kingdom, engendered an 'end of term' lightheartedness which affected even the normally punctilious senior officers. Thus *Warspite*, anchored at a buoy in Grand Harbour, was taking on stores, including potatoes, from small boats or dghaisas for the journey home. The Commander, W.H.G. Fallowfield, was pacing the deck as Duty Officer, when Midshipman Fox was startled to observe:

> He throws a potato at a dghaisa. The men in it all stand up and shout at all the other dghaisas and a little war ensues, while the Commander, very much the Commander, struts up and down the quarter-deck.(6)

Preparation for their return home continued. On Sunday 11 May 1930:

> Routine was a bit early this morning and the Vice Admiral came aboard to walk round the ship and inspect the Divisions and say goodbye. He, Admiral Kelly*, is very sphinx like and never makes a polite remark during his inspections. As a result we were rather pleased when he stood up on the quarter deck at the end of his visit and made several really pleasant remarks on the ship. He said he was sorry we were leaving the First Battle Squadron and that during our time here we had led in everything; smartness, discipline, efficiency and sport. He said that we had set an example for the rest of the Fleet, etc., etc. All very nice, especially from a man who never says anything that he does not mean.(4)

At 10.00 hours, Monday 19 May, HMS *Warspite* left for home, via Gibraltar. Her departure, as recorded by Midshipman Fox, was a ceremonial and emotional occasion:

* At that time commander of the 1st Battle Squadron, Mediterranean Fleet, to which Warspite belonged.

HMS *Bryony*, with HE the Governor on board led the way: an escort of eight picket boats and barges guarded our flanks and the Prime Minister (of Malta), in a tug, followed astern. On passing Baracca a salute of seventeen guns was fired. Both breakwaters were crowded with friends and relations fluttering handkerchiefs, and several cheering parties were fallen in. As we passed between the breakwaters, feeling very important, all the sirens of our escort hooted goodbye. When clear of the harbour we manned ship on the port side and steered towards the Fleet, who were coming towards us in perfect line ahead. We passed them on our portside at one cable's length. The Fleet was composed of five battleships (First Battle Squadron), four 'County' class cruisers (First Cruiser Squadron), four 'C' class cruisers (Third Cruiser Squadron), HMS *Cairo*, the First, Second and Fourth destroyer flotillas, HMS *Douglas*, and three submarines. There were over forty ships altogether, and the line stretched for ten miles. Each ship in turn cheered the departing Commander-in-Chief.(6)

Warspite arrived in Portsmouth on 26 May. In July she again did guard duty at Cowes Regatta Week, where Midshipman Fox was roped in to help crew a Mr Davies' private schooner *Westward*, competing in the Royal London Club race.

Mr Davies is a very strong personality who believes in driving his men the whole time. He keeps up a continual flow of words. Lord Jellicoe was sailing with us. He is a little man, quite at home with everyone, talking with us as if we were his equals. I actually had the distinction of seeing him with practically no clothes on as I was in the cabin with him when he shifted*. There are not many people who have seen Jellicoe in his pants.(6)

In the Autumn of 1930 *Warspite*, now part of the Atlantic Fleet, went to Invergordon for Fleet exercises. After the Mediterranean, the weather off Scotland in October was not to everyone's liking:

Today we should have done long range torpedo firing, but it has been very rough – too bad to pick up the torpedoes – and we have just waited and waited, anchored in mid-ocean, hoping for the weather to moderate. It was the sort of day when everyone got on everyone else's nerves, and we all felt gloomy and snappy,

* Changed his clothes.

> accentuated by a rough sea and a stuffy gunroom, and, worse than anything, all the forenoon a stupid little instructor tried to teach us electricity.(6)

After returning to Portsmouth and Christmas leave, *Warspite* sailed with the rest of the Atlantic Fleet to join up with the Mediterranean Fleet for the annual Spring combined fleet exercises. Late January 1931 found the ship and her crew at Lisbon:

> On Saturday we gave an 'at home' on board for the local aristocracy, 600 people invited and, would you believe it, there were 300 or 400 gatecrashers. Owing to the gatecrashers, of course, the tea ran out lamentably. Every single thing that was eatable in the ship was brought out. They even filled up a soup plate with little breakfast biscuits. This soup plate was seized by a vast lady who sat down in a large armchair and solemnly and systematically finished them all off ... (6)

A few days later the ship's crews started to go down with influenza, perhaps picked up from the guests, invited or otherwise:

> there is an awful lot of 'flu about and violent measures are being taken by all the ships to combat it. We have a rather humorous addition to or daily routine. Twice daily 'Clear lower deck. Hands to gargle'. Then all the hands troop out on to the jetty and gargle – I suppose nearly a thousand at a time.(6)

1931 was to be a year when the Nation was also far from healthy financially. It was a time of world-wide recession. The country had over two million unemployed, with no sign of any economic revival, and August saw the resignation of the Labour Government and the formation of a National Government under Ramsay MacDonald. The country was facing an immediate financial crisis, with a then-considered enormous deficit of over £150 million forecast. Among a range of proposed remedial actions, the May Committee on National Expenditure recommended all-round pay cuts in the Public Sector – civil servants, teachers, police and the armed forces.

The Navy had already felt the draught of the recession. In April 1930 the Admiralty, as an economy measure, had abruptly announced that pensions, given after twenty-two years service, would in future be reduced. Now two alternatives were proposed to implement the public sector pay cuts in the Navy – either an all-round reduction in pay scales, or the application of 1925 rates to all men on the higher 1919 pay scales. The latter proposal caused much concern on the lower decks. Some 75 per cent of lower deck ratings had joined the Navy before 1925 and were on the higher 'protected' pay scales (indeed some veterans of the First World War Grand Fleet were still serving). The financial position of sailors who had enlisted after 1925, when lower pay scales were introduced for new recruits, was already a cause of concern and unrest, particularly among younger married men with families to support. The worst-off were Able Seamen on the 1925 pay scale who had married while still under the age of 25, when marriage allowances were paid. For such sailors, out of a total basic wage of £1 3s 2d (approximately £1.16 in current money), plus 1s 8d (7p) in lieu of rum if an abstainer, an A.B. would have to support a wife and family as well as himself.

On 1 September 1931 the National Government decided, among other measures, to implement the proposal that 1925 rates were to apply to all ranks of the Navy, but no public announcement of this, or of other measures, would be made until the Chancellor's emergency budget to the House of Commons on 10 September. The Admiralty was, however, warned of the proposed changes. The Chancellor duly announced on 10 September that the budget deficit was £170 million. To counter this, 6d (2.5p) was put on income tax, 2d (1p) on petrol and 1d (0.5p) on beer. Teachers' pay was to be reduced by 15 per cent and that of the Police by 7 per cent. For the Navy, 1925 pay scales were to apply to all ranks with effect from 1 October 1931.

The proposed imposition of 1925 rates would produce gross anomalies; it was not a case of equal sacrifices. The announcement, when it reached the ships, was to cause very great anger and understandable concern by the lower deck, where it was considered as a complete breach of trust by an Admiralty which had no regard for its lower rank sailors. For some it amounted to up to a 25 per cent pay cut at three weeks' notice. Officers were only faced with an average 11 per cent decrease.

The Admiralty, which had advanced warning of the likely scale of the cuts, had dispatched a signal, to become known as the 'Warning Telegram', approved by the First Lord, on 3 September to its nine

Commanders-in-Chief – the three base commanders at Portsmouth, Plymouth and the Nore, and the six sea-going commanders of the Atlantic, Mediterranean, China, Cape, West Indies and East Indies fleets. Eight of them received and acknowledged the signal. There was, however, no reply from the Atlantic Fleet. The signal had been received in HMS *Nelson*, the flagship of the Atlantic Fleet, and Rear-Admiral R.M. Colvin, Chief of Staff to Sir Michael Hodges, the Commander-in-Chief, had drafted an acknowledgement and provisional reply, to await the imminent return from leave of the C-in-C. Unfortunately for all concerned, Hodges was taken seriously ill with thrombosis and pleurisy immediately upon his return, and command was hurriedly transferred to Rear-Admiral Tomkinson, the next officer in seniority. It was a time of frantic activity; the Atlantic Fleet was preparing to depart for its Autumn exercises off Scotland the next day. Admiral Tomkinson only briefly saw the Warning Telegram in the mass of detail involved in the transfer of command at such a time and agreed the draft reply. He had no time or opportunity for considered action or consultation with his ships' captains, and decided to wait for further orders on the matter.

The Fleet, now under the command of Admiral Tomkinson flying his flag in HMS *Hood*, departed from its home ports of Portsmouth, Plymouth and the Nore on 8 September, two days before the budget announcements. HMS *Nelson* was left behind in the hope that the sick C-in-C would recover sufficiently to join up later with the rest of the ships. The assembled fleet, less *Nelson*, consisted of the battleships *Rodney*, *Warspite* and *Malaya*, the battlecruisers *Hood* and *Repulse*, the cruisers *Dorsetshire*, *Norfolk*, *York* and *Centaur*, and the minelayer *Adventure*.

Thus the Atlantic Fleet was at sea taking passage to Invergordon and busily engaged on simulated 'Red Fleet *versus* Blue Fleet' exercises when the budget cuts were announced. News of the cuts reached the ships in various ways: by radio on and after 10 September, and from newspapers on the arrival of the Fleet at Invergordon on the afternoon of Saturday 12 September, two days after the budget announcement. The order announcing the cuts, plus the redirected 'Warning Telegram', reached HMS *Hood*, the flagship of the stand-in C-in-C, at about this time. To compound the communication problem the administrative office of *Hood* was closed with the relevant staff on shore leave. The papers were locked away for attention later. The men of the fleet had still not been officially informed of the cuts at this time.Rumour was rife, and morale low, among the sailors. Midshipman Fox wrote home:

> We arrived on September 11th. I landed with our running team after anchoring, but there was a marked lack of enthusiasm among the sailors, an indication that there was something wrong. This year the officers form a group in front and the remainder straggle behind. Last year it was the reverse. That evening one of the sailors in the running team confided in me that there was going to be trouble about the pay cuts.(6)

On the Saturday evening men from the different ships assembled for an *ad hoc* meeting in the canteen ashore. Discussion and argument was heated and disorganised; it was a rowdy meeting, but agreement was reached for a further meeting on the Sunday evening. The midshipmen in charge of liberty boats reported rowdiness and rebellious singing on the way back to the ships, but officers-of-the-watch, wrongly in retrospect, put it down to 'letting off steam on the first night ashore', and took it no further. It was not seen as the forerunner to mutiny.

On Sunday morning a BBC bulletin, received on lower deck radios, gave details of the naval reductions, quoting 'an Admiralty Fleet Order published yesterday', and Sunday newspapers brought on board ships by men returning from church services ashore gave accounts of the pay cuts. The radio report and the newspaper accounts, some exaggerated or containing unwarranted claims, only fuelled the growing groundswell of resentment and air of suspicion on the lower decks. Then men of the Atlantic Fleet had still not been officially informed of the scale of the cuts. On Sunday evening the brooding resentment took tangible form with serious disturbances ashore, and the crew of *Warspite* were to become involved in both its instigation and its suppression. It was a portent of the troubles to come, that were to divide the loyalties of both ships and men over the next few days.

At noon on Sunday 12 September, *Warspite*'s Master-at-Arms reported a rumour of a planned mass meeting ashore that evening to his commanding officer, Captain Baldwin Wake. It was rumoured that the Devonport contingent of *Rodney*, *Adventure* and *Norfolk*, together with the *Hood*, were heavily involved. As *Warspite* had the guard duties for that day, the officer in charge of the evening shore patrol was warned of possible trouble. The early evening ashore was quiet, but as the canteen filled up the atmosphere became more belligerent and unruly, and glasses and chairs were thrown as men vented their anger. Argument and speechmaking against the pay cuts gradually became more focused into a plan for concerted action to strike, and to refuse to man the ships. A further meeting was loosely planned for the Monday, to enable the participation of the other half of the ships' crews presently on duty. Tuesday morning seemed to be the target time for strike action, when the main units of the Fleet were due to leave harbour on exercises. Prominent among the agitators, and later named as the ringleader, was A.B. Leonard Wincott of HMS *Norfolk*.

After a bit of 'argy-bargy' the shore patrol broke up the meeting relatively easily. Although the officer in charge had taken the precaution of sending a request for reinforcements back to the *Warspite*, by the time the Commander, another officer and a duty party of seamen and marines arrived the trouble seemed to have quietened down. *Warspite*'s officers did however identify two or three of their crew who had taken a prominent role in the disturbance, or 'canteen brawl', as it was later described. The canteen was closed for the night, and the men returned to their ships in an orderly manner.

Apart from the report of the *Warspite*'s Master-at-Arms, the Fleet's senior officers and ship's captains apparently had no appreciation or prior warning of the likelihood of serious trouble over the cuts. Although they cannot have been completely insensitive to the growing air of resentment in their ships – and indeed some had privately warned senior officers in the Admiralty of their concern at the likely impact of the cuts upon lower-deck morale – the threat of possible strike action caught them completely off-guard. It was confirmation of a growing breakdown in the traditional relationships between senior officers and their men, which had been taking place since the end of the First World War. The social and economic fabric of the Navy, like that of the country, was changing.

Most of the long-serving senior N.C.O.s and the more junior officers, themselves facing heavy financial cut-backs, were sympathetic to their men. In a letter home Midshipman Fox summarised the weekend disturbances and their context, and the views of most of his fellow officers in daily contact with their men:

> The cuts in naval pay have been announced. In the evening at the canteen ashore there was trouble. The Captain of the *Hood* and our Commander landed with an extra large patrol to keep order. The cuts which hit the men hardest are those of the Able Seamen who entered the service before 1925. Their pay has been reduced from 4/- [20p] to 3/- [15p] a day. All ranks have had cuts, but they have been worked out hurriedly with the result that there is inequality and hardship. ... Of course everybody's sympathies are with the men, except over this behaviour. A lot had entered the Navy on the promise that their pay would not be reduced. An A.B. only got four shillings a day and a very small marriage allowance. An A.B. may be forty and father of several children, so, with only three shillings a day, it means nearly starvation. I don't think you can honestly blame a man for losing his head under the circumstances. It is a 25 per cent cut and no hope of restoration is held out.(6)

Monday began with no obvious continuation of the previous night's troubles. *Warspite*, flying the flag of Rear-Admiral French commanding the 2nd Battle Squadron, sailed without incident, in company with her sister-ship HMS *Malaya*, for sub-calibre firing* exercises in the Moray Firth. Everything appeared normal on the remaining ships.

Mid-morning, Rear-Admiral Tomkinson sent a message to his captains of the Atlantic Fleet ships that the pay cuts were 'to be explained without delay' as soon as copies of the official Admiralty Fleet Order, now being hurriedly duplicated, were received on board. Hoping that things would blow over, he also sent a signal to the Admiralty:

> There was a slight disturbance in the Royal Navy canteen, Invergordon, yesterday Sunday evening caused by one or two ratings endeavouring to address those present on the subject of reduction in pay. I attach no importance to the incident from a general disciplinary point of view, but it is possible it may be

* Firing with reduced charges to lessen the wear on the gun barrels.

reported in an exaggerated form by the Press. Matter is still being investigated.(7)

On *Warspite*, now at sea, Commander Fallowfield, in charge of the previous night's reinforcements of the ship's shore patrol, was conducting his own investigation to assist the C-in-C's enquiry. His manner was not now that of the end-of-term potato-throwing commander of the previous year's carefree days in Malta. This was a serious matter; it could be attempted mutiny. He questioned the three members of the ship's crew recognised by the shore patrol as taking a leading part in the previous night's disturbance: Stoker Thomas Winstanley, Marine Charlie Hall and Telegraphist Stephen Bousfield. Winstanley claimed that he was only advising men not to throw glasses, and had not mentioned pay cuts. Hall admitted that he had been discussing pay cuts but not proposing any mutinous actions. Bousfield also said that he had told men to stop throwing glasses, and advised them that passive resistance was the only way to get anything done about the pay cuts. The men were allowed to return to duties, and *Warspite* and *Malaya* continued their exercises without trouble.

At Invergordon, far from blowing over, the affair was about to blow up. Around mid-day the ships' crews were addressed by their Captains and advised to put any protests through the normal channels. How the normal channels would deal expeditiously with complaints about pay cuts due for implementation in less than three weeks' time was not convincingly explained. Admiral Tomkinson decided not to cancel evening shore leave, partly because he did not wish further to inflame the situation, and partly because he believed that the men could be trusted to let off further steam without any serious consequences. He was to be proved wrong. The men were obviously moving towards more direct action, and a further meeting took place in the canteen on the Monday evening.

It was to be a turning point in a rapidly-changing situation. The men were angry and frustrated, many were drunk, and there was talk of rebellion and plans put forward for immobilising the Fleet. They returned to their ships in a noisy, ugly mood, cheering, shouting, and scuffling amongst themselves. Mutiny was in the air. It was becoming obvious that trouble was planned for the next morning,

Tuesday, when the ships were due to sail on exercise. Admiral Tomkinson, who a few hours earlier had seemed inclined to the view that reports of the trouble ashore were exaggerated, was disturbed by the behaviour of the men returning to their ships; discipline was obviously breaking down. At 23.15 he took the precaution of sending another signal to the Admiralty:

> Further disturbances took place among the libertymen landed at Invergordon this evening. Libertymen have all returned aboard, but there is considerable unrest among a proportion of the lower ratings. The cause of the complaints appears to be the drastic reduction in pay of rates below petty officers who were on pre-1925 scales of pay. Further telegram follows.(8)

By 01.00 on the Tuesday he was very much concerned by reports from his Captains of trouble. For example, on HMS *Valiant*, things appeared to be getting so far out of hand that the Captain of Marines wanted to parade his men fully armed at 06.00 in preparation for serious trouble threatened for the next morning. Admiral Tomkinson sent another signal:

> Having received reports from flag and commanding officers I am of the opinion that it may be difficult to get ships to sea for practice this morning, Tuesday. I have made the following general signal to the Atlantic Fleet in company. Begins: 'The Senior Officer, Atlantic Fleet, is aware that cases of hardship will result in consequence of the new rates of pay. Commanding Officers are to make a thorough investigation and report to me typical cases without delay in order that I might bring the matter at once to the notice of the Admiralty.'(8)

The Commander-in-Chief's message, due to be read out when the men were called for duty in the morning, was to fall on deaf ears; it was too late for mediation. The new rates were to be introduced in three weeks' time and would be in effect when the men returned home from exercises. The married men in particular had not been given an opportunity to discuss the cuts with their wives to try to adjust family budgets. For many, with rent to pay and hire-purchase commitments, there was the real prospect of eviction and repossession of property and furniture. Many of the men feared destitution and family break-up. The Government and the Admiralty had arbitrarily imposed their sanctions on the lower deck: now the sailors would impose their own. There were sufficient men on most of the ships who were determined that the ships would not sail in the morning; they would simply 'down tools' and refuse duty. Rear Admiral Tomkinson decided to carry on with the ships' departures as planned. The sailing schedule was for *Repulse* to sail at 06.30 to join *Warspite* and *Malaya* on firing exercises. *Valiant* would sail at 08.00, to be followed by *Nelson*, *Hood* and *Rodney* in that order. The cruisers would not sail, but remain in harbour for exercises on board ship.

Everything on HMS *Hood*, Tomkinson's own flagship, appeared to be normal when the men fell in at 06.00 and commenced duties. The officers did not know that the crew planned to 'down tools' at 08.00. HMS *Repulse* left harbour at 06.30 without incident. However, mutiny was already breaking out on other ships. On HMS *Rodney* only 75 men out of 1200 reported for duty, and from the *Valiant* came an urgent message that the ship could not sail because stokers were refusing duty. On the *Nelson* a gathering of men was clustered around the port bow cable, preventing the raising of the anchor. Then, around 08.00, some 200 men on *Hood* refused duty. Reports of mutiny or refusal of orders were now coming in from most ships; it was becoming obvious that the ships would not depart according to schedule. Admiral Tomkinson informed the Admiralty, postponed the sailings and recalled the ships on exercise to harbour.

As the day wore on the situation deteriorated. On the cruiser HMS *Norfolk*, which was being seen as the focus of rebellion, the Executive Officer asked the men for a clear statement of their grievances. A.B. Wincott, already noted as a ringleader in the canteen disturbances of the previous weekend, volunteered to produce a collective statement. This was to become known as the 'Mutineer's Manifesto'. It read:

> We, the loyal subjects of His Majesty the King, do hereby present to My Lords Commissioners of the Admiralty our representations to implore them to amend the drastic cuts in pay that have been inflicted upon the lowest paid men of the lower deck.
>
> It is evident to all concerned that this cut is the forerunner of tragedy, misery and immorality amongst the families of the lower

> deck, and unless we can be guaranteed a written agreement from the Admiralty, confirmed by Parliament, stating that our pay will be revised, we are still to remain as one unit, refusing to serve under the new rate of pay.
>
> Men are quite willing to accept a cut, which they the men, consider in reason.(7)

Admiral Tomkinson informed the Admiralty of the grounds for the unrest in the flurry of signals now passing between London and Invergordon. A copy of the manifesto was smuggled to a *Daily Mail* reporter in Invergordon, on to his editor and then on to Captain W.E. Hall, the Labour MP for Portsmouth North. The mutiny was now starting to come very much into the public domain, with lurid newspaper accounts, emergency questions in the House of Commons and the start of a serious run on the pound in world markets.

Admiral Tomkinson was worried as to whether the three recalled ships would obey orders, but they returned in proper order in the early afternoon. Their return was to evoke pride in one ship's officer and shame in another. From a later letter of Midshipman Fox on *Warspite*:

> The ships out exercising came in on Tuesday p.m. by special order, and, although it was in working hours, as we passed *Nelson* and *Valiant* their hands were on the forecastle yelling at us. In other words, discipline had broken down. Our ship's company behaved perfectly.(6)

From the *Valiant*, Lieutenant Elkins, who had been in charge of the Monday night shore patrol observed:

> *Warspite* passed, hands fallen in. Ours on the forecastle. We sounded alert*; for a moment there was silence, then our sailors gave three cheers. Few naval officers could have felt more ashamed. I noticed that neither the Captain or the Commander came onto the upper deck.(7)

By now an impasse had been reached. The sailors had 'downed tools' and effectively immobilised the Atlantic Fleet. Admiral Tomkinson had sent a number of situation reports and signals urg-

* The call as a preliminary to the paying of courtesies between passing ships.

ing an immediate reconsideration of the scale of the pay cuts, and had despatched his Chief of Staff to London to report at first hand to the Admiralty, and the Admiralty was vacillating between appeals to the men's loyalty and demands that discipline be reinstated and the exercises continued. They continued to vacillate for the rest of the day and the following morning.

By mid-day on the Wednesday discipline had seriously deteriorated on some of the major units of the Fleet. With the idle crews confined to their ships and isolated from each other, they made their continuing defiance clear by inter-ship jeering, or cheering, in responses to the on-deck activities on nearby ships. Admiral Tomkinson reported:

> No work on *Rodney*, *Norfolk*, *Adventure*, *Valiant*. Rushton says Devonshire affected by *Hood*, fears work will cease, *Hood* same. Continually subjected to subversive encouragement and abuse from men on the forecastle of *Rodney*.(8)

The abusive catcalling and intimidation was having an effect on ships which had so far played no part in the mutiny. *Malaya*, *Warspite* and *Repulse* had lowered stages over the side in order to occupy the men in painting the ship. The sailors on *Malaya* were subjected to a barrage of abuse; to cries of 'blacklegs', 'You dirty West Country scabs'. *Warspite*'s were similarly abused and work was abandoned.

> The only time we had trouble was the following morning [Wednesday]. About sixty men refused to work. The remainder, who should have painted the ship's side, asked if they could do something else, as if other ships saw them at it their lives would be forfeit when they got ashore. All around us were yelling mobs on the forecastles; picket boats and other boats could not be manned. *Valiant* had to borrow our picket boat for urgent jobs. The Captain of the *Hood*'s own boat was refused him. We heard ugly stories of snotties* being thrown overboard, but maybe they were made up. In any case things were very serious and at the back of our minds hovered the very ugly word 'Mutiny'.(6)

During the afternoon there were some signs that the mens' collective will for rebellion was crumbling. Some ships' Captains ordered

* Midshipmen.

a 'make and mend', effectively a free half day. This was something of a gamble which paid off, with many of the men electing to go to sleep rather than go to the forecastles and join the groups of cheering or jeering men. Midshipman Fox records the positive lead being shown by the crew of the *Warspite*:

> Our ship's company did a splendid thing at 13.15 on Wednesday. They were piped to fall in for work on the port side of the Boat Deck i.e. the side not visible to the other ships. Every man jack fell in, and voluntarily, on the starboard side in full view of the Fleet.(6)

Even on the rebellious *Hood* the mens' mood was changing: around 17.00 hours a complete engine room watch fell in for duty. On most of the ships, however, there was still a very strong mood of mutiny.

Finally in the late afternoon the Admiralty, caught between the men and the Government, came to a positive decision. It ordered all ships to return to their home ports forthwith, to enable investigation of their complaints with a view to their alleviation where it was found to be necessary. The signal was relayed to the ships and their crews. Then the doubt arose as to whether the ships, collectively or individually, would accept the olive branch and obey orders. There were grave doubts among officers of all ranks. The Commander-in-Chief signalled the Admiralty: 'I am not sure that all the ships will leave as ordered but some will go.'(8) Admiral Tomkinson was not alone in his doubts about the Fleet's response. Midshipman Fox's letter sets out the misgivings of his fellows:

> The Fleet was ordered to disperse to home ports. Until the last minute we did not think *Valiant* or perhaps *Hood* and *Rodney* would be able to put to sea. However they did.(6)

The departures were not without incidents and stubborn resistance from pockets of still-mutinous sailors. The captain of the *Valiant* had to order his Captain of Marines to clear the forecastle using armed force if necessary, and men on the *Hood* had sat on the anchor cable, at risk of serious injury, to prevent the raising of the anchor. However, the sight of *Warspite* departing finally dowsed the fire of mutiny in Admiral Tomkinson's flagship, and she began her journey home. At around midnight Admiral Tomkinson was able to signal to the Admiralty:

> Atlantic Fleet ships have all sailed from Invergordon except HMS *Centurion* which is boiler cleaning and will sail with the HMS *Shikari* at 1100 tomorrow, Thursday.'(8)

The mutiny had lasted for thirty-six hours, from 06.00 on Tuesday 15 September to 18.00 on Wednesday 16 September. Its repercussions were to last much longer.

After the rebellion came recrimination and retribution, as Government, Admiralty and Press sought solutions to the national financial crisis and scapegoats for the mutiny. The consequences of Invergordon were to be far-reaching. The run on the pound had been very serious. The world at large still regarded the Royal Navy as a major bastion of Britain's power and prestige, and to read in the international press of mutiny among its sailors had helped shatter confidence in Britain's financial state. On Monday 21 September the Government was forced off the gold standard and the value of sterling plunged by 20 per cent. The same day the Government, as part of a reassessment of how to deal with the financial crisis, cut back on its proposals for the reductions in public sector pay.

The letter from Midshipman Fox to his parents, written from *Warspite* at Portsmouth on the same day, succinctly sums up the situation:

> It was announced today that the cuts in pay for the Police, Defence Forces and London Schoolmasters were to be 10%. There are a few special cases. This seems a fairly sensible way out of the difficulty. It admits that a mistake was originally made in having the sacrifices greater in some cases than in others. The Cabinet was probably so busy that it did not foresee the results of its first announcements. Had it done so it would have saved the Navy from a serious disgrace and would have prevented the flight of money from London which followed the announcement abroad that the British Navy had mutinied.
>
> It is worth mentioning that no more than three or four thousand men had a share in the unrest at Invergordon and there are 96,000 men in the Navy as a whole.(6)

The Government of the day, with a general election looming, was looking to draw a line under the affair. In the House of Commons Sir Austen Chamberlain, whose wife Ivy had launched *Warspite*, and who had only taken up the post of First Lord of the Admiralty nineteen days before the start of the mutiny, announced that there would be no recriminations against those who had taken part in the mutiny:

> The past is past. It is in the interests of everyone in the Navy – and out of it – to forget it. I am not going to look back. I am going to look forward and I count confidently on the traditions of the service and of the men of today to loyally uphold them.(8)

He also complimented Admiral Tomkinson on his handling of the situation:

> The Admiralty have already conveyed to him [Tomkinson] their full approval of the action which he took and of his service during these times. The compliment is well deserved and will be well-received by the men of the Fleet.(8)

They were fine words from the politician, but in the Admiralty the cutlasses were already being sharpened.

When the ships had returned to their home ports one hundred and twenty ratings, identified as having played a prominent part in agitating or inciting the protest action, were removed from their various ships and confined to naval barracks. Seven weeks later, the day after the General Election of 27 October, two dozen ratings were dismissed from the Navy 'Services No Longer Required'. 'S.N.L.R.'. does not count as a punishment, and hence does not require to be promulgated by courts martial. It was a convenient way of quietly getting rid of people considered to be undesirable. Among those dismissed, the only one from the *Warspite*, was Stoker Tom Winstanley.

The Admiralty now needed to regain the confidence of the lower deck; it needed a firm positive hand to rebuild morale. The opportunity came with the resignation of the Commander-in-Chief, Admiral Hodges, on health grounds following his thrombosis. Rear-Admiral Tomkinson could have been promoted, but was passed over and reverted to Rear-Admiral of the Battlecruiser Squadron. Admiral John Kelly, a bluff 'sailors' sailor' popular with the lower deck, was given the appointment of Commander-in-Chief Atlantic Fleet. He immediately set off on a series of fact finding/public relations visits to the major ships of his fleet. *Warspite* was visited at Rosyth where she was exercising in early October:

We have been at Rosyth for three days and are now going on to Invergordon, exercising for a further three days on the way. The Commander-in-Chief called on the ship's company on Monday and was introduced to all the officers. He had a long chat with me, asking when I was getting home again. I felt like saying 'That depends on you, Sir'.

He made a speech to the ship's company, starting off with several anecdotes and then getting serious. He said that two or three months ago the Admiralty had said to him in so many words, 'Sorry, old bean, but we don't want you any more'. He said he turned round and said (pause) 'Well, on second thoughts perhaps I'd better not tell you what I said'.

The serious part was good. He told us that he had been talking for two hours to the King before taking up his command. Among other things the King showed him that his mind was still completely naval and that he understood sailors as well as anyone. He was broken-hearted over the recent unrest. Admiral Kelly then explained that the sailors were absolutely loyal to HM's person and crown, as well as to their officers, but he honestly thought that they had been tried too hard. A sailor, he said, did not mind any hardship, death, or anything else, but if his wife and family were tampered with he put his foot down. I can't get the feeling into this that was behind the Admiral's words, but you could feel that every man was touched. J.D. [Admiral Kelly] was ashore watching soccer matches this afternoon in full Admiral's uniform. He cut a very fine figure.(6)

If reconciliation was to be the Admiralty's approach to the lower deck after Invergordon, then its dealings with some of the senior officers involved bore the stamp of recrimination and retribution. Five months after the mutiny, Rear-Admiral Tomkinson, sailing with his ships in the West Indies, heard in a BBC bulletin that he was to be replaced as Commander of the Battlecruiser Squadron. He had not been officially informed of the decision before the public announcement. Two days later he received two letters from the Admiralty. The first posted carried a mixture of good and bad news. He was promoted to Vice-Admiral, but would only retain his present appointment for a further six months. His replacement had been named. The second letter, one of censure, effectively finished his naval career by putting the blame of Invergordon onto him:

> After making every allowance for the difficult and unusual circumstances in which you were placed, Their Lordships are unable to relieve you of responsibility for a serious error of judgement in omitting to take any decided action on the 13th and 14th September, when dissatisfaction had begun to show itself amongst the men. If the situation had been well handled on those two days, instead of being allowed to drift, Their Lordships consider it improbable that this outbreak would ever have occurred.(8)

On the same day the captain of the *Hood* also heard that he was to be relieved of his command, as well as the captains of the *Rodney*, *Valiant*, *Adventure*, *Nelson*, *Norfolk* and *York*. Their naval careers too were effectively finished.*

Two letters from Captain Roskill, the naval historian who served on *Warspite*, written forty years after Invergordon to the daughter of one of the senior officers involved, contribute other retrospective views of the mutiny. In the first letter, observing that the Mediterranean Fleet had not mutinied at the time of the pay cuts of mid-September 1931, when he was serving at Malta on the battleship HMS *Royal Sovereign*, Captain Roskill wrote:

> I remember very well the long queue of requestmen waiting to place their complaints about pay cuts before the Captain. And I also remember very well how Sir William Fisher† visited every ship in the First Battle Squadron and told the men how proud he was that they had all presented their grievances in a lawful manner and how he himself was fighting to get the worst hardships rectified.(9)

In the second letter, Roskill put the mutiny into an historical context:

> The real tragedy of Invergordon to me is that it gave Hitler and Mussolini encouragement to believe that as the British Navy had

* On the outbreak of the Second World War all the Captains who had lost their commands were recalled to duty from their enforced retirement. Vice Admiral Tomkinson, at the age of sixty-two, was recalled as Flag Officer, Bristol Channel, a shore appointment which he held for three years before finally retiring through ill-health. He lived on in retirement for many years, dying in 1971 at the age of ninety-four.

† Commander-in-Chief, Mediterranean at that time.

been shown to be disloyal they could safely defy this country. And that led to all the diplomatic successes they scored right up to Munich 1938. I am convinced that had Beatty still been First Sea Lord it would not have happened because in spite of his wife's great wealth, he always fought the lower deck battle against the 'Treasury'.[10]

Early 1932 found *Warspite*, after completing her interrupted training schedule and Christmas leave, off the north-west coast of Spain *en route* for the combined Spring exercises with the Mediterranean Fleet. It had been a rough passage through the Bay of Biscay:

> We have now got to Arosa Bay after the most stupendous buffeting. It was by far the worst gale I have ever seen and even opened the eyes of the Captain and the Admiral. The sea was all over the forecastle and both the for'ard turrets; and I might exaggerate a bit and say that it was breaking on the bridge. Actually there were great hard lumps of spray beating on us where whenever there was a big wave. It was a fine sight, *Nelson* ahead of us and *Malaya* astern, pounding up and down. Looking down from the bridge, we saw spray right up by the funnel top and all the guard-rails were bent for'ard and a paravane broke loose from the upper deck. We were pumping for'ard and tons of water got in.
>
> Tomorrow morning we do general drill and can expect some fun with J.D. Kelly. You remember the poached egg one ('Send poached egg to Flagship') at a general drill at Invergordon? Another one was 'Send Butcher with ship's cat'. These signals make people move quickly and laugh.[6]

At Gibraltar in mid-February for a respite from the often arduous training round, it was time for the social round of reciprocal entertaining of the local populace.

> Last Friday some of the gunroom gave a children's party. We had about thirty, most of whose names we did not know. It was a huge success. The table broke in two under the excitement and we turned it into a very successful children's slide. We had two pugnacious small boys to whom we gave boxing gloves, so that they were happy for about half an hour fighting. Then one of them went out on the half-deck and punched the sentry.[6]

Warspite returned to Portsmouth from her combined spring exercises in March; it was also the time for Midshipman Fox* to leave the ship. *Warspite* left for the Mediterranean again on 13 January 1933 for the usual round of training exercises and 'showing the flag' visits. She was now the flagship of the 2nd Battle Squadron, flying the flag of Rear-Admiral R.M. Colvin who had replaced Rear-Admiral W.F. French in December.

The reports from the Rear-Admiral to the Commander-in-Chief Home Fleet (the Atlantic Fleet having been redesignated 'Home Fleet' after Invergordon), perhaps show that the social round could not be taken lightly by the sailors. They had to be on their toes, and keep their wits about them, if the British Navy's good name was to be restored. Thus on a visit to Tangier:

> 3 February. Arrived at 10.30 according to programme and saluted the country with 21 guns. The simple fact that the ship anchored at the actual time announced was much commented on by the Moors and others, and provided material for comparison with ships of some other nationalities.[11]

The danger of the social gaffe had always to guarded against:

> 5 February. [Admiral] gave a lunch party on board at which [were] entertained the Consul General and diplomatic representatives. Included among the party was Sir Medhi el Menebhi, G.C.M.G., a prominent local Moor and British subject whose prestige in Morocco was considerable. Swathed and hooded in voluminous blankets, his gigantic figure presented a striking contrast in deportment to the remaining guests at the table.
>
> Sir Medhi el Menebhi is an enlightened Mohammedan and accustomed to European manners and customs, but even so it was perhaps an unfortunate incidence that ham featured in the luncheon menu, and that he should have been nearly served therewith. No contretemps, however, occurred.[11]

It seems ironic, or perhaps appropriate, that the next day some of the ship's officers should have been taken on a pig-sticking expedition as part of the reciprocal hospitality of the hosts.

---

* Midshipman Fox had been promoted to Sub Lieutenant. After further training courses he was posted to the cruiser HMS *Danae* in the West Indies Squadron in November 1933. He was then aged twenty-two. He had begun his naval career at Dartmouth in 1925 at the age of fourteen. He ended it in 1946 in command of the new destroyer HMS *Ulster*.

Warspite then moved on to Palma, Majorca, where, in company with HMS *Malaya*, the annual ship's inspection took place. It was spit, polish and sand-stoning of the decks time for the crew. As relaxation they watched the Squadron Boxing Championships, held on board *Warspite*, on the evenings of 15 and 16 February. Then it was more training exercises and back to Gibraltar, where, on 19 March: 'Embarked a wild sow from Morocco for passage to Portsmouth for London Zoo.'(11) The ship was not going to be allowed to forget its luncheon *faux pas*, and the pig was soon to be introduced to the foibles of *Warspite*. Only two days after leaving Gibraltar with HMS *Valiant* on passage home she had yet another collision:

> 21 Mar. 0850. Collision off Lisbon in dense fog with Rumanian S.S. *Peles*. *Warspite* hit amidships. W.R. anteroom wrecked, bulges holed. Effected temporary repairs and proceeded at noon.(11)

While the damage done to *Warspite* was superficial, SS *Peles* fared worse. She was towed stern first into Lisbon by *Valiant* for major repairs.

Not all the peacetime 'showing the flag' visits were confined to the Mediterranean ports. In the summer of 1933 HMS *Warspite*, following short visit to Denmark, paid a visit to Great Yarmouth. The social divide between officers and men was maintained.

> On Monday 20 June, the Corporation gave a ball in the Town Hall which was attended by about forty officers from the ship. On 29 June similarly 150 ratings and their lady friends were invited to a dance in the Town Hall.(11)

Some of the crew were unable to attend the dance, however:

> At about 19.30 on the 29 June a large fire broke out in a fish curing establishment on the River Yare. A fire party of one hundred men was landed and conveyed to the fire by motor buses and motor lorry. At about 03.00 it was clear that the fire was confined to the building itself and that there was nothing left but to allow it to burn itself out, *Warspite*'s party was therefore withdrawn.(11)

After Great Yarmouth, *Warspite* moved on to the seaside towns of Margate, Deal and Eastbourne on the way back to her base at Portsmouth.

While the workday and social round continued, naval policy was changing. Although the London Naval Treaty of the early 1920s, which restricted the construction of new capital ships, did not expire until 31 December 1936, the Government, faced with the growing threat of nationalistic European dictatorships, particularly Germany and Italy, and the expansionist ambitions of Japan, started in the mid-1930s to modernise Britain's existing capital ships and to plan a programme of new building. All the major maritime powers were also modernising and rebuilding their battleships. The U.S.A., Japan, Germany, France and Italy were all to possess new capital ships by the outbreak of war in 1939. Great Britain in 1939 possessed none newer than *Nelson* and *Rodney*, whose keels were laid down in 1923.

HMS *Warspite*, like most of Britain's battleships, was of First World War vintage. She was twenty years old and becoming obsolescent in modern ship terms, and was the first to go forward for modernisation. Thus on 7 November 1933 *Warspite*'s complement was reduced to 40 per cent of normal strength, and on 12 December 1933 squadron command was transferred to HMS *Malaya* at Devonport and *Warspite* moved into Portsmouth Dockyard. She was to remain there for three years.

The previous modifications to *Warspite*, carried out some ten years earlier, while giving her a much-changed appearance, were merely a facelift compared with the major reconstruction that she was to undergo. She was almost completely gutted amidships and rebuilt. The major objective of her reconstruction, and that of her sister-ships of the *Queen Elizabeth* class, was to improve underwater and upper deck protection against mines, torpedoes and bombs. It had to be achieved, and the additional weight absorbed, without sacrificing her speed and hitting power. The 23-knot speed, comparable at her commissioning in 1915 with any capital ship of her day, was now inferior to that of the new capital ships being constructed by foreign powers, notably Japan, Italy and the U.S.A.

The weight savings to allow for the additional protection were achieved by replacing her engines with modern high-pressure boilers and geared turbines; the heavy bridge was replaced with a tower control structure and single mast, and four of her 6in secondary armament guns were sacrificed. Amidships she was given two hangars to house two Walrus observation planes* and a cross-deck catapult to launch them. Her 15in guns were 'cocked up' by increasing their maximum elevation from 20 degrees to 30 degrees. The effect of this was to increase their range, using a new shell with a modified nose profile, from 23,400 to 32,000 yards or 18 miles. The envisaged naval strategy and future role of battleships meant that *Warspite*'s torpedo capability was now obsolete. The torpedo chambers were discarded and the space released used for the stowage of extra ammunition. Four eight-barrelled 'pom-poms' and twin 4in anti-aircraft guns, plus multiple heavy machine guns, were fitted. These were considered adequate defence against air attack, given *Warspite*'s increased armour protection and the capabilities of the aircraft of the day.

The downside of *Warspite*'s modernisation was her increased displacement, now some 32,000 tons. This meant a lower freeboard and resulting wetness and impaired ventilation below decks, particularly in bad weather. The later increase in her wartime complement would aggravate these accommodation problems, compounded by overcrowding on mess decks and strains upon washing and cooking facilities, and less-than-satisfactory eating arrangements. The officers ate in the wardroom on the port side of the upper deck, while the seamen's food, cooked in the ship's galley on the forecastle deck, had to be sent via a lift down to the servery below and hence distributed to the various messes. The cooking of food had, of necessity, to take place hours before it was consumed. Eggs and bacon fried at 3am was not at its best when served at 7.30am. The crew still had to sleep in hammocks slung on the messdecks and in any available spaces or compartments around the ship.

While *Warspite* was being modernised events were taking place which were to hasten the drift to war and fully stretch the Royal Navy for the next decade. First there came the Abbyssinian Crisis, brought about by Italy's invasion of that country in order to increase its African empire and influence in the Horn of Africa region. It left Britain in an awkward position, since the Italian

* In later years, with advances in the range of land-based reconnaissance planes and increased aircraft carrier use, the Walrus planes were removed and one of the hangars used as a ship's cinema. She was, however, re-equipped with Walrus spotter planes while serving with the Eastern Fleet in 1942.

actions threatened communication links, via Suez, the Red Sea and Aden, with India, Australia, New Zealand and the Far East. Short of a unilateral declaration of war against Italy, there was not much Britain could do. The League of Nations, to which the U.S.A., Germany and Japan were not party, decided upon 'Collective Security' by means of economic sanctions against Italy. It was very much left to Britain to implement this strategy. France's fleet was, according to its Government, 'not ready for sea'. In any case France, after years of disagreement, now had a non-aggression pact with Italy, and was much more preoccupied with the growing threat from a re-arming Germany to its Eastern border.

Britain's response was to move its naval base from Malta, within easy reach of Italian aircraft, to Alexandria, and to assemble there as big a fleet as it could muster in the path of Mussolini's ships, to harry them and those carrying contraband to Abyssinia. To do so Britain, now much reduced in naval strength, had to draft what ships could be spared from the Atlantic and Pacific Fleets and from the China Station, now itself under pressure from the threat being offered to China by Japan. When the Abyssinian crisis abated – after Italy had defied the League of Nations and conquered the country – a new crisis in the form of the Spanish Civil War arose. This drew the Mediterranean Fleet 1000 miles to the western end of the Mediterranean, to take off refugees and keep watch against gun running and prevent other contraband reaching the Spanish mainland. The Royal Navy was to be involved in these tasks from 1936 to 1938.

HMS *Warspite* emerged, virtually a new ship, from Portsmouth Dockyard on 8 March 1937 after a major reconstruction costing £2.3 million. Although much changed physically she soon showed that what had not changed was her capriciousness. On 12 March, while carrying out contractors' trials prior to her handover to the Royal Navy, her helm jammed hard over while she was undergoing full-power speeding trials. The fault corrected, she performed impeccably three days later in steaming for eight hours on full-power trials, achieving over 80,050hp and attaining a speed of just under 24 knots.

On 18 March *Warspite* underwent her gunnery trials. This involved firing each gun at maximum depression and at the new maximum elevation of 30 degrees. It was an opportune occasion for another mishap. She was test-firing her 15in guns at the now-extended range of some sixteen to seventeen miles, in very misty conditions, on a designated firing range of the English Channel, when a large Royal Mail liner, carrying some 800 passengers, passed unseen in the mist across her line of fire at the moment of firing. *Warspite*'s crew knew nothing of this. Some days later a letter from the captain of the liner, via the Commander-in-Chief and the captain of *Warspite*, was brought to the attention of the newly appointed Gunnery Officer, Lieutenant-Commander S.W. Roskill. The liner captain's letter described how, at the critical moment, a loud explosion had occurred followed by a great column of water about 400 yards on the port bow of the ship. The officer of the watch had promptly altered course,

> thus avoiding a second similar explosion two hundred yards away. ... As the passengers were at breakfast at the time the effect was very disturbing.(12)

What had happened was that with visibility from *Warspite* down to about eight miles, Roskill had had a destroyer placed, just visible, that far away down range, on the assumption that the destroyer would be able to see a further eight miles and thus be able to relay the fall of the shot. Alas, it had been a false premise; as it turned out the destroyer could not see, from her position, a further eight miles in the mist. It was a close call. In Roskill's own words:

> It was, indeed, lucky that we had only near missed her; for a fifteen inch shell, even a solid practice one, could have done a lot of damage. By such ill chances can a Gunnery Officer's career be jeopardised.(12)

The Gunnery Officer was not the only senior officer whose career was to be in jeopardy. The run-up to the recommissioning of the ship had not gone smoothly. The officers and men had been driven hard and heavily worked for several weeks, training, cleaning and preparing the ship for sea as well as having to deal with numerous teething problems in the machinery and equipment. All the time the senior officers had been under pressure from the Admiralty which, with war clouds looming and ongoing troubles in the Mediterranean, wanted *Warspite* commissioned, out of the dockyard and back in service. Dockyard space was at a premium and needed for other ships scheduled for modernisation or modifications, and HMS *Nelson* was due to arrive at Portsmouth for an extensive refit at the end of June.

Nevertheless, the temptation to cut corners and let things slide had to be resisted; as witnessed by one small boy, son of the then Commander or Executive Officer:

> She was a great ship. My father* served on her twice, in the Mediterranean as Torpedo Officer in 1932 and again as Commander for a short time while she was being rebuilt in Portsmouth Dockyard. I went aboard when I was about eight and can remember him being angry at finding a hatch going down to the depths of the ship without ladders that had not been roped off.(13)

To compound the troubles the bulk of the ship's crew was raw and inexperienced, with a large proportion of new recruits, as the Navy rapidly expanded its numbers to match the new ship construction in the rearmament build-up. Among them was a large draft from the Chatham depot, made up of sailors drawn from London and the Midlands and with some from as far afield as Scotland. Stoker F.W. Earridge was in this draft. He had joined the Navy on 4 January 1937 at the age of eighteen:

> The buzz soon spread about the drafts and the ships available, two cruisers *Sussex* and *Emerald*, and the *Warspite*. ... A motley crew set off for Portsmouth, this was to be their home for many years, and they were to make history with her, as she had done at Jutland during the First World War.(14)

Many of the officers were also new to the ship, and there had been a late change in one of the senior appointments, with Commander D.H. Everett taking over as Executive Officer in the crucial final run-up to commissioning, when the previous holder of that position was posted to *Nelson* for her refit.

Eventually the ship was commissioned on 29 June 1937 under the command of Captain V.A.C. Crutchley, V.C., for service as a flagship of the Mediterranean Fleet. She had a full wartime flagship

* Later Admiral Sir William Andrewes.

complement of 1218 officers and men, a very considerable increase on her original design complement of 993, with consequent increased pressures on the living space and conditions of the men. The next day, 30 June, trouble broke out amongst a proportion of the crew when, in an effort to finish the ship's preparations for sea, it was announced that the weekend leave period was to be shortened. For the Chatham men, especially those living further afield, it meant only a few hours at home at a time when, with war looming and the future so uncertain, every hour with loved ones was precious. The marines had to be called out to try to quell the disturbance:

> The mutiny was caused over leave, ...which had been cut from Friday – Monday, to Saturday – Monday. The Scots ratings ... would just get home, say Hello and Goodbye. Why this happened nobody knows, but when the Marines were called out to quell it, they sided with the sailors.(14)

Captain Crutchley addressed the men on the grievances and made clear his annoyance with regard to their somewhat impetuous actions, and reported the incident to the Commander-in-Chief, Portsmouth. There the matter may have rested, but the story was leaked to the Press. The upshot was a Court of Enquiry conducted by Sir Max Horton, Commander of the Reserve Fleet. The findings were that the handling of the situation could not be regarded as entirely satisfactory; some officers were commended, some censured. The Commander, First Lieutenant and Captain of Marines were relieved of their appointments*, three ratings were discharged 'S.N.L.R.' and ten others posted to different ships.(15)

Warspite's troubles did not end there. On 5 July she sailed for her final acceptance trials prior to final inspection and departure for the Mediterranean, where the Commander-in-Chief, Admiral Sir Dudley Pound, was awaiting the arrival of his flagship with some impatience. Tipped off by Captain F.H.W. Goolden, his predecessor, who had been in charge of the ship during her reconstruction and trials, that *Warspite*'s steering was still a bit uncertain, Captain

* The three officers received other sea-going appointments later. One of them, Commander Everett, served as Senior Executive Officer on HMS *Ajax* during the Battle of the River Plate against the *Graf Spee* in December 1939 and was awarded the D.S.O.

Crutchley ordered full war-time manoeuvring trials at high speed against an imaginary attacking enemy. It was make or break time for *Warspite*; and her steering jammed in a high-speed turn. This caused some commotion on the mess decks:

> We went to sea today at about 10.00 for full power and rudder trials. The rudder trials caused a certain amount of havoc among the gunroom crockery, because when steaming at full speed and the rudder was put over all the glasses and plates started charging down the table and quite a number were broken. Those of us in the gunroom at the time spent most of our time pouncing on the crockery before it crashed onto the deck and broke.(16)

All appeared well when the steering was released, but on return to harbour one set of the turbine gearing failed and inspection showed severe damage to the coupling mechanism. These were repaired within a month and on 27 August *The Times* reported that the Commander-in-Chief's office at Portsmouth had announced that *Warspite*:

> ... will leave the floating dock in the dockyard at 3.45pm and will proceed to Spithead. Tomorrow she will sail at 8am for eight hours thorough repair trials and afterwards she will anchor at Spithead. On Monday the *Warspite* will return to harbour and berth at Pitch House Jetty preparatory for sailing at 11.15am on Friday 3 September for the Mediterranean Fleet.(17)

Alas, the programmes of planners and the whims of the *Warspite* did not necessarily match. The trials showed that there was a recurrent steering problem when *Warspite* was turning on full rudder at high speed. According to Midshipman McNeile's log for Saturday, 28 August:

> The couplings have all been put back by now and we sailed today at 08.15 for an eight hour full power trial, which we are all hoping will be successful. During most of the forenoon the engine-room department seemed to be having some difficulty with the safety valve which lifted every other minute. After steaming backwards and forwards for eight hours we eased down and came to anchor at 20.00. Everything seemed to have gone alright in the engine room , but of course we cannot tell until they [*sic*] have been opened up.(16)

Unfortunately all had not gone well with the trials, and the Midshipman's log entry of 30 August records that:

> In the evening it was announced that the sailing of *Warspite* is indefinitely postponed, as exactly the same defects have occurred as before. This announcement left rather a gloom over the ship.[16]

It took from August 1937 to January 1938 to find and rectify the problem.

On 5 January 1938 HMS *Warspite* finally sailed for Malta, arriving at Grand Harbour Valetta on 14 January. After their mishaps and misdemeanours of the past six months the ship's crew were keen to show the Navy and the Commander-in-Chief what the new *Warspite* could do. The audience did not have long to wait. While 'working up' to peak wartime condition proficiency *Warspite* had been carrying out close-range anti-aircraft drill, using the brand new rapid-firing weapons against a target towed by a low-flying aircraft. The Gunnery Officer had rung the 'cease firing' bell and the ship had turned towards Valetta Harbour and home, when the pilot flew low over the ship once more to allow the gunners to see the results of their efforts on the towed target. Perhaps because he was confused, or it was too much of a temptation, a young midshipman immediately opened fire again with one of the multiple 'pom-poms'. As the man in charge, the jinxed gunnery officer Lieutenant-Commander Roskill, explained:

> I stopped him as quickly as I could, but since these weapons fired about eight hundred two pounder shells a minute there were quite a lot of them already in the air. I said to my Captain that they must have fallen in Malta and remembered, uneasily, how densely populated that island is. I felt distinctly uncomfortable as we picked up our buoys, though I was at least relieved to see that the town of Valetta was not in a state of uproar, and that there were, apparently, no punctures in the roof of the Opera House. To my surprise, for several days nothing happened, and I began to think that we had got away with it, when my Captain sent for me one morning. He showed me a letter from the Commander-in-Chief, forwarding one from the Governor, enclosing one from the General, covering one from the Commanding Officer, 2nd Battalion The Green Howards. The real meat was at the bottom of the pie. It was a description by a platoon commander of the

Green Howards who had been exercising his men on a rifle range not far outside the town: 'when the sound of firing was heard from a warship out at sea [and] a rain of shells began to fall on the beach and creep up to the rifle range'. The platoon commander had ordered his men to take cover immediately, Corporal Brown had shown commendable promptitude in getting this order obeyed (I wondered why there should have been any laggards!) and there were no casualties or injuries. The report, and especially the last sentence, took a great weight off my mind, even though I realised that the matter was unlikely to end there. I wrote the official explanation and the Captain dealt with the errant Midshipman even as I had been dealt with many years earlier. Meanwhile I suggested to the Fleet Gunnery Officer that, since no damage had been done, we might help to liquidate the affair by calling on the C.O. of The Green Howards at an appropriate time for liquidations – such as after Church Parade on the following Sunday – and tendering suitable apologies. I also had a brainwave and got my Ordnance Officer to burnish up a two-pounder shell, mount it on an ebonite base, and inscribe it suitably 'From HMS *Warspite* to the 2nd Battalion, The Green Howards; to commemorate the Bombardment of Pembroke Rifle-range' with the date. We also made a tiny miniature for Corporal Brown – he having been the 'best performer'. This idea appealed to the Fleet Gunnery Officer, who had a strong sense of humour, and we accordingly proceeded to The Green Howards' barracks on the Sunday, made our apologies, and asked the Commanding Officer to accept the presentations. It was a huge success with the soldiers, the presentations were joyfully accepted, champagne was opened, and we were invited to their next regimental guest night at which the model occupied the place of honour on their table.* Unfortunately someone dined out on this story a little too freely, and it came to the attention of certain higher authorities who did not have as much sense of humour as the Fleet Gunnery Officer or the Commanding Officer of the

* In fact it was the 1st Battalion of the Green Howards; the 2nd Battalion were on operations on the North West Frontier of India at that time. The trophy is no longer in the possession of the 1st Battalion, although 'an elderly Sergeant's mess member says he can recall it in the 1950s'.[17] The Green Howards Gazette records at that time the football field exploits of a Cpl Brown, thought to be the same Cpl Brown. He was captain, and a prolific goal scorer, of the cup-winning battalion team. Obviously he was as lively a performer on the football field as he was on the firing range on the day *Warspite* uninvitedly joined the activities.

Green Howards. It was deemed to have treated a serious matter with unseemly levity and they were 'not amused'. But apart from that the story ended happily for all the players.(12)

On 6 February, Admiral Pound* came aboard his flagship for the first time. It had been a long wait and initially he was somewhat hostile to the ship's crew; her delays and mishaps had plainly upset him. After inspecting the ship he 'gingered them up' with an abrasive address. Later Captain Crutchley added his own 'kick up the backside'.

> The Captain had us all on deck to address us, and because of the mutiny, called us all a shower of b******s. ... This man came to be the feared of men. To explain this, we were all young tearaways in some respects, but we knew there would be no mercy for any indiscretions; this was a man in the Nelson mould. We heard sailors' yarns about him, but I pity the man to approach him; and yet in my life, with political and trade union work, I have never met a man that held the respect which he had. His ship's company actually believed that no harm could come to them when 'Crutch' was there, myself included.(14)

Although the ships of the Navy were now working towards peak efficiency in anticipation of an escalation of the growing international crisis, the ships of the Mediterranean Fleet still held to their routine of spells of rigorous training interspersed with relaxing goodwill visits to foreign ports. After intensive combined Spring exercises with the Atlantic Fleet, the two fleets returned to Gibraltar for a few days of analysis and debriefing. Here the ship's crew of *Warspite* entertained the two fleets with performances of a self-mocking satirical review, at the same time taking a sly knock at the Commander-in-Chief, entitled 'What's the Delay?'. The ship then left on a goodwill visit to the French Riviera.

> We were looking forward to it. ... Our favourite was the South of France and the Italian Riviera. We anchored in Ville Franche Bay, in the immediate vicinity of Nice, Monte Carlo, Monaco and Mentone and Grasse. Grasse was the home of the scent industry, and we paid a visit. But with only a twenty four hour pass, except

---

* Later Admiral of the Fleet Sir Dudley Pound, First Sea Lord.

> for a conducted tour of the Casino at Monte Carlo which was out of our price range, Nice was our main port of call. It was possible to drink the night through. There was no shortage of female company. Some of the girls openly said that the money they earned was being saved for a dowry for their marriage. One of our stokers actually married one, her name was August, a German girl ... but after a lot of goings on a Diplomatic level, the marriage was annulled. San Remo was a beautiful place, but even at that stage one could feel that war was not far away. Several of the lads had offers of £250 just to marry a German Jewess, to get her to Malta and British Nationality.(14)

In the drive towards achieving full fighting efficiency the Admiralty ordered the Mediterranean Fleet to carry out extensive gunnery practice off Malta under simulated wartime conditions in the late summer of 1938. *Warspite* was required to try out her main armaments and new anti-aircraft guns. For the main armament, the test involved prolonged bouts of firing against practice targets towed at high speed by light cruisers, opening up at a range of about fifteen miles. The results of the shoot were spectacular; the Commander-in-Chief, Captain and crew were delighted, and it did much to foster a much better relationship with the Commander-in-Chief.

> The first salvos, fired at about 21,000 yards, fell just over the target, and a good air report* at once corrected the range. From then on, for forty salvos, *Warspite* hardly ever stopped hitting. The first target was quickly shot away, so she shifted to the second 'enemy', and at once began to score hits on it as well. Meanwhile a towing aircraft represented a bombing attack, and was engaged by the anti-aircraft armaments. ... Admiral Pound was delighted, and himself attended the lectures on the results given to the ship's company. From then on there was no looking back for *Warspite* – only forward to greater deeds and services.(19)

Stoker Earridge was equally delighted, proudly remembering that with the 15in salvo there were forty hits, two misses and two misfires. He reported Captain Crutchley telling the crew: 'I hope the Italians had spotter planes up watching that.'(14)

* *Warspite* was using one of her own spotter planes, with Lt-Cmdr. W.L.M. Brown as observer to report on the fall of the shot.

Although justifiably proud of their achievement, such prolonged ship's trials under wartime conditions were a severe test of the crew's determination and endurance:

> We did a forty eight hour War Exercise off Malta. It was always hot on the Mess Deck, worse so down in the Boiler or Engine Rooms. They battened down all the hatches. Stokers never wore anything bar shorts, vests and overalls. Hammocks were out of the question, we slept on mess tables, stools and the bare Corticene on the deck. At times the temperature rose to 148 degrees. When getting up the imprint of the body was left on the deck in sweat.(14)

Off duty and back in harbour, there were always the attractions of the Gut in Valetta:

> A bottle of Blue [light ale] cost 2½d [1p] and for five shillings [25p] a good time could be had by all. This included Big Eats and Head Down.(14)

In June 1939 Admiral Sir Andrew Cunningham* replaced Admiral Pound† as Commander-in-Chief on the latter's promotion to First Sea Lord. *Warspite* continued as the Commander-in-Chief's flagship. The immediate threat of war was temporarily averted by the signing of the 'peace in our time' Munich Agreement of September 1938. Life continued as normal for the Mediterranean Fleet, albeit with training increasingly on a wartime footing. The Fleet was gradually shifting its main base to Alexandria, since it was considered that Malta was too vulnerable to attack from Italy, now becoming very aggressive towards Albania and the Balkans, and openly siding with Hitler's Germany.

In July the new Commander-in-Chief sailed with *Warspite* on an official goodwill visit to Turkey. The ship was escorted by four of the new, formidable, 'Tribal' class destroyers – *Cossack*, *Zulu*, *Maori*

---

* Admiral of the Fleet Viscount Cunningham of Hyndhope, 'A.B.C.' to the Navy, was C-in-C Mediterranean Fleet from 1939 to 1942, served on the Combined Chief of Staffs Committee in Washington and was appointed Allied Naval Commander in the Mediterranean in September 1942. He became First Sea Lord following the death of Admiral Pound in October 1943 and served in that capacity until 1946.

† Admiral of the Fleet Sir Dudley Pound served as First Sea Lord from 1939 to 1943. Overburdened by the pressures of his wartime office, he suffered a major stroke whilst at the 1943 Quebec Conference between Churchill and Roosevelt, and died shortly afterwards on Trafalgar Day, 21 October 1943.

and *Nubian*, only launched in 1937.* It was an impressive show of strength for an important visit. Turkey had fought on the German side in the First World War, with disastrous results for the Allies in the Gallipoli Campaign, and intense diplomatic efforts were being made to encourage Turkey not to repeat the alliance with Germany in any coming conflict. By all accounts it was an outstandingly successful visit:

> We were royally entertained. Everyone seemed genuinely pleased to see us, and the sailors were well looked after, being taken out to some of the big houses on the Bosphorus. The British Ambassador [Sir Hughe Knatchbull-Hugessen] set a very high standard in his entertainment of 300 sailors. The basis of it was 1,200 bottles of beer and a troupe of dancing girls, both of which were most popular.(2)

Although the lower deck sailors were perhaps initially sceptical of what Turkey might have to offer they enjoyed the visit and its memorable sights and experiences:

> The cruise which we had to the Dardanelles and Istanbul always sticks in my mind. A beautiful moonlit night, the sea like a sheet of ice, a brilliant starlit sky. We saw a lot of sea and sailed many miles, but this was one time that stood out. Istanbul was, according to 'Jack', Hells, Bells and Smells. We visited the Venereal Disease Museum, and the exhibits on what terrible things could result from sexual intercourse shook even the most hardened sailor. The drinking habits varied. ... In Istanbul a drink like Pernod appealed to some. It was cheap, and with a glass of water in the morning they got the same effect all over again.(14)

The visit had been equally memorable for the Turkish people of the ports of call. The *Daily Mail* of 7 August 1939 reported the departure of the British ships:

> ... huge crowds of Turks lined the shores of the Bosphorus and Sea of Marmora to cheer the British battleship *Warspite* and their four escorting destroyers as they left Istanbul after their five day visit. The ships now go on to Cyprus.(20)

---

* The 'Tribals' had a hard and eventful life. Of the sixteen built for the Royal Navy only four survived the coming war. Only HMS *Nubian* survived of the four destroyers that escorted *Warspite*.

Elsewhere war and storm clouds were gathering. On that same day British newspapers reported that, on the other side of the world, Japanese warplanes had bombed Chinese installations on the River Yangste at Ichang, hitting two merchant ships owned by Jardine Matheson and Co. of Hong Kong. The crew of the British gunboat HMS *Gannet*, 310 tons, attempted to put out the ship's fires but were beaten back by the flames. In Japan a crowd of 100,000, including German and Italian residents, attended an anti-British demonstration in Kobe, the fourth largest city in Japan. Back in Europe, Goering flaunted the strength of his German Luftwaffe at a speech at Dessau. At home, plans were announced for a trial black-out for the following Wednesday night, including a twenty-four hour postponement in case of bad weather; and at Glamorgan on a rain-affected pitch Austin Matthews took 7 for 21 to help to bowl out the touring West Indies cricket team for 96 in their first innings.

By the late summer of 1939 the political crisis had worsened. On 22 May Hitler and Mussolini had committed the Axis powers of Germany and Italy to a military alliance, and Italy had invaded Albania. With war seemingly inevitable, the Allied Powers of Britain and France began actively to prepare for conflict, and the Royal Navy was mobilised on 31 August. Britain and France, seeking to stop further territorial aggression by the Axis powers, had given guarantees of military assistance to Poland, Greece and Romania. When Germany invaded Poland on 1 September, and refused an Allied ultimatum to withdraw, 'a state of war' with Germany was officially declared on Sunday 3 September 1939.

CHAPTER 4

The Second World War: The Opening Year

Warspite went to war lying at anchor in Alexandria harbour, Egypt. In company with all the other major units of the Mediterranean Fleet, she had gathered there on mobilisation:

> Lying in harbour was pretty boring for all the younger ratings, nothing to do, entertainment was scarce. ... Entertainment on board, except for the occasional film, consisted of the Tannoy system. The favourite was, guess who, Vera Lynn. ... I will never forget Chamberlain's announcement of being at war with Germany. A lot of us congregated in the recreation space, some played games. Others got their heads down. When somebody switched on the Tannoy speaker, a momentous time in history was nigh. But Jack was not impressed. By general consent the cry went up 'shut that bloody thing off'.(1)

The higher ranks of the Mediterranean Fleet were equally *blasé*:

> During the last days of August and the early days of September the fleet was holding the squadron regattas in Alexandria harbour. It was actually while standing on the foremost 15-inch turret of the *Malaya* watching the finish of a race that I was handed the signal stating that Great Britain had declared war on Germany. There was little to be done. So far as possible all our preparations had been made. As I wrote to an aunt, I never expected when war was declared to have nothing to do but go ashore and have tea with my wife.(2)

There was little that the Mediterranean Fleet could do at that time. Their main concern was Italy, posturing and threatening but keeping out of the war. If she did declare war, Italy could cause serious trouble for Britain's interests in the Mediterranean, particularly Malta, Egypt, and the shipping passing close to her shores on the way to and from the Far East via the Suez Canal. Besides her air force, she had a formidable navy, far stronger than the Mediterranean Fleet. While France was responsible for the western end of the Mediterranean, she was understandably more concerned with the land war being fought on her eastern borders, and the main Italian threat was seen to be focused on Malta and the Eastern Mediterranean Basin. But for the time being Italy was keeping out of the war; and the Mediterranean Fleet, with *Warspite* as flagship, could only remain alert and 'trail their coat' in a cruise to the west of Crete between 11 and 16 September.

On paper, at the outbreak of war, the navies of Great Britain and France were more than a match for their German, and potentially Italian, opponents. This superiority was most apparent with regard to capital ships, but the reality was somewhat different. Great Britain, with twelve battleships and three battlecruisers, appeared to be able to field a very formidable force; but they were all old ships and, in modern terms, slow. Ten of the battleships, the *Queen Elizabeth*s and the 'R' class, had served in the First World War nearly a quarter of a century before. The two newest, *Nelson* and *Rodney*, had commenced construction in 1923 and, though powerful, being the only British battleships to mount 16in guns as main armament, had design weaknesses and were painfully slow. *Warspite* was a prize gem in this collection of ships. After her complete reconstruction she was virtually a new ship, even if in reality some twenty-five years old; she was as fast as any in the Navy, with a firepower and gun range to match any other existing battleship. Her services were soon to be in great demand. In contrast, Germany and Italy had fewer capital ships, but they were all either new, or, in the case of Italy, had undergone recent major reconstruction.

The nature of naval warfare had also drastically changed since the First World War. The days of the set-piece action between fleets of capital ships had gone, and the role, and indeed the value, of battleships was being increasingly questioned. The Germans, geographically bottled-up in their North Sea or Baltic ports, had no intention of engaging in another Jutland. They saw the role of their capital ships, acting alone or in pairs, as sea raiders, breaking out of their ports and, in conjunction with a protracted U-boat campaign, preying on the merchant shipping lanes bringing food and war supplies to the Allies. In the days before air surveillance and present-day detection techniques, the spectre of powerful German ships roaming the oceans, picking off lone merchant ships and attacking convoys, was an on-going nightmare for the Admiralty. Thus the Allied capital ships in the early months of the war had to be thinly deployed, protecting convoys against possible attack and trying to find and destroy the raiders.

The Germans had already deployed their two pocket battleships *Graf Spee* and *Deutschland* in the South and North Atlantic respectively. These ships, of a class novel to British naval thinking and ostensibly built to comply with the pre-war treaty 10,000-ton construction limits, were in fact of 12,000 tons and very fast and powerful for their size. Capable of 26 knots, they were armed with six 11in guns and eight 5.9in guns as secondary armament. When built and designed in the early 1930s they were given enough speed to escape from any warships which they could not overcome with their heavy guns. It was thought by their German designers that the only potential enemy ships which they had to fear were the British battlecruisers *Hood*, *Renown* and *Repulse* and the French fast battleships *Dunkerque* and *Strasbourg*.*

A further threat was that offered by the two fast and powerful German battlecruisers *Scharnhorst* and *Gneisenau* breaking out of their home ports into the North Atlantic via the North Sea and the Denmark Strait between Iceland and Greenland. These two ships were each of 32,000 tons, the same displacement as the *Warspite*. Built some twenty years later than most of the British capital ships, *Scharnhorst* and *Gneisenau* were each armed with nine 11in guns, twelve 5.9in, and fourteen 4.1in anti-aircraft guns. Perhaps more importantly they were capable of 31.5 knots, making them ideal 'hit and run' raiders against convoys of merchant ships protected by

---

* They were mistaken. Although initially successful in the early months of the war, sinking nine Allied ships totalling 50,000 tons, the *Graf Spee* was eventually found on 13 December 1939 by a hunting pack of three smaller cruisers, the 8390-ton *Exeter*, mounting six 8in guns, and the sister-ships *Ajax* and *Achilles*, each 7000 tons and mounting eight 6in guns. Although outgunned and outranged, and badly damaged in the process, the cruisers succeeded in inflicting heavy damage on the *Graf Spee*, driving her to seek refuge in neutral Montevideo harbour, Uruguay. Given seventy-two hours to repair her damage, treat or offload her wounded and leave, and fearing that heavier British units were waiting for her over the horizon, Captain Langsdorff chose to scuttle the *Graf Spee* outside Montevideo harbour. Her crew were interned and Captain Langsdorff committed suicide.

small escorts. It was essential therefore to give these convoys 'big ship' protection, capable of defending against raids by German battlecruisers and pocket battleships.

It was against this threatening background, and with things quiet in the Mediterranean with Italy still not showing her hand, that *Warspite* was recalled home for convoy escort duties on 27 October 1939 by Admiral Pound, the First Sea Lord. She arrived at Gibraltar on 6 November and left almost immediately for Nova Scotia. After the relatively calm waters of the Mediterranean her crew found the Atlantic very rough. *Warspite* ran into violent gales and heavy seas and only arrived at Halifax, in the midst of a snow blizzard, on 14 November. On 18 November she left with convoy HX 9:

> We left harbour in company with some forty to fifty merchant ships. The speed of the convoy was arranged beforehand, and to conserve fuel, it was at an economic speed, but for some of the older ships it was difficult to keep up with the rest, and they were left to get home on their own, with all the attendant risks. However, we left the lot this time to chase the *Deutschland*, or to keep her safely away from the convoy.(1)

The reason for *Warspite*'s sudden departure from her convoy was indeed to meet the challenge of German surface raiders. On 23 November 1939 the patrolling armed merchant cruiser *Rawalpindi** encountered what was originally thought to be the pocket battleship *Deutschland* in the straits between Iceland and the Faroes. It turned out to be the *Scharnhorst* and the *Gneisenau*. *Rawalpindi* gave battle but, inevitably, was sunk with the loss of 270 lives. *Scharnhorst* and *Gneisenau*, having given away their position without breaking out into the Atlantic, returned home. Alerted, and unaware of their return, heavy British units commenced a search to bring the German battlecruisers to account. *Warspite* was ordered to leave the convoy she was escorting on the afternoon of 24 November to search the Denmark Strait. Finding nothing, *Warspite* swept down the west coast of Scotland before docking at Greenock. Her unexplained departure from the convoy caused some resentment among the seamen of the convoy ships:

* A merchant liner armed with 6in guns as an emergency wartime measure.

> On reaching Greenock, the comments came thick and fast, 'Where the ****** Hell did you get to?' We heard that the Canadians, who were being brought over in numbers, were under the impression that they were on their own, but in fact, the Fleet was screening them, out of sight.(1)

Social life for the sailors in blacked-out Greenock was not the same as in peacetime Malta:

> At that time we were none too happy with leave arrangements, which were four hours ashore every other night, and if the sea was in any way rough it took the drifter one hour to get us ashore. The pubs shut at 9pm so it became a case of shove as much down as you could. Jack always looked after the least able, even to the point of lowering them into the drifter on a rope. The weather was so bad one evening that we had to sleep on the seats in Greenock Town Hall. Another memory of that Hall was a concert by Gracie Fields, quite an occasion. ... The Scots were very good to the sailors. ... Greenock was to play quite a part in my life, as on one of our shore runs a fellow stoker, who was not a regular going ashore mate of mine, and I both met our future wives in the Blackout. This, as you may guess, has led to many a witty remark. Also both of my daughters were born there, after the marriage of course. But that was some time off.(1)

For the remainder of 1939 and the early months of 1940 *Warspite* was based at Greenock, working with the Home Fleet out of the Clyde on patrol and convoy protection duties. On 4 December 1939 HMS *Nelson* was badly damaged by an acoustic mine off Loch Ewe and *Warspite* became flagship. She thus had the distinction, within just over a month, of serving as flagship to both the Mediterranean and Home Fleets.(3)

April 1940 signalled the end of the so called 'Phoney War' on land, and attention suddenly switched to Norway, whose strategic position was attracting growing attention from both the Allies and Germany. The key issue was the supply of iron ore to Germany, which was importing some 10 million tons of Swedish ore a year via the port of Narvik and through the territorial waters of the Inner Leads, a chain of islands along the long coastline of neutral Norway. Almost simultaneously both sides acted, to curtail or to protect, this trade in a highly strategic war material. The British

Home Fleet had moved back to Scapa Flow to be nearer the new focus of activity, and began minelaying in Norwegian waters on 8 April. On the previous and same days Germany attacked and overwhelmed Denmark and invaded Norway with a five-pronged attack on Narvik, Trondheim, Bergen, Kristiansand and the capital Oslo. The Allies, preparing for seaborne landings in northern Norway, sent units of the Home Fleet to intercept, attack and – it was hoped – destroy much of the invading forces. *Warspite*, who had transferred her flagship duties to HMS *Rodney*, was due to return to her interrupted posting in the Mediterranean, but was ordered to remain.

It was to become a messy operation for the British and the French, whose troops were ill-equipped and prepared, and whose air forces were inadequate for the demands placed upon them. For the Royal Navy it was to prove an arduous but ultimately triumphant campaign; for the German Navy it was to prove a disaster. *Warspite*'s contribution, almost entirely confined to the Narvik sector of the campaign, was to prove decisive.

The sequence of events, focusing upon those affecting the Narvik sector, began in early April when German planners assigned ten destroyers collectively carrying 2000 troops to secure Narvik as Group I of their five-pronged attack. They would be supported by the battlecruisers *Scharnhorst* and *Gneisenau* which, after escorting the destroyers and troops to the mouth of the Vestfjord, the fjord leading to Narvik at its head, would sail on into the Arctic to divert heavy British units. The German destroyers *Wilhelm Heidkamp*, *Anton Schmidt*, *Hans Lüdemann*, *Georg Thiele*, *Bernd von Arnim*, *Wolf Zenker*, *Erich Giese*, *Erich Koellner*, *Hermann Kunne* and *Dieter von Roeder*, would be supplied by three oil tankers. In the event only one was able to deliver the fuel supplies necessary for the ships to return to Germany.

Throughout the weekend of 6 and 7 April squadrons and units of both German and British naval forces sailed or rendezvoused. On Sunday 7 April German movements towards Norway were confirmed by British air reconnaissance. In response, *Rodney*, *Repulse*, *Valiant*, the cruisers *Sheffield* and *Penelope*, and ten destroyers left Rosyth at 20.30 and, a little later, two cruisers and fifteen destroyers left Rosyth. Four cruisers loaded with troops also lay at Rosyth, awaiting orders to deploy to Stavanger and Bergen. Already at sea, far to the north, was Admiral Whitworth flying his flag in the battlecruiser *Renown*, accompanied by nine destroyers. They were there to deal with any threat to Narvik. Late on the Sunday Admiral Whitworth received a signal: 'Most immediate. Concentrate on preventing any German force proceeding to Narvik.'(4)

He was not able to comply immediately. The weather conditions were foul, with heavy seas and snow storms from a severe Arctic gale. He replied that he would patrol the entrance to Vestfjord when the seas moderated. It was already too late. By sailing in the more protected Norwegian coastal waters the *Scharnhorst* and *Gneisenau*, with the ten destroyers, screened and defended by four U-boats (*U 25*, *U 46*, *U 51* and *U 64*) allocated to Group I by Admiral Doenitz, had reached the entrance to Vestfjord at 8pm. The destroyers immediately started making their way up the fjord, capturing or destroying any opposition to their progress towards the port and town of Narvik. It was not until the early hours of 7 April that the seas calmed sufficiently for the British ships to move towards their Vestfjord position; in doing so, at 03.37, they encountered the *Scharnhorst* and *Gneisenau* at some 20,000 yards range. The two battlecruisers, commanded by Admiral Gunther Lüjens, turned north-westward to draw *Renown* and her escorts away from Vestfjord. *Renown* and her destroyers immediately gave chase, but the destroyers were unable to keep pace in the heavy seas and *Renown* ploughed on alone. A fierce running battle, at high speed and long range, ensued. The exchanges continued, with extensive damage to the main armament control of the *Gneisenau* and less severe damage to *Renown*, until 08.00 when *Renown*, with her inferior speed, finally had to abandon the chase.

It was time for *Renown* and her destroyers to reform and, belatedly, concentrate upon the given task of protecting Narvik from German occupation. It was at about this time, in a rapidly changing situation, that Captain Warburton-Lee, in command of the ten escorting destroyers, received a direct order from the Commander-in-Chief, Home Fleet: 'Send some destroyers up to Narvik to make certain that no enemy troops land.'(4)

Then at mid-day a further signal, direct from the Admiralty in London, was received by Warburton-Lee:

> Press reports state that one German ship has arrived Narvik and landed a small force. Proceed Narvik and sink or capture enemy ship. It is at your discretion to land forces if you think you can recapture Narvik from number of enemy present.(4)

The Admiralty obviously had no idea of the extent of the German penetration of the Narvik sector. Admiral Whitworth, in view of the threat still posed by the nearby *Scharnhorst* and *Gneisenau*, would need some destroyers to accompany the *Renown*, so he and Warburton-Lee decided to split up their destroyer force. The five destroyers of the 20th Flotilla would remain with the *Renown*, while Captain Warburton-Lee would take *Hardy*, *Hotspur*, *Havock* and *Hunter* into Narvik fjord in accordance with, and in the light of, the Admiralty's instruction and erroneous intelligence report. The First Battle of Narvik was about to begin.

At this time both sides were bedevilled by lack of firm intelligence as to the other's dispositions and intentions. During the morning of 9 April it became increasingly apparent that German forces had arrived, and possibly landed, at Narvik and the neighbouring inlets. Not that all was going well for the German ships. They were very low on fuel and the tankers, intended to replenish their fuel supplies for the return 900-mile journey to their bases, had not arrived. In consequence they were in increasing danger, with British ships gathering in the Norwegian waters, of being trapped in the long narrow fjord with its single outlet to the sea.

Captain Warburton-Lee, his force increased to five destroyers by the arrival of HMS *Hostile*, released from escort duties with the cruiser HMS *Birmingham*, signalled the Admiralty that he intended to attack at dawn on 10 April, when high water conditions would reduce the damage from any moored mines. The Admiralty agreed, but, during the night, still unclear as to the exact position in the Narvik locality, became ambivalent:

> Norwegian coast defence ships *Eidsvold* and *Norge* may be in German hands; you alone can judge whether in these circumstances attack should be made. We shall support whatever decision you take.(4)

In fact both the Norwegian ships had already been torpedoed and sunk at their moorings by the invading German destroyers.

Captain Warburton-Lee decided to press on with his attack, and in the early hours of 10 April, the destroyers *Hardy*, *Hunter*, *Havock*, *Hotspur* and *Hostile* made their way up the fjord in a heavy snowstorm. As dawn was breaking at 04.20, and the snowstorm lifting, the torpedo and gun fight began. The German ships, which had not been alerted by their U-boat patrols, were taken completely by surprise; but the British ships were equally surprised to find themselves facing, eventually, ten German destroyers. The German ships had more than numerical superiority. Individually they were also considerably larger, at 1625 tons, and better armed, each carrying five 5in guns and eight torpedo tubes, compared with the 1340-ton British 'H' class destroyers, each carrying four 4.7in guns and eight torpedo tubes.

In the confused close-quarter exchanges in the confines of the fjords, losses of life and ships were heavy on both sides. The German side received a massive blow at the outset:

> On the Commodore's ship, the *Wilhelm Heidkamp*, the alarm had hardly been sounded when a torpedo blew away her stern. Commodore Bonte was killed on the spot, and with him fell his First Officer, Lieutenant Commander Heyke, [and] the flotilla's Chief Engineer, Commander Maywold.(5)

By the end of the battle the German side had had the *Wilhelm Heidkamp* and *Schmidt* sunk, while the *Roeder*, *Thiele*, *Armin* and *Lüdemann* had received damage beyond complete local repair, and the *Kunne* had her engines temporarily disabled. Only the *Zenker*, *Koellner* and *Giese* were undamaged, but had used up over half of their ammunition. The German's repair and supply position was further worsened when the retiring British destroyers encountered and sank the enemy's large supply ship *Rauenfels*, bringing much-needed ammunition and stores to the invading Narvik force.

The British lost the *Hardy* and *Hunter*, and the *Hotspur* was badly damaged. The two ships sunk were lost towards the end of the action as the retiring British ships, having fired off nearly all their torpedoes, were surprised as they withdrew by three fresh German destroyers which had been berthed in a side fjord, not seen by the British in their dawn dash up the main fjord. The British force also lost at this time their inspirational leader. Captain Warburton-Lee was mortally wounded, and everyone with him on the bridge of the *Hardy* killed or wounded, when a 5in German shell landed there. His last signal, flown just before the bridge of the *Hardy* was demolished, was: 'Keep on engaging the enemy.'(4) He was posthumously awarded the Victoria Cross for his inspired leadership of the outgunned British destroyer force.

Thus the First Battle of Narvik ended indecisively, but with the German destroyers badly mauled, low on fuel and supplies, and confined to the narrow fjords and side inlets of the approaches to Narvik. The loss of their commander and senior engineering officer had also been a demoralising blow, particularly in view of their now isolated position. They had however landed some 2000 troops and had the support of a number of U-boats to report on Allied activity in the approaches to Vestfjord and constitute a major deterrent to Allied ships venturing into the narrow confines of the fjord. They also had three days of grace while the Allies held off and considered their overall position in the campaign which, apart from the Narvik stalemate, was now running strongly in the Germans favour in other parts of Norway. The indecisiveness and lack of co-ordination between the Allied naval, air and military activities was to be an unfortunate feature of the short-lived Norway campaign.

The Germans used the three days to try to get their ships in a seaworthy condition, carrying out such local repairs as they could and sharing out the available fuel for an attempted dash out of the trap. Unfortunately two of their undamaged destroyers grounded themselves while manoeuvring in the narrow confines of the fjord and thus worsened the overall position. They were well aware of their dangerous situation; the U-boat *U 64* arrived on the afternoon of 12 April and reported: 'Strong enemy destroyer patrols are cruising off the entrance to the fjord. Narvik threatens to become a trap.'(6) All that the German High Command could do, with their surface ships fully stretched by the campaign, was to send as many U-boats as possible to make the Allies pay heavily for any attempt to finish off the German forces at Narvik. Admiral Karl Doenitz,*

---

* Later Grand Admiral Doenitz. Commanded the German U-Boat Fleet from 1939 to 1943 and was then appointed C-in-C of the German Navy. His baton, personally presented by Adolf Hitler in 1943, is now on display in the Shropshire Regimental Museum at Shrewsbury Castle.

the German Commander-in-Chief of their Submarine Fleet, related how:

> On 12 April, signals and U-boat sightings indicated that the enemy intended to make a landing somewhere north of Narvik, probably with the object of launching an attack there on Narvik itself. In my opinion this made it highly desirable that we should have U-boats operating in Vaagsfjord*, and I accordingly detailed three boats (*U 47*, *U 48* and *U 49*) to proceed at once to Vaagsfjord.(7)

Later, German Supreme Command were informed that:

> Every available ship in the German Fleet has been committed. All available U-boats are in action. Three U-boats are in Vaagsfjord, five in Westfjord, three are proceeding to Narvik with ammunition and stores. (6)

Finally, on 12 April the Admiralty decided to send a strong force up the Westfjord to finish off the German ships and bombard the forces ashore prior to an allied landing to take the town. It was decided not to risk using HMS *Renown*. The *Renown*, *Hood* and *Repulse* were the only British capital ships with a chance of both catching and engaging in single combat the *Scharnhorst* and *Gneisenau*, still lurking in northern waters. *Renown* was deemed too precious to be risked in the confined waters of the fjord with its attendant dangers from mines, U-boats and air attack. It was a case of 'send for the *Warspite*' with her big guns and thick skin. Admiral Whitworth transferred his flag to *Warspite*:

> The transfer of myself and staff from *Renown* to *Warspite* in the middle of the night, in a very big swell, turned out to be the most hazardous and difficult part of the operation.(8)

The Admiral was making light of what was, in the event, to prove a hazardous and dangerous operation for the British and Germans alike.

At 07.30 on 13 April 1940 *Warspite* and nine destroyers – the four 'Tribals' *Bedouin*, *Cossack*, *Eskimo* and *Punjabi*, and five smaller destroyers *Hero*, *Icarus*, *Kimberley*, *Forester* and *Foxhound* –

---

* A fjord to the north of Westfjord.

rendezvoused just inside Westfjord, approximately 100 miles from the town of Narvik. The Second Battle of Narvik was about to begin.

On board the British ships, preparations were well-advanced and morale was high. The crews had a right to be confident; for once they were meeting the enemy on equal or better terms. The man in charge of the operation, Admiral Whitworth, was also more confident than he had been of late. He had recently undergone an unhappy period on *Renown*; the ineffectual chase of the *Scharnhorst* and *Gneisenau*, and the interference and actions of the Admiralty in dealing directly on tactical matters with his subordinate ships' captains, had obviously had some effect upon his confidence:

> Once on board *Warspite* there was a complete change of atmosphere. The relief was immense. The plan of attack and the forces placed under my command were both entirely to my satisfaction. I had complete confidence in the outcome of the operation. The Captain of *Warspite*, Victor Crutchley VC, and myself saw eye to eye.(8)

The Admiral's confidence was shared by the officers and men who appreciated the care and attention that was being paid to their welfare,:

> As before the previous action, medical officers were warned of impending events. The morale of the ships' companies was superb and they are reported to have faced the action in a spirit of pleased expectancy.(9)

The medical arrangements had been particularly well-prepared and contingency plans made. For Boy Seaman Roy Emmington and his comrades:

> We were all told we were going into Narvik with nine destroyers the next day; us boys were told by our instructor to bathe and put on clean gear and overalls.(10)

Clean bodies and underwear before a battle was a naval tradition going back to the time of Nelson and the Napoleonic Wars. It was a basic precaution to minimise the risk of infection of the quite horrific wounds suffered in a naval engagement, but in taking care of the men's bodily needs the cleansing of their souls was not forgotten:

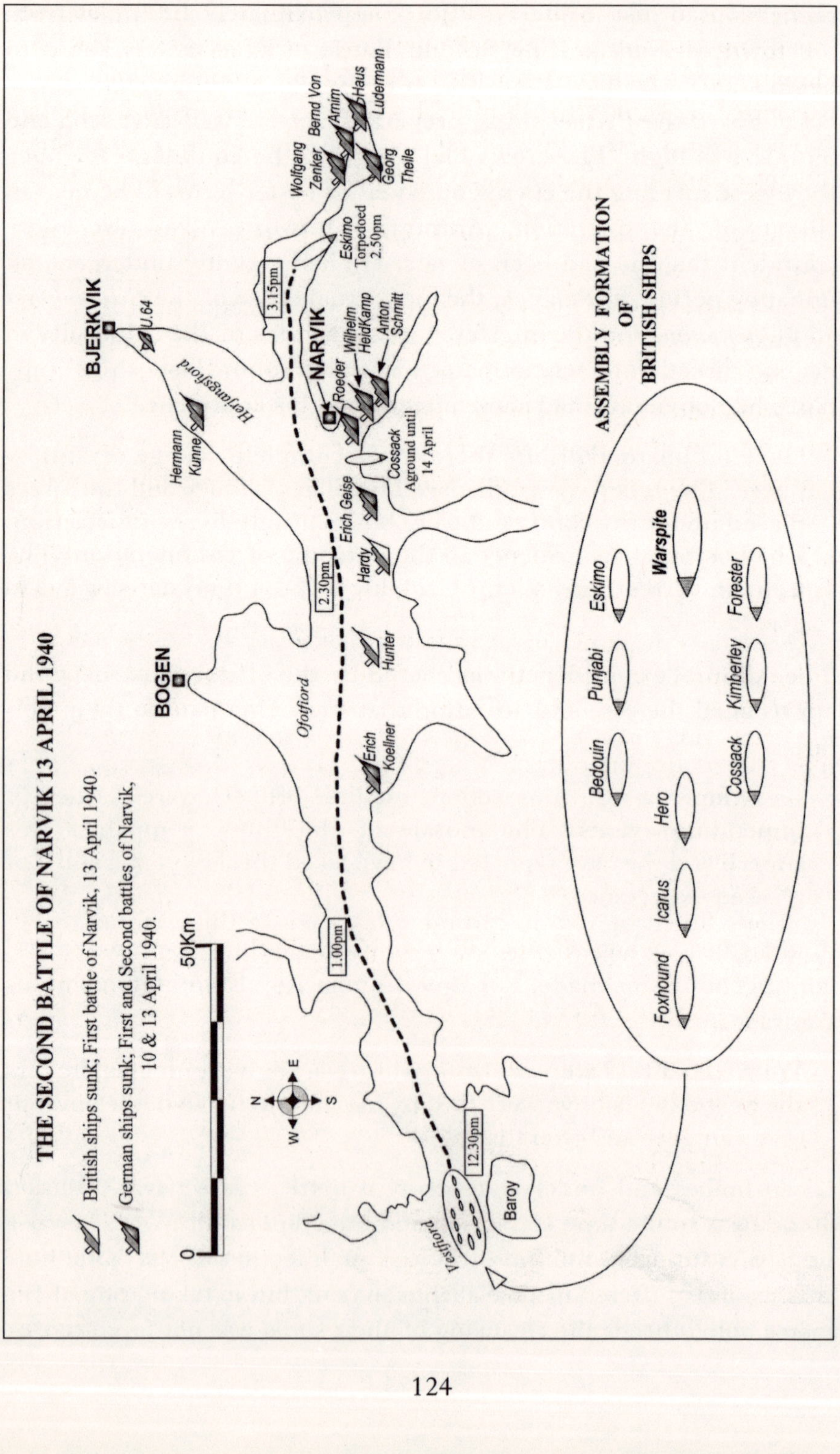
THE SECOND BATTLE OF NARVIK 13 APRIL 1940
British ships sunk; First battle of Narvik, 13 April 1940.
German ships sunk; First and Second battles of Narvik, 10 & 13 April 1940.
0
50Km
N
E
S
W
BOGEN
BJERKVIK
U.64
Herjangsfiord
Hermann Kunne
NARVIK
Roeder
Wilhelm HeidKamp
Anton Schmitt
Wolfgang Zenker
Bernd Von Arnim
Haus Ludermann
Georg Theile
Eskimo Torpedoed 2.50pm
3.15pm
Cossack Aground until 14 April
Erich Geise
Hardy
2.30pm
Hunter
Ofotfiord
Erich Koellner
1.00pm
12.30pm
Baroy
Vestfiord
ASSEMBLY FORMATION OF BRITISH SHIPS
Eskimo
Punjabi
Bedouin
Warspite
Forester
Kimberley
Cossack
Hero
Icarus
Foxhound

> The Captain accordingly addressed the Ship's company on the plan and also the attendant dangers that would ensue on the following day which started with a special Holy Communion at 8am attended by some three hundred, the average of a Sunday being about twenty. How often was one to see in the future celestial insurance policies being taken out before impending danger.(11)

Morale remained high as the ships cautiously made their way up the Westfjord. *Warspite* was screened ahead by *Foxhound*, *Icarus* and *Hero*, with mine-clearing sweeps streaming to clear a path through any minefields. *Bedouin*, *Punjabi* and *Eskimo* were on the starboard bow, and *Cossack*, *Kimberley* and *Forester* on the port. All the destroyers had to keep a sharp look out for torpedo attack from the damaged, but still highly dangerous, German destroyers deployed in ambush in the side fjords and inlets, and from the unknown number of U-boats waiting for an opportunity to sink the ultimate prize of *Warspite*. On the flagship, Petty Officer Reardon, Gunner's Mate, in 'A' turret, recalls:

> We are passing some land now and it looks very snow covered and forbidding. An early dinner today before going to Action Stations.(3)

His Officer Commanding, Lieutenant Hoare, in charge of the Forecastle Division of about 150 men including 'A' turret, remembered that:

> At about 11.30 we were given the standard constipating action stations lunch of two hard boiled eggs and a thick corned beef sandwich, and by noon we were waiting for things to happen.(11)

The crew were confident and relaxed:

> My own [gun] crew are on the fo'c's'le [*sic*] for a smoke; some wag rolls a snowball and one of 'B' turret crew gets it in the neck. This is the general signal for a snowfight between the two turrets when 'Action Stations' sounds ...'(3)

Although unsure about the German U-boats' strength and deposition, the Admiralty and Admiral Whitworth were well aware of the threat posed by torpedo attacks from submarines in the narrow confines of the fjord. There was little room for manoeuvre or the taking of evasive action for a big ship like *Warspite*. Fortunately the screening destroyers were by now on full alert. On HMS *Icarus*:

> Once or twice we saw torpedo tracks heading towards her, but quick signalling from our bridge enabled her to avoid them.(12)

Warspite's anti-torpedo tactics were not solely defensive. The Admiral also took an aggressive stance, using *Warspite*'s Swordfish float plane in an offensive role. Petty Officer Airman F.C. Rice recalled how:

> Lt. Cdr. W.L.M. Brown and myself were briefed by the Admiral, Captain Victor Crutchley VC and Commander Currie:-
> (i) Carry out a general reconnaissance for the fleet advancing up Ofotfjord, with particular reference to the presence of German warships inside fjords, the movements of German forces, and the positions of the shore batteries.
> (ii) Bomb any suitable targets.
> We were catapulted [off] at 11.52 on Friday 13 April 1940, in Swordfish Floatplane L9767 (Lorna). The crew:
> Self, Petty Officer Airman. Pilot
> Lt. Cdr. Brown. Observer
> Leading Airman Maurice Pacey. Telegraphist/Air Gunner.(13)

The Swordfish carried an assorted bomb load; two 250lb high-explosive bombs, two 100lb anti-submarine bombs and eight 40lb anti-personnel bombs. 'Lorna' was ready for any eventuality and action was not long in coming:

> *U 64* was seen on the surface at the top of Herjangsfjord near Bjrevkvik. I selected the two anti-submarine bombs and put the Swordfish in a dive and released the bombs at 200 feet. I couldn't see the bombs fall as we pulled out, but Pacey saw the starboard bomb fall close alongside and the port one hit just abaft the conning tower; the U-boat was already sinking when I could see her again. She hit us in the tail with one shot. I think it was from her 37mm gun.(13)

U 64, the first German submarine to be sunk from the air in the Second World War, was a brand new Atlantic class submarine and had had her sea trials curtailed to take part in the Norwegian operation. Thirty-six of her crew, who had put up a spirited resistance to the Swordfish attack, survived the sinking. For their parts in the action the pilot was awarded the D.S.M.*, the observer the D.S.C.†, and the telegraphist/air gunner was Mentioned in Dispatches. Despite the damage she had received, the Swordfish and her crew continued their reconnaissance, sending back vital information on the positions of enemy ships, before landing alongside *Warspite*, which had stopped off Narvik, at 16.00 hours and being hoisted in.

While the vigilance of the destroyers and her own aircraft undoubtedly saved *Warspite* from a number of torpedo attacks, pure luck was also to play its part. For once it was on *Warspite*'s side. Lieutenant Erich Topp, lieutenant and watchkeeping officer of one of the attacking U-boats, reflected how:

> Suddenly, through the periscope a number of destroyers came into view, steaming in three columns towards us; and behind them the grey shadow of a battleship. It was the *Warspite*, a giant among giants, steaming inevitably into our sights. The atmosphere on board was electric. It was as though the U Boat had clenched its teeth in its excitement. One or two men glanced nervously at the hydrophones as we turned to pass beneath the column of destroyers. No reaction from the enemy. We ourselves could hear his Asdic operating as it groped to find us. But he failed to locate our position ... We waited ... still no depth charges ... still no depth charges. They probably took the Asdic echo to denote submerged rocks. Tubes one and four had long been cleared for action. On these two torpedoes depended the fate of the whole expedition. If *Warspite* sank, Narvik was saved. And not only that; if we could sink the *Warspite*, with her would sink too the morale of the British troops landed at Andalsese – five thousand of them! If we could destroy the *Warspite*, Allied resistance would collapse and with it the belief in the invincibility of the British Navy. We went slow ahead, very slow. But we had to keep moving in order to maintain periscope depth. We waited. Forty-eight hearts beat so furiously that we could almost hear them. Then this nervous tension was shattered by a jolt that caused the whole vessel to shudder. From beneath the keel we heard a dull thudding and scraping. At the same instant we began to rise and the boat was down by the stern. The Commander

* Distinguished Service Medal

† Distinguished Service Cross.

acted like lightening. 'Aft hydroplanes hard down. Flood ballast tanks'.

In the periscope there appeared just the net cutter, and then the bows of the ship, foaming through the water. A moment later the upper edge of the turret and the loop aerial of the direction-finding gear mounted on it became visible. Further out British destroyers were approaching at speed. Some six hundred yards on the beam was *Warspite* firing at Narvik. As filthy bad luck would have it, she came straight into our line of fire. But we were no longer capable of firing, and a great, unique, chance is lost forever. An impish submerged rock had been the cause of the trouble. We had run straight into it and had been thrust upwards by it. Both motors were put to full astern to pull us off. The destroyers took not the slightest notice of us. Could it be that they had not seen us? In all the welter of misfortune that had overtaken us, this was our one piece of luck.(6)

It is perhaps not surprising that the escorting British destroyers had missed finding or seeing the U-boat. The surface ships were all at full stretch dealing with the German destroyers lying in ambush, and a series of sharp and bloody running encounters between individual ships were taking place on the run into Narvik. The defending German destroyers, tucked away in side fjords and inlets, were in strong positions to deal with the British ships as they passed by or rounded headlands. The exchanges between *Cossack* and the German destroyer *Roeder* were a case in point, as Cossack's captain explained:

Owing to the headland ... I could not get a visual sighting of the German ... but by the time my director was on, the German had several seconds to aim at *Cossack*'s large forepart coming round the point. The net result was that he scored several hits before I could get in a shot at him, and in the process cut my main steampipe, so killing one boiler-room crew and temporarily cutting off steam to the main engines. The way I had on carried me to a point where *Cossack* grounded*, but by this time I was going very slow, and so in due course after lightening the forepart and having the nasty experience of being fired at much too accurately

* According to Admiral Whitworth, '*Cossack* fouled and got caught up in the wreck of a merchant vessel, and was not aground in the ordinary sense of the word.'(8)

Above: The launch of HMS *Warspite*, Devonport, 26 November 1913. (By permission of the Trustees of the Imperial War Museum: Q113056)

Below: HMS *Warspite* undergoing repairs after the Battle of Jutland in No. 8 Dock, Devonport, 1916. (By courtesy of the Plymouth Naval Base Museum)

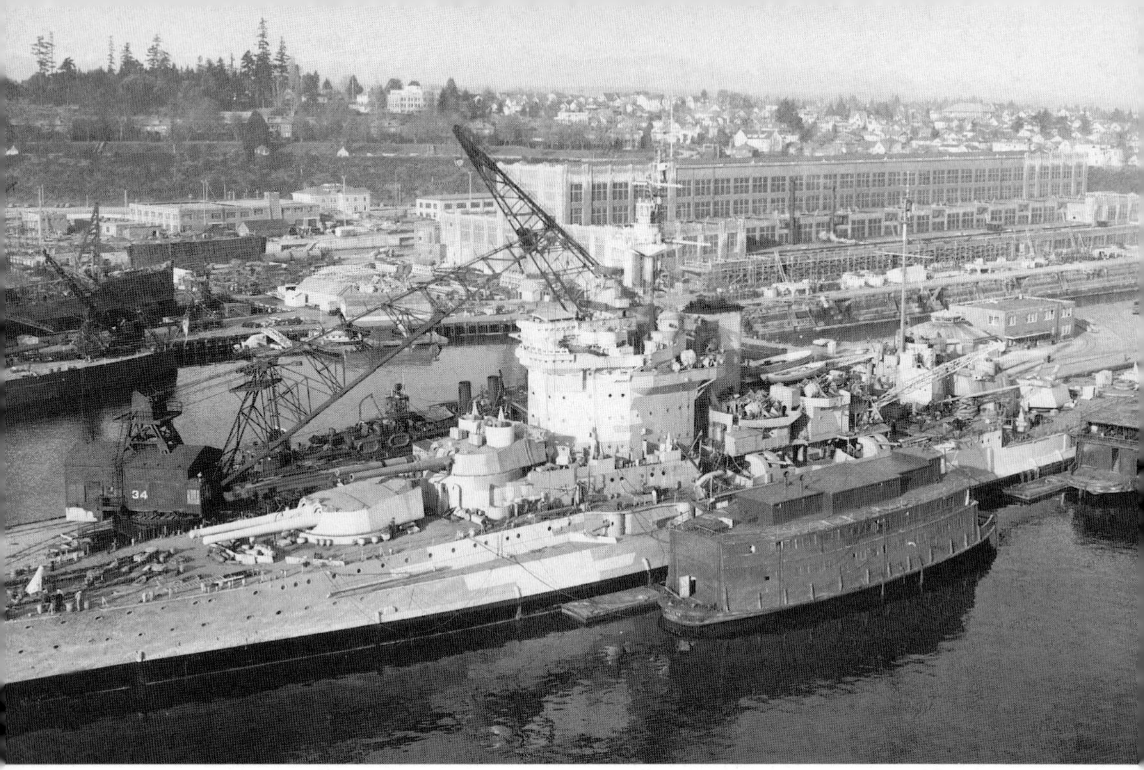

Above: HMS *Warspite*, her repairs after Crete nearly completed, at Bremerton Navy Yard in 1942. (By courtesy of Puget Sound Naval Shipyard)

Below: The loading gate of one of HMS *Warspite*'s 15in guns. (By permission of the Trustees of the Imperial War Museum: FL22140)

Above: HMS *Warspite* firing her main armament. (By permission of the Trustees of the Imperial War Museum: FL22131)

Below: The deck of the Italian battleship *Giulio Cesare* after being hit by a 15in shell from HMS *Warspite*, 8 July 1940. (By courtesy of Ufficio Storico della Marina Militare, Rome)

Above: HMS *Warspite* *c*1942. (By permission of Mrs J Stockton)

Left: Captain and officers of HMS *Warspite*, Valetta Harbour, Malta, December 1940. (By courtesy of Commander P Hoare)

Right: Able Dog Pluto. (By courtesy of Purfleet Heritage and Military Centre)

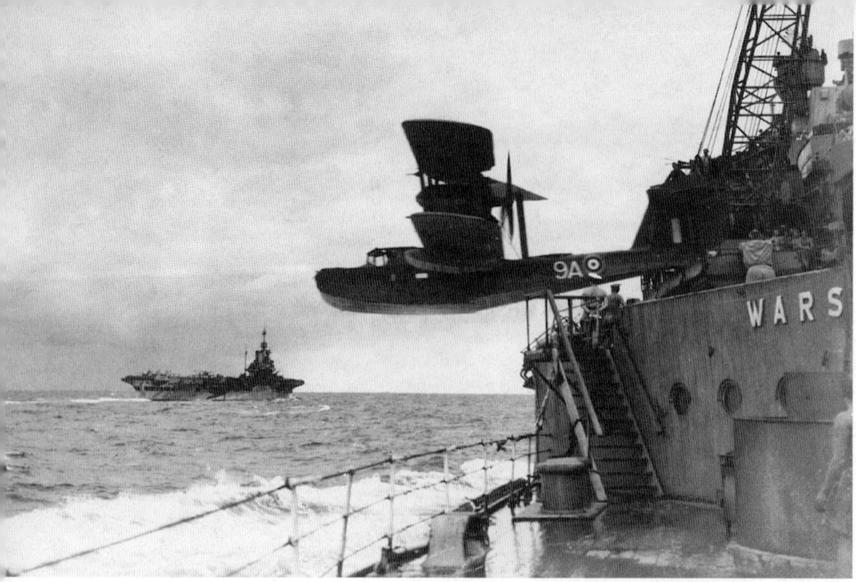

A Walrus aircraft being catapulted from HMS *Warspite*, with HMS *Formidable* in the background, 28 June 1942. (By permission of the Trustees of the Imperial War Museum: A11027)

The Commander-in-Chief, Admiral Cunningham inspecting the crew of HMS *Warspite*, his old flagship, August 1943. (By permission of the Trustees of the Imperial War Museum: A19001)

Captain H Packer (right, with telephone to ear), directs *Warspite*'s bombardment of Reggio, 2 September 1943, while the Navigator (centre) and the Officer of the Watch stand by. (By permission of the Trustees of the Imperial War Museum: A19248)

Loading four 15in shells into the after shell room of HMS *Warspite*; Far Eastern Fleet, 29 May 1942. (By permission of the Trustees of the Imperial War Museum: A10654)

View from the *Warspite* as HM Rescue Tugs *Jaunty*, *Oriana*, *Nimble* and *Restive* tow the 'Old Lady' to Gibraltar, 1000 miles away. (By permission of the Trustees of the Imperial War Museum: A27632)

HMS *Warspite* aground in Prussia Cove with the Penlee lifeboat, the *W & S*, manoeuvring under her stern. (By permission of the Morrab Library, Penzance)

A view of the partially dismantled *Warspite* seen from the ramparts of St Michael's Mount, *c*1951. (By permission of the Morrab Library, Penzance)

by a German mortar, which we could not see, we got off. We were very close to the dry land, and I remember a Norwegian coming down on skis and giving us some helpful information about the strength of the German garrison and their movements.(14)

The *Roeder*, who from her position had been mistaken for a shore battery, had received damaging hits from *Warspite* and, burning and irreparably damaged, was abandoned and blown up by her crew. It took twelve hours to repair the damage to *Cossack* caused by eight hits from the 5in guns of *Roeder*, get her off the obstruction and afloat. She was eventually able to make her own way, stern first and under the escort of HMS *Forrester* to Skjdfjord for the repairs necessary to get her home to the UK. HMS *Eskimo*, having avoided seven enemy torpedoes, was struck by the eighth, which blew away her bow:

> Finally only the *Thiele*, in the Rombaks Fjord, was still armed with two torpedoes. The first was let off by mistake and exploded against the rocks; the second was launched by the torpedo officer, Lieut. Sommer, in person and blew away the bows of the British destroyer *Eskimo*. With that the *Thiele* too was compelled to give up the unequal struggle. To save his crew, her captain Lieut.-Commander Max Eckardt Wolff, ran his ship at full speed onto the rocks.(5)

HMS *Eskimo* was towed to the Lofotens by HMS *Punjabi* and later to safety by HMS *Vindictive*.

While the destroyers were engaged in their deadly duels the *Warspite*, finding no shore batteries to attack, joined in the destroyer fights, with the sound of her 15in guns reverberating among the mountains surrounding the fjord. It was the first time that *Warspite*'s main armament had fired in anger since the Battle of Jutland nearly a quarter of a century before. For her gun crews, training and routine took over:

> We report to control and the Turret Officer tells me I can load. We hear the order repeated to the men down below, the cages come up with a thud, and out go the rammers. ... Suddenly comes the order 'Salvos', and the right hand gun comes to the ready. Then 'Enemy in Sight', and the sight setters chant out the ranges. It is like a practice shoot. Our guns are nearly horizontal, so the

> range must be short. Then the 'ding ding' of the fire gong, the right gun moves a little, comes steady and there is a 'Woof' which rocks the turret. The left gun is now at the ready and fires while the right gun is re-loading. B Turret, firing over our heads, blow away our 'blast bags' and the turret fills with smoke – like London on a November night. The Turret Officer calls out 'Tell the crew we have hit a destroyer and she is burning nicely.'(3)

For the crew at action stations entombed below decks, such news updates were a welcome relief:

> My own action station was in a small compartment that housed two air compressors that produced 4500 lb of pressure, and were used for clearing the 15-inch guns of burning cordite, which could, if not removed, ignite material being made ready for next firing. The noise they made was terrific. To reach my eventual tomb was through one armour plated door, down through a hatch of some six inches of steel that was wound shut, as all hatches and doors were, after ratings had reached their action stations. This took place at 11.00am approximately, and I was to be on my own for some 7-8 hours. There was a running commentary over the Tannoy System, which if it had been recorded at the time, would have been worth hearing again. I heard some of it, and had phone communication with the Engine Room, but it was almost impossible to hear with the noise in the compartment. After the operation had been completed successfully we were de-tombed and allowed on the upper deck. Wonderful fresh air, and a beautiful light.(1)

Other members of the crew were also allowed a breath of fresh air and a view of the effects of their actions:

> After a while 'Check fire' is ordered and the ship seems to be stopping. 'Crews may go on top of turrets', and up there is a sight – burning and sinking enemy ships all around us, and our own destroyers searching into every little corner that might hide something ... '(3)

The effects of *Warspite*'s guns had indeed been awesome. The German destroyer *Erich Koellner* was one that had felt the full effects of *Warspite*'s withering fire when, at 13.22 hours, the battleship passed the burning but still dangerous destroyer. Her crew were manning their torpedo tubes and, because of this threat, she received full point-blank broadsides at two miles range from all four 15in turrets and the starboard 6in guns. The *Erich Koellner* was completely torn apart, rolled over and sank.

By mid-afternoon *Warspite* and her attendant destroyers, less the damaged *Cossack* and *Eskimo*, were at the head of the fjord; and:

> By 5pm we had reached Narvik town with not only the [German] destroyers sunk but a submarine in the bag as well. And then came a majestic moment; we had not received any air attack or seen any sign of activity, and we anchored off the town on a beautiful spring evening surrounded by snow-capped hills, and all the turret's crew clambered through the man-hole in the roof of the turret and in a state of high elation ate our post-action tea of guess what – two hard boiled eggs and a corned beef sandwich.(11)

With all the men of the *Warspite* safe, it was time to start taking care of the wounded; there were large numbers to be seen to from the earlier actions:

> ... at 14.00 hours HMS *Punjabi* was in close action with the enemy for some fifteen minutes. This ship sustained much damage and was on fire in three separate places when she retired from the action. ... In HMS *Cossack* there were heavy casualties. This ship was struck by eight shells and most of her casualties occurred through explosions around the guns and in the boiler rooms. HMS *Eskimo*, having avoided seven enemy torpedoes was struck by the eighth. The explosion carried away the bows of the ship and the forward medical station disappeared with its staff. The ship remained afloat and turned in uncontrolled circles while her medical officer crawled about in water and oil fuel to attend to casualties trapped in the wreckage. The casualties from HMS *Eskimo* were taken on board HMS *Forester* which already had a small number of casualties of her own. ... It was not until June 5, at Barrow-in-Furness, that it was possible to remove many of the dead from the wreckage. Other destroyers taking part in the action – *Foxhound*, *Icarus*, *Bedouin*, *Hero* and *Kimberley* – all escaped with a comparatively light list of casualties, which is accounted for, to some extent, by the fact that the action was fought at very close range, so that many of the shells passed clean through a number of destroyers without exploding. In HMS

> *Foxhound* there were a few casualties from rifle bullets fired from the shore by German snipers.
>
> HMS *Warspite* had no casualties, but she took on board casualties from *Eskimo*, *Cossack*, *Punjabi*, *Foxhound* and *Forester*. *Warspite*'s sick bay had been damaged, so the forward medical flat was converted into an operating theatre in which fifty-nine major surgical casualties were treated. In due course the walking casualties from HMS *Warspite* were transferred to the SS *Franconia*. Cot cases were kept on board for twelve days* and were then transferred to HMHS *Isle of Jersey* on April 26. In due course these casualties arrived at the Royal Naval Auxiliary Hospital, Kingseat, Aberdeenshire. ... in this action HMS *Warspite* virtually performed the duties of a hospital ship for some time, which meant that the numerous casualties were subjected to far less handling and hardship than those in the First Battle of Narvik when there was no major ship present to perform such duties.(9)

The presence of so many wounded comrades on board had a profound effect upon the sailors of *Warspite*'s crew:

> The ship has stopped and *Forrester* and *Bedouin* are secured alongside with their bows to our quarterdeck. A little further up the fjord can still be seen three big fires, the remains of enemy destroyers burning away, and the smell of burning paint and flesh is horrible. *Forrester* and *Bedouin* are now transferring wounded and prisoners to us; the wounded are mainly from *Eskimo*; some nasty sights.(15)

Twenty-one year old Stoker Earrridge remembers how:

> They were laid out on our mess decks, and we heard that there had been over forty operations performed that night. To us young stokers, who had to step over them to reach the hatches to our own boiler or engine rooms etc, you knew this was definitely for real, especially when a young fellow asked me to cover his legs as they were cold, and you had to make believe, as he had lost both of them.(1)

After having achieved an overwhelming naval victory Admiral Whitworth now found himself in something of a dilemma. His ships and aircraft had sunk eight destroyers and one U-boat at the

---

* *Warspite* was still engaged in close action with the enemy for that time.

expense of two badly damaged and one less badly damaged destroyers. The Germans had no surface warships left in the fjord. He had at his disposal eight 15in guns, twelve 6in guns and nearly fifty 4.7in guns, and for the moment there seemed to be no worthwhile opposition. On the other hand his crews were tired and he had many wounded men on board. He was still uncertain about the number of U-boats still lurking in the fjord or at its mouth, and the threat of attack by enemy aircraft seemed imminent when German reconnaissance planes flew overhead at 18.00 hours. He was opposed by some 2000 enemy troops ashore and could, at best, only muster a landing party of some 200 sailors and marines to attempt to take the town and resist inevitable counterattacks. To use his naval guns to overwhelm and drive out the enemy troops from the town would result in many civilian casualties and heavy damage to their property. The Admiral was tempted to make the attempt, but decided against it.

Later that evening of the 13th, on the understanding that the arrival of Allied troops was imminent, he signalled:

> My impression is that enemy forces in Narvik were thoroughly frightened as a result of today's action and that presence of *Warspite* was the chief cause for this. I recommend that town be occupied without delay by main landing force.(4)

There is little doubt, had a properly-equipped Allied landing force been available and ready to land, that Narvik could have been taken at that time. When it became clear that no troops were immediately available it was thought prudent not to further expose the *Warspite* to the risk of air and U-boat attack in the very narrow confines off Narvik. Accordingly, in the early hours of the 14th *Warspite* withdrew, escorted by five destroyers, leaving two destroyers to keep an eye on developments and assist *Eskimo* and *Cossack*.

> The ship got underway again around 03.00 on 14 April and heads to sea again. On Sunday morning at 09.00 we held burial service for three ratings who had died since being brought aboard and again at 18.00 that evening for another who died.(9)

Warspite remained in the area of Westfjord in anticipation of assisting an allied landing to take Narvik, which, for a variety of reasons, became increasingly delayed. Her patrolling presence, together with that of her escorting destroyers, acted as a deterrent to any attempt by the Germans to reinforce their Narvik garrison from the sea. On 19 April *Warspite* had a narrow escape when attacked by *U 47*, commanded by the German ace Gunter Prien who had sunk the British battleship HMS *Royal Oak* at her moorings at Scapa Flow six months before on 14 October 1939:

> Sighted *Warspite* and two destroyers and attacked the battleship at a range of 900 yards. No success. As a result of the explosion of one of them at the end of its run I was placed in a most awkward predicament and was pursued by destroyers coming from all directions.(7)

Final analysis by the German High Command showed that in all four unsuccessful attacks had been made by U-boats on *Warspite* during the Narvik campaign. The failure of these attacks, and others on Allied ships, was due to complete failures in German magnetic torpedoes:

> Soon after the beginning of the war it became apparent that magnetic firing pistols, which should detonate the torpedo when it reached a position beneath its target, had by no manner been perfected. Very frequently the pistol detonated too early while the torpedo was still on its way to the target; or it detonated at the end of its run; or it failed to detonate at all, even when passing beneath its target. The depth at which the torpedo ran was also found to be considerably greater than the depth at which it had been set. In addition, the contact firing pistols, too, did not always function properly.(7)

The result was a complete failure of the German U-boat campaign in Norway; with the exception of *U 39*, not one German U-boat had a single success throughout the whole of the Norwegian operations. It was not the fault of the commanders, of their crews or of the boats themselves. The new magnetic torpedoes had proved a failure. 'The torpedo crisis is a national disaster'(6) declared a disillusioned and horrified Admiral Raeder.*

The crews of the British ships were not to know this good fortune, and of the handicap that the U-boats were operating under,

* Commander-in-Chief of the German Navy, 1938-1943.

when, on 24 April, *Warspite*, the cruisers *Aurora*, *Effingham* and *Enterprise*, and destroyers, supported by aircraft from the aircraft carrier *Furious*, were ordered back to bombard Narvik. The purpose was to attempt to dislodge or sufficiently disable the enemy forces, so that Allied troops could land virtually unopposed. Lack of suitable landing craft and assault weapons, plus deep snow, ruled out any consideration of attempting an opposed landing. For the wounded still on board *Warspite* it was not a welcomed return:

> ... I've often wondered just what went through the minds of these men, when as we did, they learned, being only 24 hours from [home] port, that we were going back to Narvik. ... Some of the injured were screaming when they heard gunfire again. After the event, one often breaks out in a cold sweat recalling some of these happenings.(1)

Any misgivings of the men were shared by some of the officers, sceptical that the objective could be achieved by naval gunfire alone. Meredith Dewey*, Chaplain on HMS *Effingham*, recorded in his diary entry of 23 April:

> ... unfortunately we have no H.E. shells – only anti-ship ones – nor have sea ammunition [*sic*] nor landing boats. ... Evidently Cork† determined to make a noise somehow. Glad to find no intention of sending a landing party which would be machine-gunned on the beach by the Germans – 2000 of them. All seems a bit pointless; no-one can tell whether any Germans in the town or forts or whether they have left for the hills. All hope that we shall make such a horrid noise that even if we do not hit a machine gun – we shan't fire at the town – the Germans will surrender. Seems little chance of this. But there will undoubtedly be a shindy tomorrow with the *Warspite* firing 15-inch at 1000 yards range. See that first lesson tomorrow Matins is the Fall of the Walls of Jericho.(16)

On 24 April the 15in and 6in guns of the *Warspite*, and the 6in of the *Effingham*, *Enterprise* and *Aurora* pounded away for three hours. It was to little effect; targets could not be seen under the covering of

---

* Later Dean of Pembroke College, Cambridge.

† The Earl of Cork and Orrery, Admiral of the Fleet, in charge of the naval operations in the Norwegian Campaign.

deep snow and few worthwhile results were obtained. A wireless station was destroyed together with some sheds and rolling stock in the railway marshalling yards, and a ferry steamer was sunk, but that was about all. The German garrison was not dislodged, despite having received some 150 rounds of 15in shells at 1000 yards range from *Warspite*, plus all the lesser calibre rounds of the other ships. On *Effingham*, Padre Dewey's diary records his impression of the day:

> Wednesday 24 April. Woken at 4.30am for breakfast and went on deck to see a magnificent sight. *Warspite* just astern with all 15-inch guns pointing to starboard and nine destroyers on either side. Narvik three miles up the fjord. A tedious five [*sic*] hours of bombardment though not as much noise as expected. Orders were to keep below, which I did. ... Popped up once though to see the small ship at the pier we had sunk and shells bursting round the railway and behind Narvik. The masts of several large ships could still be seen sticking up out of the water. We did our stuff after *Warspite*, *Aurora* and *Enterprise* had fired. Not a soul to be seen and only one reply from the enemy guns. Prevailing impression after that very little use, and in the Ward Room some aversion to the whole proceedings, it being bound to destroy some homes.(16)

It was becoming apparent that the Norwegian campaign as a whole was by now bogged down and that the struggle to take Narvik was degenerating into a prolonged siege rather than the prompt seizure recommended by Admiral Whitworth on the 15th. The Admiralty, with Winston Churchill the then First Lord, was nervous about the continued exposure of the modernised *Warspite* to air and U-boat attack, and decided to replace her with a slower, unmodernised 'R' class battleship, HMS *Resolution*, which was equally capable of carrying out bombardment duties.

Accordingly *Warspite* withdrew from the Norwegian campaign and returned to Scapa Flow and then Greenock. Even in home waters there was no escape from the dangers of war:

> We all knew that we would not stay in home waters for very long, but an event was to occur when we were ammunitioning ship one day with hatches open. After a large bang, bits of metal fell around the ship, we automatically thought of an Air Raid. However it was the French destroyer, the *Maille Brieze*, which

> had blown up. My girl friend heard the noise in the town centre where she was working in Woolworth's. The French, we were told, used rarefied air in their torpedoes, and one, upon being charged, shot along the deck, exploded in the entrance to the forward mess-decks, and trapped all the ratings there. The portholes of all destroyers at that time were too small to climb out of. ... All the small boats in the harbour converged on the destroyer to assist, and an Engineer and Stoker from the *Warspite* were sent over with oxy-acetylene cutting gear to try to weaken a patch by the portholes to enable the trapped men to force a way out. However, the heat was terrific, and eventually rescue attempts were abandoned, and she sank.(1)

About this time, on 27 April, Captain Crutchley was relieved of command of *Warspite*:

> We lost our Captain, Victor Crutchley VC. He was to become Commodore of Devonport Barracks, and in his farewell speech he gave us the impression that he was going to a job for a man with no arms and no legs.(1)*

He was replaced by Captain D.B. Fisher, CBE.

Back in Norway, the struggle for Narvik and the stalemated campaign continued. By early May events in the Low Countries and northern France had effectively reduced the Norwegian campaign to an expensive side-show. In mid-May the Germans had overrun Holland and Belgium and were making inroads into northern France. The Allies were in retreat, France was reeling and the British Expeditionary Force threatened with annihilation. On 20 May Churchill, now Prime Minister, proposed the abandonment of the Narvik campaign; and on 24 May, even before its final capture on 27 May, had ordered the evacuation of the Narvik area after the destruction of its port facilities. On that same day, 27 May, the evacuation of the British Expeditionary Force from Dunkirk began. Italy, seizing the moment, declared war on the Allies, and on 21 June France capitulated.

Great Britain, now alone, faced the imminent threat of invasion by the rampant German army. A major factor which prevented this

* Admiral Sir Victor Crutchley, VC, KCB, DSC, later commanded cruiser squadrons in the Pacific. He died on 26 January 1986.

was their shortage of warships to guard and oversee the passage of their army across the channel. Vice-Admiral Ramsey*, in charge of the Dunkirk evacuation, had no doubt as to the dangers of the situation and, ironically, of the part played by the Navy in the aborted Norwegian campaign in thwarting the German invasion of Britain:

> The menace of the invasion was very real. ... It was generally believed that Hitler would follow-up his successful advance to the coast by invading England while the British Army was short of equipment. The German Army and Air Force were free of all major commitments and now, if ever, was the moment for them to launch the full weight of their might against England. The British Naval losses had been heavy, and the Fleet was stretched to the limit in disputing Mussolini's bid for control of the Mediterranean while at the same time defending the vital supply lines in the North Atlantic. We did not know at the time how severely the German Navy had been hammered in the Norway campaign. Only two of their cruisers and about eight destroyers were fit for service.(17)

Warspite had played no small part in helping to reduce the number of available German destroyers, but now her services were required in the Mediterranean to help thwart Italian ambitions.

Thus on 30 April *Warspite* left Greenock for Gibraltar, sailing unescorted but taking a passage well out into the Atlantic to avoid prowling U-boats, and then onto Alexandria. She arrived on 10 May and immediately became the flagship of Admiral Cunningham, still Commander-in-Chief, Mediterranean:

> The *Warspite* arrived that night, and I moved over to her next day, May 11th ... and very glad we all were to be back in our old quarters. I think the men were glad to see us also. There is a cachet about being fleet flagship which extends to the most junior rating on board.(2)

His predecessor, Admiral Sir Dudley Pound, now First Lord of the Admiralty, remembered with nostalgia his own time as Com-

* Later Admiral Sir Bertram Home Ramsey. Was to become, as Allied Naval Commander, a key figure in the planning of Operation 'Overlord', the 1944 Allied invasion of Europe. Died in an aircraft accident in northern France in January 1945.

mander-in-Chief with the *Warspite* as his flagship when he wrote to Cunningham:

> You must be very glad to find yourself back in *Warspite*. I have not envied you in the last eight months but I do now.(3)

It was also time for new crew members to start a new life on the flagship:

> After a lengthy train journey along the Suez Canal we arrived at the port of Alexandria. I was a boy seaman at the age of sixteen when I boarded the *Warspite*.(19)

He was to have an eventful time on the *Warspite*. After dockyard repairs for blast damage from the action of her own guns, sustained in the Norwegian Campaign, *Warspite* was ready for sea and action on 24 May.

By 9 June the Admiralty had managed to assemble what was, on paper, a respectable fleet for Cunningham to command. He had the 15in gun battleships *Warspite*, *Malaya*, *Royal Sovereign* and *Ramillies*. The latter was undergoing a refit in the floating dockyard at Alexandria, and only the *Warspite* of the four 1915-vintage ships had been modernised. She was Cunningham's only battleship with anything like a respectable turn of speed and the increased range of her 'cocked-up' main armament was to prove crucial. The Commander-in-Chief also had the aircraft carrier *Eagle*, transferred from the China Station; the 7th Cruiser Squadron, consisting of *Orion*, *Neptune*, *Sydney*, *Liverpool* and *Gloucester*; and the 3rd Cruiser Squadron of *Capetown*, *Caledon*, *Calypso* and *Delhi*. All his cruisers had 6in guns; he had no heavy 8in gun cruisers. He also had a mixed bag of twenty-five destroyers and some twelve submarines. In early June Admiral Cunningham also had the support of one French battleship, the *Lorraine*, four French cruisers and three French destroyers based in Alexandria. Their support was to be in question after the French capitulation on 21 June.

Ranged against him was the more modern Italian fleet. Initially it was weaker in provision of capital ships, with only two battleships, the *Conte di Cavour* and the *Giulio Cesare* in commission in early June. Admiral Cunningham had had the opportunity to see at first hand these two future opponents during a pre-war goodwill visit that they had made to Malta:

> The two battleships were fine examples of old ships modernised, and the work had been most skilfully done. They had been rearmed with ten 12-inch guns and a good anti-aircraft armament. Some sixty feet had been added to their length and this, with modern boilers and machinery, gave them a reputed speed of 26 or 27 knots as against the 21.5 when they were completed in 1915.(2)

The Italians had another four battleships nearing service availability; the two First World War vintage battleships *Andrea Doria* and *Caio Duilio*, nearing completion of extensive reconstructions, and the two brand new *Littorio* class battleships, the *Littorio* and *Vittorio Veneto*, nearing completion and due for commissioning. A further two ships of this class, the *Impero* and *Roma*, were under construction. These latter four ships were of first class quality and would be formidable opposition. Each of 41,000 tons displacement, they carried nine 15in and twelve 6in guns and substantial anti-aircraft armament. They each had a speed of 30 knots. In the smaller classes of ship, the Italians were roughly on equal terms with the British although they had an advantage in 8in gun cruisers. The Italian air force, with large numbers of land-based planes, posed an as-yet undetermined additional threat to the Mediterranean Fleet. 'And so the stage was set.'(2)

On 11 June, *Warspite*, *Malaya* and *Eagle*, accompanied by seven cruisers and nine destroyers, carried out a sweep north-west of Crete. There was no response from the Italian Fleet or air force. For the newer crew members of the *Warspite* it was a somewhat disappointing introduction to war, but there were memorable moments for one young seaman:

> We were at sea 'closed up' in the A turret. It was a practice run when we had a 'misfire' in the left hand gun. After the strict procedure, the breech was opened and the cordite bags had to be retrieved. Being the smallest of the gun crew I had a rope tied to my leg and was shoved into the breech. With my arms outstretched, one arm each side of the bag and squeeze while I was pulled out. I do not remember how many bags. Upon inspection it was found that there were too many thicknesses of foil which prevented the charge from igniting the cordite. (18)

In late June the ambivalent position of the French ships not yet in German hands created a crisis of confidence between the former allies. In a nutshell, in order to avoid these ships falling into German hands, the British gave the French the alternatives of continuing to fight on the British side against the Germans, sinking the ships, decommissioning them, or, in the case of ships based in Oran, of sailing them to a French colony in the West Indies. It was a confused time for Frenchmen everywhere; on the ships there were, in varying degrees, pro-Allied and neutral factions. It was also a worrying time for the British. At Oran, where the two fast French battleships *Dunkerque* and *Strasbourg* were based, together with two further battleships and other vessels, an impasse in the negotiations was reached. On 3 July 1940, the *Hood*, *Valiant* and *Resolution* of Force H based at Gibraltar under the command of Admiral Somerville, a one-time captain of *Warspite*, bombarded the French ships at their moorings. There was much loss of life and the creation of a long-lasting bitterness between the former allies.

At Alexandria, Admiral Cunningham, under orders not to allow the French ships to leave, was able to persuade the officers and crews of the battleships and cruisers based there to effectively decommission their ships. It was a tense and suspicious time. Stoker Earridge remembered that:

> During this period, three French cruisers were in Alex harbour and not wishing to assist us. We had to ensure that they did not get away to assist the other side.(1)

With French honour having been called into question and decommissioning grudgingly accepted, and with simmering anger among the French crews caused by the British treatment of their Oran comrades, an uneasy relationship continued for sometime. Boy Seaman Hatch remembers:

> ... an incident involving the French battleship that was moored at the outer perimeter of the harbour. Apparently they were entertaining at night with all lights ablaze. For obvious reasons they were asked to darken ship. They were very reluctant; then they were informed that all guns from the Fleet were trained on them.(18)

It is a tribute to the patience and goodwill of the officers and men of both the French and British ships that major incidents and bloodshed were avoided at this time of minimal trust between the former allies.

Within a few days of the truce *Warspite* was to be called into serious action. Admiral Cunningham's plan was to bring two convoys safely to Alexandria from Malta: the first, a fast one of three merchant ships carrying civilians and non-essential personnel from the soon-to-be-besieged island, the second a slower one of four ships with stores and equipment. He determined to protect these convoys by aggressively sweeping into the eastern and central Mediterranean with virtually the whole of his fleet, in the hope of drawing out and engaging the Italian fleet and thus sufficiently distracting them from paying any serious attention to the convoys.

Flying his flag in the *Warspite*, Cunningham and his fleet left Alexandria harbour during the evening of 7 July. In addition to the *Warspite* he had the *Royal Sovereign* and *Malaya*, the aircraft carrier *Eagle*, the cruisers *Orion*, *Neptune*, *Sydney*, *Gloucester* and *Liverpool*, and seventeen destroyers. At 08.00 on 8 July the submarine *Phoenix* reported that at 05.15 she had sighted the two Italian battleships *Conte di Cavour*, flagship of Vice-Admiral Campioni, and *Giulio Cesare*, with an escort of four destroyers, some 200 miles east of Malta. The Italian force had not in fact been lured into battle but were part of a strong force which, in addition to two battleships, consisted of five 8in cruisers, twelve 6in cruisers and a total of twenty-four destroyers. They were, like their British opponents, covering convoy movements of their own, in this case five troopships sailing from Naples to the Libyan port of Benghazi.

Throughout the day Cunningham's force, travelling at a best speed of 20 knots in an attempt to engage the enemy, was subjected to high-level bombing attacks by land-based planes of the Italian airforce. The cruiser HMS *Gloucester* was hit on the bridge and her captain killed. Later intelligence reports on the movements of the Italian ships indicated that, although widely scattered, they were heading for the base of Taranto. By noon on 9 July the two opposing forces were still some ninety miles apart, with the Italians nearing home and safety and the British increasingly at risk as they neared the Italian mainland. Despite the dangers Cunningham was determined to bring the Italian fleet into action. In an attempt to damage and slow down the Italian heavy ships, the Commander-in-Chief ordered air strikes at 11.45 and 15.45 by torpedo bombers from *Eagle*. Neither were successful. He also took a calculated risk at noon of splitting his force. The Commander-in-Chief decided to leave the slower battleships, *Malaya* and *Royal Sovereign*, and the *Eagle*, to follow at their best speeds, while he forged ahead on the *Warspite*, screws churning the water, at her best speed of some 24 knots in support of his four cruisers which were racing ahead at 30 knots. The damaged *Gloucester* was ordered back to provide support for the *Eagle*.

> It was not quite the moment I would have chosen to give battle. They had a huge number of cruisers, and we, because the damaged *Gloucester* was not fit to engage in serious fighting, had no more than four which had little more than 50 per cent of their ammunition remaining.* Moreover the speed of approach was limited by the maximum speed of the *Royal Sovereign*. However, any opportunity was welcome . . .(2)

By 15.00 hours the four cruisers, under the command of Vice-Admiral John Tovey and now ten miles ahead of the *Warspite*, sighted the enemy light forces, and some ten minutes later HMS *Neptune* reported 'Enemy battlefleet in sight'. The cruisers were outnumbered, outgunned and outranged and they and the closing *Warspite* were hotly engaged over the next few minutes, at extreme ranges, by the enemy heavy units.

> It required a few salvos of 15-inch from the *Warspite* to redress the balance when the enemy's preponderance became too pressing.(2)

At 15.30 the enemy turned away under cover of a smoke screen and *Warspite*, now flat out at 24.5 knots, turned, deliberately this time, a complete circle to allow the *Malaya*, now forging ahead of the *Royal Sovereign*, time to catch up. On the *Royal Sovereign*, struggling to keep in touch, it was a time of frustration:

> I took a quick look through the layer's telescope and away out on the starboard side were our cruisers and destroyers, steaming at full speed with Battle Ensigns streaming out in the wind. It was quite a sight. Although *Warspite* and *Malaya* opened fire and the Italian shells were dropping close to us we did not return fire.

* In the first year of the war the Mediterranean fleet was frequently short of full ammunition stocks on its ships.

> The reason being that our ship was too slow and could not keep up with *Warspite*. *Malaya* was ordered to take over our place in the line.(10)

At 15.53, coming out of the turn, *Warspite* opened fire on the leading Italian battleship at a range of 26,000 yards. The Italians replied and, shooting well, straddled the British ship but without securing any hits. Then came the moment when a battle is both won and lost:

> The *Warspite*'s shooting was consistently good. I had been watching the great splashes of our 15-inch salvos straddling the target when, at 4pm, I saw the great orange coloured flash of a heavy explosion at the base of the enemy flagship's [*sic*] funnels. It was followed by an upheaval of smoke and I knew that she had been heavily hit at the prodigious range of thirteen miles. This was too much for the Italian Admiral, my old friend Riccardi, whom I had entertained in the *Hood* in 1938 and who kept The Life of Nelson on his bed table. His ships turned away, and having discharged seventeen salvos in all, the *Warspite* ceased firing at 4.04, the whole western horizon being overlaid with a thick pall of smoke behind which the enemy became completely hidden. From this time until about 4.40 we, in the *Warspite*, engaged a cruiser at long range which disappeared behind a smokescreen and let go a few salvos of 6-inch at enemy destroyers dodging in and out of the smoke.(2)

The British destroyers, now concentrated on the disengaged bow of the *Warspite*, and Vice-Admiral Tovey's four cruisers, were being hotly engaged by the enemy cruisers, scrapping to cover the retirement of their battlefleet. The British destroyers were ordered to counter-attack by Admiral Cunningham, himself an old destroyer man who was still full of fight and enjoying the cut and thrust:

> From *Warspite* it seemed a most unconventional battle. Leaning over the bridge, the Commander-in-Chief laughingly indicated each enemy ship as it darted out of the smoke with a variation of the remarks: 'There's another b*****!' 'Shoot that b***** up.' *Warspite*'s guns, therefore, engaged a variety of targets, but few of these waited for a second salvo. They preferred that bank of smoke.(19)

Keen though he was to continue the fight, Cunningham was not so reckless as to plunge through the smoke screen in pursuit of the

Italian ships. He was fully aware of the risk of being drawn into a set trap of submarine and aircraft attacks. The British fleet therefore began working its way windward and northward of the smoke. In doing so they were subjected to heavy bombing attacks from large numbers of Italian aircraft with the *Warspite* and *Eagle* singled out for particular attention. By 17.00 hours, when the British ships had worked around the area covered by the smoke, no Italian ships were in sight, having retired towards the Straits of Messina. Thus effectively ended the encounter off Calabria, or Punta Stilo, with Cunningham and his ships now only twenty-five miles from the Calabrian coast.

It was clear that the British had won the scrap and that the 15in long-range shell hit upon the Italian flagship had been pivotal in the encounter; nevertheless Admiral Cunningham was unhappy at the outcome:

> The action was most unsatisfactory to us. I suppose it was too much to expect the Italians to stake everything on a stand up fight. Yet, if they had timed their attacks better with all types of arms they employed they might have given us much trouble. The one 15-inch hit they sustained from the *Warspite* had a morale effect quite out of proportion to the damage. Never again did they willingly face up to the fire of British battleships, though on several subsequent occasions they were in a position to give battle with a great preponderance of force.(2)

The shell had wrecked secondary armament on the *Cesare*, killing and wounding over 100 men. It caused a fire below decks and, as the smoke circulated through the ventilators, caused a group of boilers to be extinguished with a consequent loss of speed from 26 to 19 knots. *Warspite*, although sustaining no casualties, had, as usual, not gone unscathed:

> Observers on the *Cesare* thought that a hit had been scored on the *Warspite*, whose after turrets ceased firing amidst rising flames. It was learned later from British reports however that the *Warspite*'s reconnaissance plane had caught fire from the flash of the ship's own salvos over the stern.(20)

Warspite's crew resolved the problem by dumping the aircraft overboard.

In fairness the Italians had their point of view on this encounter:

> At this time the *Cavour* and *Cesare* were the only Italian battleships in service. It must have appeared to the enemy, who had many battleships in reserve, to be a splendid opportunity to eliminate the *Cavour* and *Cesare* before the other Italian battleships were ready for service. The Italian Fleet on the other hand, had exactly the opposite interest – to avoid fighting against superior forces. It was the Italian Navy's hope that the Air Force would be able to cripple the enemy battleships before surface contact was made, with the result that there would be some equality of forces.(20)

The Regia Aeronautica certainly tried hard, both before and after the battle, to sink the British Fleet. Moving first towards Malta and then on to Alexandria as defence cover for the two convoys, the ships were subjected to almost continuous air attack.

Back in Malta, the Vice-Admiral responsible for the passage of the two convoys to Alexandria had been delaying their sailing pending the outcome of Cunningham's sortie to entice the Italian Fleet. On learning that the two Fleets were joined in battle, and deciding that the Italians would be too preoccupied to offer much naval opposition, he had sailed the fast convoy of the three merchant ships, *El Nil*, *Knight of Malta* and *Rodi*, at 23.00 hours on 9 July with an escort of four destroyers. Cunningham, meanwhile, heading towards Malta, sent off *Royal Sovereign* and her screening destroyers to refuel at Malta and then to escort, together with *Malaya*, *Eagle* and remaining destroyers, the slow convoy to Alexandria. The cruisers were divided between the two convoys as additional protection. Admiral Cunningham, who needed to attend an important conference with his fellow Army and Air Force Commanders-in-Chief, pushed on ahead to Alexandria, with the *Warspite* and escorting destroyers.

Both the slow convoy and its heavy escort, and *Warspite* and her accompanying escorts, were subjected to continuous attack until sunset on 12 July by Italian aircraft from Libyan airfields. Despite the determination of the attacks there was little damage and few casualties among the ships:

> In all, during our five days at sea on this occasion, the *Warspite* and the five destroyers with her were attacked thirty-four times

> in four days, something over four hundred bombs being dropped. Particularly do I remember a most virulent attack on July 12th during our return passage to Alexandria when twenty-four heavy bombs fell along the port side of the ship simultaneously, with another dozen on our starboard side, all within two hundred yards, but slightly out on line. Other ships had much the same sort of experience. On this day I saw the *Sydney*, which was in company, completely disappear in a line of towering pillars of spray as high as church steeples. When she emerged I signalled 'Are you alright?' to which came the rather dubious reply from that stout-hearted Australian Captain J.A. Collins, now a Flag Officer in the Royal Australian Navy, 'I hope so.'(2)

Back on *Warspite*, the Air Defence Officer had particular reason for trying to remain 'cool under fire' during this time:

> Bombs, bombs, bombs; yet surprisingly few ships were hit. ... In my memory I can only reach back to the sounding of alarm bells, to the whine of the forced-draught fans as the ship rapidly increased speed, and to the wide swathes of bombs as they crossed and re-crossed the fleet. Action Stations, Defence Stations and much more rarely Cruising Stations (the lowest degree of readiness). One after the other, day in, day out. On one occasion, in an interval between air attacks, a tired bridge messenger accidentally tripped up, and shot a jug of scalding cocoa down the back of my neck. My roar of pain coincided with the 'Air Raid Red' alarm bells. Captain Fisher turned round and said to me 'We seem to be rather noisy in our closing up today A.D.O'.(3)

For the Commander-in-Chief at least, there was both a benefit and a personal blessing resulting from the concentrated air attacks upon the fleet and the slow convoy:

> The attention the Italians paid to the fleet and the slow convoy caused them to entirely overlook the fast convoy carrying the personnel from Malta. For that I was supremely thankful, as my wife and two nieces were on board [the *El Nil*]. Their convoy arrived safely at Alexandria at 9am on July 13th, the *Warspite* having reached harbour three hours earlier. Knowing we had been in action, they were delighted to see the flagship, though somewhat perturbed to notice she was heeled over. In point of fact she had

> been purposely listed to examine the bulges to see if they had been damaged by near misses.(2)

Although Cunningham and his ships had been undoubted victors in the encounter off Calabria, he had serious reservations as to the capabilities of his ships in any future encounter. He was particularly concerned about the vulnerability of his older, unmodernised battleships to air attack, their lack of speed and inferior gunnery capability. Too much depended upon the *Warspite*. The Italian battleships and heavy cruisers had comfortably straddled the British ships at a range of 26,000 yards and only the *Warspite* had been able to match the range and accuracy. On the way back Cunningham's ships had been bombed throughout the hours of daylight by some hundred planes and been lucky to escape without heavy losses. The *Eagle* and the *Royal Sovereign* in particular had borne charmed lives. The Mediterranean Fleet badly needed reinforcements and air cover.

On 17 August 1940 *Warspite*, with the Commander-in-Chief on board, *Malaya*, *Ramillies*, the 8in cruiser *Kent* and an escort of twelve destroyers set out to bombard Italian installations and troop concentrations close to the Egyptian border. The targets were the port of Bardia and Fort Capuzzo near Sollum. While *Malaya* and *Ramillies* concentrated upon Bardia, *Warspite* and *Kent* dealt with Fort Capuzzo some ten miles away. It was a satisfactory bombardment, with *Warspite* firing sixty 15in and nearly fifty 6in shells. It was a pity that the cruiser *Effingham**, a bombarding partner at Narvik, was not in company; it would have been an appropriate occasion for that ship's chaplain to re-read the lesson on the Fall of the Walls of Jericho:

> The *Warspite* did one bombardment on Fort Capuzzo. The walls were said to be thirty feet thick, and they went.(1)

Cunningham's request for reinforcements following the action off Calabria was quickly met by Pound. The Mediterranean Fleet received the 8in cruiser *Kent* and lost the *Royal Sovereign* which had left for Durban, South Africa, for docking to repair underwater bomb damage. More reinforcements were on the way. *Warspite*'s sis-

---

* HMS *Effingham* was lost in the Norwegian campaign, becoming wrecked and having to be destroyed by other ships of the Royal Navy on 21 May 1940.

ter ship, the modernised *Valiant*, together with the aircraft carrier *Illustrious* and the anti-aircraft cruisers *Coventry* and *Calcutta*, left the United Kingdom on 20 August *en route* for Alexandria via Gibraltar, which they left on 30 August. The plan was for the reinforcements to be escorted by elements of Force H – the battlecruiser *Renown*, the aircraft carrier *Ark Royal* and the cruiser *Sheffield*, plus seven destroyers – half way across the Mediterranean. Cunningham also left Alexandria on 30 August, flying his flag in *Warspite*, accompanied by *Malaya*, *Eagle*, the cruisers *Orion* and *Sydney* and nine destroyers to meet up with the reinforcements. A convoy of two merchant ships and an oil tanker also left Alexandria for Malta at the same time, with a close escort of four destroyers. Air reconnaissance showed that the Italian Fleet was also at sea on 31 August: two battleships, seven cruisers and eight destroyers were steering towards Cunningham's force, but at a distance of some 130 miles. However the Italian Fleet turned away towards its base at Taranto, and, with Cunningham's first priority being to shield the convoy and not to be lured away to leave it open to attack, there was no encounter. On the morning of 2 September, with *Warspite* in sight of Malta, the reinforcements met up with Cunningham's force and joined the Mediterranean Fleet. So ended *Warspite*'s first year of the war: the combined Fleet returned to Alexandria on 5 September.

The Italians began a long-expected offensive in the Western Desert against the Egyptian frontier on 13 September, and on 28 October invaded Greece. The need to support the Greeks and assist the Army in the Western Desert, as well as continuing to escort convoys to and from Malta, now placed great strain upon the ships and men of the Mediterranean Fleet. Cunningham received much-needed further reinforcements in the shape of *Warspite*'s sister ship *Barham*, the 8in cruiser *Berwick* and the 6in cruiser *Glasgow*. Numerically, the Mediterranean Fleet was now much more of a match for the Italian Fleet.

Numerical superiority over the Italians in terms of capital ships was achieved, at least in the short term, on the night of 11 November 1940 when Swordfish aircraft from *Illustrious*, supplemented by aircraft and aircrew transferred from the temporarily disabled *Eagle*, carried out a torpedo attack on the Italian Fleet at their base in Taranto. It was an outstanding success, which overnight changed the balance of power in the Mediterranean. The *Conte de Cavour* was sunk by the bows in shallow water and, although raised, took no further part in the war, the *Caio Duilio* was so badly damaged that she had to be beached to stop her from sinking, and the *Littorio* was put out of action for a year.

Warspite spent the last few months of 1940 escorting convoys passing to and fro between Alexandria and Malta and Crete. These sorties were almost invariably carried out under heavy bombing attacks. During her return from one sortie *Warspite* had on board, in addition to the Commander-in-Chief and his staff, an American War Correspondent who, with an air attack imminent, was sitting typing in the wardroom. A young lieutenant was sent down to invite him on deck so that he could write a good eye-witness story. The invitation was met with: 'No, sir. My people want a live story not a dead correspondent.'(2)

In addition to being bombed by day, at sea or in Alexandria harbour, the fleet was now also being subjected to night bombing attacks:

> They were nerve-racking and dangerous, particularly as they were thrown in at dusk after our aircraft carrier had flown on all her fighters for the night. We had no specially equipped night fighters. However we realised how lucky we were that they had not started when we were entirely without radar. The *Illustrious*, so fitted, now picked up the attackers at a good distance and they were met with a heavy barrage at five miles.(2)

Throughout these sorties during the early part of the war, Cunningham was very much the sea-going Commander-in-Chief, accompanying the battlefleet whenever possible and directing operations at first hand. He had a fixed routine:

> In the *Warspite* I carried out my usual routine. I never took my clothes off at sea except for my daily bath, and never left the close proximity of the bridge. I had a sea cabin and bathroom one ladder down, and here I had my meals unless some urgent situation compelled me to have them in the Commander-in-Chief's chart-house on the bridge. The five Commanders on the staff, Dick, Carne, Barnard, Brownrigg and Power, kept watch day and night and conducted the routine movements of the fleet. By day I was practically always on the bridge and if I was not the Chief of

> Staff, Rear Admiral Willis was there. If things were quiet he would be on the bridge until midnight, when he was relieved by the Captain of the Fleet, Richard Shelley, until 3 or 3.30am. Then I came up, and was always on the bridge at dawn. I was on call, of course, at any time during the night. Everything was reported to me, and I was invariably up for any alterations of course other than the normal zig-zags.(2)

However his presence, and that of his staff, did cause some problems and tensions on *Warspite*. Cunningham had with him when at sea, in addition to the above-mentioned senior staff, some two dozen, mainly reservist, paymaster executive officers. Senior in age, experience and outlook to the majority of *Warspite*'s officers, there were tensions caused by the shortage of adequate accommodation, particularly over wardroom overcrowding at mealtimes:

> There was soon a muttering about the quality of the food. The Commander, Charles Madden, who was then President of the Mess, accordingly announced that all officers' names would be put in a hat, and whoever's name was pulled out would arrange the menus for the following week, thereby presumably ensuring at least one satisfied customer. Alas, the first name out of the hat was a newly joined young Surgeon Lieutenant who the previous season had been a Scottish second row rugby trialist. On the first morning at breakfast all these newly acquired senior officers sat down to breakfast and had an acute seizure when they found they were being offered mutton chops and beer! The experiment proceeded no further.(11)

The invasion of Greece by the Italians had made the island of Crete, off the southern coast of that country, of major strategic importance because of its commanding position in relation to the Eastern Mediterranean and the Suez Canal. Suda Bay, an excellent natural deep water harbour on the north-western coast of the island, thus became an increasing focus for the fleet's activities as an advanced base for the support of Greece. With this facility, and with the Italian battlefleet severely mauled at Taranto and having dispersed their remaining heavy units to more distant ports such as Naples, Cunningham was able to take a more offensive stance against the Italian forces. Thus on 18 December, after having covered Malta-bound convoys for two days, Cunningham's battlefleet refuelled at Suda Bay and sailed into the Adriatic to bombard the Albanian port of Valona, the main supply port for the Italian offensive against Greece. The bombardment took place in very bad weather, with *Warspite* and *Valiant*, accompanied by the cruisers *Gloucester* and *York* and a destroyer escort, firing 100 15in shells into the port and nearby airfield. It was later found that some twenty enemy aircraft had been destroyed or damaged on the airfield.

After the bombardment *Warspite*, with the Commander-in-Chief on board, sailed on to Malta. It was the first time that she had been able to do so since May and was indicative of the ascendancy that the Navy and Royal Air Force had managed to achieve over their enemy counterparts. The ship had a tremendous welcome:

> ... the *Warspite* steamed into the Grand Harbour during the early afternoon of December 20th. It was our first visit since May, and news of our arrival had been spread abroad. As we moved with our band playing and guard paraded, the Barracas and other points of vantage were black with wildly cheering Maltese. Our reception was touchingly overwhelming. We stayed in Malta about forty hours completely undisturbed by any air attack. It was a most useful visit.(2)

Warspite returned to Alexandria, after an uneventful passage, on Christmas Eve. Meanwhile, in the Western Desert the Army had made major territorial gains, and, in the Mediterranean at least, 1940 ended on a high note. It was all to change in 1941.

CHAPTER 5

1941: Nadir of the Navy

1939 and 1940 had been bad years for the Royal Navy. It had lost one battleship, two aircraft carriers, two cruisers, thirty-seven destroyers and twenty-four submarines, plus thousands of irreplaceable experienced seamen, in trying to protect the country and cover its wartime commitments. 1941 was to prove even worse and would become arguably the year when the Navy's fortunes, and those of *Warspite*, reached their lowest ebb.

Warspite's working year began early when, on 2 January 1941, she bombarded the Libyan port of Bardia in support of the advancing British Army. The port fell shortly afterwards. A week later *Warspite*, *Valiant* and *Illustrious*, plus escorts, were out on Operation 'Excess', to meet up with an eastern-bound convoy out of Gibraltar off Malta. The objective of Operation 'Excess' was the safe passage of four merchant ships through the Mediterranean, three bound for Piraeus with supplies for the Greek Army and the other with supplies, including much-needed anti-aircraft ammunition, for Malta. At the same time, the opportunity was being taken to cover the running of two merchantmen with supplies, fuel oil and petrol from Alexandria to Malta and of an oiler to Suda Bay, Crete. During the afternoon of 10 January the battlefleet was subjected to a ferocious air attack by a mixed force of Italian and Luftwaffe aircraft. The German aircraft were part of the newly-arrived X Fliegerkorps, an elite force of anti-shipping attack specialists. Their well-rehearsed dive-bombers were a new feature in the Mediterranean theatre:

> One was too interested in this new form of dive-bombing attack to be really frightened, and there was no doubt we were watching complete experts. Formed roughly in a large circle over the fleet they peeled off one by one when reaching the attacking position.

We could not but admire the skill and precision of it all. The attacks were pressed home to point blank range, and as they pulled out of their dives some of them were seen to fly along the flight deck of the *Illustrious* below the level of her funnel.

I saw her hit early on just before the bridge, and in all, in something like ten minutes, she was hit by six 1,000lb bombs, to leave the line badly on fire, her steering gear crippled, her lifts out of action, and with heavy casualties.

The *Warspite* was hit once, on the fluke of the starboard bower anchor. Actually I saw the bomb burst, but fortunately the detonation was incomplete and we suffered no great harm. One of the staff officers who saw it hurtling over the bridge from astern told me it looked about the size of the wardroom sofa.(1)

Other ships were not so lucky; the cruiser *Southampton* was sunk and the *Gloucester* damaged.

It was on this day of setback in the Mediterranean that the Navy, and the country, received a very welcome lifeline from the United States, the value of which was not realised at the time, when, back in London:

Very annoyed at being disturbed early by the P.M. He is delighted by the new American bill which allows British warships the use of American ports and contains wide powers for the President in every sphere of assistance for us. He says this is tantamount to a declaration of war by the United States. At any rate it is an open challenge to Germany to declare war if she dares.(2)

Warspite was urgently to need such assistance before the year was out, but the first beneficiary was to be the *Illustrious*. Despite her damage the aircraft carrier was able to limp into Grand Harbour, Malta, for emergency repairs, carried out amidst almost continuous air attacks. *Illustrious* left on 23 January and reached Alexandria safely two days later before going, via the Suez Canal, to the safety of the United States for more permanent repairs. She would be out of the war for many months. *Warspite* had another of her mishaps when, on the night of 31 January, she was rammed by the destroyer *Greyhound* on her way out of Alexandria harbour. The damage to her bulges was slight and soon repaired, using the dockyard facilities.

By the early months of 1941 it was becoming increasingly obvious to the Germans that their Italian allies were not making much headway in the struggle for Greece and the Western Desert. At sea the Royal Navy was in the ascendancy, with the Italian Navy, following the action off Calabria and the raid on Taranto, preferring to keep its heavy units dispersed in their home bases. The German High Command was becoming disenchanted, contemptuous even, of their ally's naval capability. In the opinion of Field Marshal Kesselring*:

> As might be expected from a nation of southern temperament, the Italian armed forces were trained more for display than for action ... The Italian navy was regarded as a piece de resistance and was therefore used sparingly – an attitude which caused special internal difficulties. Yet three times we managed to overcome these and get it to put to sea. A further trouble lay in its being stationed in different harbours; to assemble it cost time and wasted fuel. Finally, one or other battleship was either not ready to put to sea, or was not fuelled, or was in dock. Exercises in large formations could not be carried out mainly because of this same shortage of fuel. Gunnery practice was a rarity. On top of this there were extraordinary technical deficiencies which deservedly earned the Italian navy the nickname 'Fine-weather Fleet'. Its doubtful seaworthiness called for increased air protection, and that, with the limited strength of the Axis air forces in the Mediterranean, imposed ridiculous demands on the German Luftwaffe, whose hands were already full protecting convoys. If the Italian fleet by any chance ever came within extreme range of the British fleets and a few shots were actually exchanged, it had to break off the engagement at the approach of dusk because of its inability to fire in the dark, and run for the nearest port – Taranto or Messina.(3)

The entry of the Germans into the Mediterranean theatre in support of their faltering Italian allies was to have a major impact upon operations in the Mediterranean throughout 1941, and at times would push the British to the brink of defeat there. The running of convoys to Malta and Greece became increasingly difficult and costly in terms of ships and men; and these tasks, plus the bom-

* German Commander-in-Chief, South, which embraced the Mediterranean theatre, from 1941 to 1945.

barding of Libyan ports and installations in support of the Army, were to keep the Navy, including *Warspite*, fully occupied in the early months of 1941. Between the sailings there were some compensations ashore to help the sailors relax. For the crew of *Warspite*, justifiably proud of their record and exploits, and of their status as flagship of the fleet, some of these compensations were humbling:

> There was of course much opportunity for recreation in the gaps between these goings-on, and one of these was the Inter-service/Inter-unit seven a side rugby tournament. HMS *Warspite*, of whose team I was a member, drew some obscure New Zealand army unit in the first round, which became rapidly less obscure when we met on the field of play, for it transpired that the whole of the team had been members of the last All Blacks touring party. It seems hard to believe, but we achieved, in a game that only lasted eight minutes each way, to lose by over sixty points to nil.(4)

As part of the German build-up some intrepid U-boats braved the treacherous waters of the eight-mile-wide Straits of Gibraltar, slipping past the British patrol boats, The presence of these U-boats, plus the bombers, and especially the dive-bombers, of the Luftwaffe, made it increasingly difficult, if not impossible at times, to sail convoys from end to end of the Mediterranean and to supply Malta and Alexandria from Gibraltar. Supplies had increasingly to come via the Cape and Suez Canal, with consequent shortages and delays. Food supplies were difficult to maintain and diets became somewhat monotonous; on *Warspite* one wag could not resist decorating the galley's menu-board:

> Supplies were short and we were eating corned beef and rice. Someone sketched what looked like a potato and under it was printed 'this is a potato'. We must have been out of potatoes for some time.(5)

By the end of March increased Axis activity in the south-eastern Mediterranean and top secret ULTRA* intercepts indicated that a German-backed attack upon Greece was imminent. In anticipation of an attack upon supply convoys sailing to and from Greece and Crete, Admiral Cunningham and his staff made preparations to

---

* ULTRA was a top-secret Allied code-breaking activity run from Bletchley Park, England.

position the battlefleet to the west of Crete to meet any such threat. He doubted, however, that the Italian Fleet would show up:

> ... I bet Commander Power, the Staff Officer, Operations, the sum of ten shillings* that we would see nothing of the enemy.(1)

Elaborate plans were made to mask the fleet's departure, with the C-in-C, in civilian clothing, making his intentions of spending the night of 27 March ashore obvious around the dockside, after playing golf in the afternoon on links where he knew the Japanese consul would be playing. This gentleman, ostensibly then neutral, was suspected of reporting British warship movements to the Axis powers. Late that evening he hurried back to *Warspite* and sailed under cover of darkness:

> What the Japanese consul thought and did when he saw the empty harbour next morning was no affair of mine.(1)

Warspite of course chose to have one of her mishaps on leaving harbour. She was sailed too close to a mudbank and stirred up the mud, contaminating her condensers. This reduced her speed, and hence that of the battlefleet, to 20 knots, which was later to cause some difficulty.

The Italian Fleet was also stirring; it looked to be one of the occasions when it was going to come out of its harbours to do battle. It had already made the first move. On 26 March, in a very daring raid, Italian one-man explosive motor boats succeeded in evading the rudimentary harbour defences at Suda Bay and so badly damaged HMS *York* that she had to be beached and became a total loss. At that time she was the Mediterranean Fleet's only 8in cruiser.

The next morning, air reconnaissance from Malta, aided by the ULTRA intercept information, found three Italian cruisers and a destroyer some eighty miles off the south-eastern corner of Sicily, sailing in the direction of Crete. The Italian Fleet was out, and, unbeknown to Cunningham at that time, in considerable force. It had assembled from its dispersed home ports to attack Allied supply lines to Greece and Crete in support of a German land attack upon Greece. From Naples, and flying his flag in the *Vittorio Veneto*, Admiral Iachino had a brand-new 35,000-ton battleship,

* 10 shillings was equivalent to 50 pence.

armed with nine 15in guns and with a speed of 30 knots. The *Vittorio Veneto* also had a form of 'internal bulge' bulkhead running the length of the ship, designed to absorb the shock of a torpedo explosion without serious damage to the vitals of the ship, and so to enable her to continue steaming after being struck by torpedoes. It was to prove a godsend to the Italians in the forthcoming engagement. From Messina came the three 10,000-ton heavy cruisers *Trieste*, *Trento*, and *Bolzano*, each armed with eight 8in guns; and the two 8000-ton cruisers *Abruzzi* and *Garibaldi*, each armed with ten 6in guns, from Brindisi. The Italian Admiral was further reinforced by the three 10,000-ton cruisers *Zara*, *Fiume* and *Pola*, each armed with eight 8in guns, sailing from Taranto. There was also a screening force of thirteen 1600-ton destroyers, each armed with between four and six 4.7in guns. This very strong Italian fleet was split into three groups. That designated Force Y by the British consisted of the *Vittorio Veneto* and four destroyers. Force X, the Italian 3rd Cruiser Division, was made up of the three *Trieste* class cruisers plus three destroyers, while Force Z consisted of the three *Zara* class cruisers, the two *Abruzzi* class cruisers and six destroyers.

Opposing them, Cunningham's fleet consisted of the battleships *Warspite*, *Barham*, and *Valiant*, the aircraft carrier *Formidable*, and nine destroyers – *Jervis*, *Janus*, *Nubian*, *Mohawk*, *Stuart*, *Greyhound*, *Griffin*, *Hotspur* and *Havock*. The 6in cruiser squadron of *Orion*, *Ajax*, *Perth* and *Gloucester*, under Vice-Admiral H.D. Pridham-Wippell* flying his flag in *Orion*, with the four destroyers *Ilex*, *Hasty*, *Hereward* and *Vendetta* in company, was already at sea and was ordered to rendezvous off the island of Gavdos. The one convoy already at sea was ordered to reverse its course and clear the area.

Moving to rendezvous with the battlefleet, Pridham-Wippell reported the presence of Italian cruisers to the north of him at around 08.00 on the morning of 28 March. It turned out to be the Italian 3rd Squadron of heavy cruisers, or Force X: the message was passed to Admiral Cunningham, and ten shillings was passed to Commander Power.

> This made it clear that the enemy fleet was at sea, so I cheerfully paid up my ten shillings.[(1)]

* Later Admiral Sir Pridham-Wippell.

Cunningham's battlefleet was closing Pridham-Wippell's cruisers, some ninety miles away, at a best speed of some 20-22 knots, dictated by *Warspite*'s condenser trouble. Facing three 8in cruisers with four 6in cruisers, heavily outgunned and outranged, Pridham-Wippell decided to turn away and try to draw them towards Cunningham's approaching battlefleet. In this he succeeded. Unaware that the British battlefleet was even at sea, the Italian cruisers followed and opened up an accurate fire at a range of thirteen miles, but without scoring any hits. At 08.55 the Italian cruisers gave up the chase and altered course to the westward:

> After about an hour of fighting, Admiral Iachino, at 08.50, ordered the 3rd Division to reverse course, and shortly thereafter the entire Italian formation was on its way back to its base. It seemed, all in all, a useless task to continue this vain fire fight, particularly since the Italian ships had already gone far beyond Gavdos and were almost halfway to Tobruk. Furthermore it was logical to expect British air attacks at any minute, and no friendly fighters had as yet appeared to protect the Italian units. Also the reconnaissance flights of the RO43s* had turned up no British convoys in the area, and the missions could thus be considered at an end.(6)

The British cruisers also reversed course and, keeping out of range, shadowed the retiring Italian ships in order to maintain contact.

The Italians were retiring, but some two hours later the Italian Admiral on the *Vittorio Veneto* had second thoughts. No British aircraft had put in an appearance and there seemed to be no British units in the vicinity other that the shadowing cruisers. He reversed the battleship's course at 10.35:

> He hoped by this manoeuvre to catch the British cruisers between the *Vittorio Veneto* and the 3rd Division. At 10.50 the *Vittorio* came within sight of Pridham-Wippell's ships, which were taken completely by surprise. Iachino now ordered the 3rd Division to reverse its course to form the other half of the pincers, and at 10.56 the *Vittorio Veneto* opened fire with her heavy guns at a range of about 25,000 metres.(6)

* Italian reconnaissance planes.

The British cruisers, straddled by 15in shells fired at a range of some sixteen miles and thus completely outgunned and outranged, had no option but to turn away under cover of a smoke screen. They were in great danger, and with the *Vittorio Veneto* capable of 30 knots and the British battleships struggling along at only 20-22 knots it was doubtful if they could reach the cruisers in time to help them.

> Something had to be done, and the *Valiant* was ordered to go on at her utmost speed to support Vice-Admiral Pridham-Wippell. It had always been my intention to hold back the air torpedo striking force until the enemy battlefleet was close enough to ensure that if one of their ships were hit, our battlefleet would be certain of overtaking and destroying her. But in this emergency my hand was forced. The striking force was already in the air, and I ordered *Formidable* to send them in. Their attack relieved the pressure on Pridham-Wippell, but had the unfortunate effect of causing the enemy battleships to turn away and make off while some eighty miles distant. This meant that we had no chance of bringing her to action during daylight, if at all.(1)

The air strike, although unsuccessful, had indeed relieved the pressure on Admiral Pridham-Wippell's cruisers:

> ... at 11.00, shortly after the *Vittorio Veneto* opened fire, she sighted six British torpedo planes Admiral Cunningham had sent to attack from his aircraft carrier immediately after the cruisers had notified him of the dangerous situation in which they found themselves. ... By 11.15 the British torpedo planes had manoeuvred into an attack position, and the *Vittorio Veneto*, at the very moment that its guns were about to reap the harvest of their fire, was forced to manoeuvre to defend itself against this new threat. In the face of heavy anti-aircraft fire the enemy planes launched their torpedoes from 2000 metres, but the *Vittorio Veneto* manoeuvred successfully to avoid them.(6)

The air attack and the threat of further, but possibly more successful, strikes caused Admiral Iachino to change his mind again and to reverse course. He turned his force north-westwards on a bearing of 300 degrees and retired at a speed of 28 knots. His cruisers of Force X were stationed some twenty miles south of the battleship. With

Warspite and her two sister-ships still some 40 miles away and struggling to maintain 22 knots, the portents for a successful outcome did not look promising. By 12.30 Admiral Pridham-Wippell's cruisers were in sight of Cunningham's battlefleet and sanctuary, and the Commander-in-Chief set about the chase of the Italian ships. He needed to speed up his own force and slow down that of his opponents; so *Warspite*'s condenser trouble had to be put right, and quickly:

> I knew that the Commander (E) was sick ashore; but was aware that the Fleet Engineer Officer, Engineer Captain B.J.H. Wilkinson, was aboard. So I sent for him and told him to do something about it. He went below and in a short time I was gratified to see that the *Valiant*, which had been coming up at full speed from astern, was no longer gaining. We pressed on together.(1)

Cunningham had also decided on a second airstrike with *Formidable*'s aircraft. Shortly after midday, a force of three Albacore and two Swordfish torpedo planes, with an escort of two Fulmar fighters, was flown off from *Formidable*. The aircraft were led by Lieutenant-Commander J. Dalyell-Stead. It was not an entirely one-sided air battle; at about this time *Formidable* was herself attacked, unsuccessfully, by two Italian torpedo bombers. *Warspite* also flew off her two spotter planes; for one of them, piloted by Petty Officer Rice, D.S.M. with Lieutenant-Commander A.S. Bolt,* D.S.C., as observer, and Petty Officer M.G. Pacey as Telegraphist/Air Gunner, it was to be a long day.

While all this activity around the fleet's aircraft carrier was taking place, a reconnaissance aircraft from Malta found what turned out to be the Italian Force Z, consisting of the three *Zara* class heavy cruisers, the two *Abruzzi* cruisers and six destroyers. Their presence was relayed to Cunningham at 13.42 hours. Throughout the afternoon Swordfish torpedo planes from Crete, and Blenheim high-level bombers from R.A.F. bases in Greece and Alexandria, harried the retiring Italian ships, while the British battlefleet ploughed on, still hoping to be able to get to grips with their opponents.

---

* Later Rear-Admiral A.S. Bolt, CB, DSO, DSC.

The First Lieutenant of HMS *Hotspur*, one of the *Formidable*'s screening destroyers, noted how:

> ... all the time we were forging ahead at our greatest speed; the *Warspite*, the *Valiant* and the *Barham* – the three great veterans, all at Jutland a quarter of a century before, and yet all capable of knocking hell out of anything Italian.(7)

Then, in mid-afternoon, the air attacks paid off. In a simultaneous co-ordinated attack by high-level medium bombers of the R.A.F., and low-level strikes by two separate waves of Swordfish and Albacore torpedo planes, the *Vittorio Veneto* was hit. While concentrating upon the Blenheim bombers' high-level attack, the Italian battleship's crew were caught unawares by the simultaneous attack from different angles of the three Albacores and two Swordfish planes from *Formidable*. While the Blenheim's bombs were exploding close alongside, torpedoes were coming in from different directions, and the two escorting Fulmar fighters were machine-gunning the Italian lookout and anti-aircraft gun platforms on her decks. The leading Albacore, piloted by Lieutenant-Commander Dalyell-Stead, pressed in particularly close and only released its torpedo at a range of some 1000 yards before turning away. As it did so it was caught by a full blast of anti-aircraft fire from the ship and crashed into the sea, killing Dalyell-Stead and his crew. From the Italian viewpoint:

> One plane was shot down, but the great hull of the *Vittorio* could not be swerved in time to escape the torpedo which the plane had launched from a short distance away. The screws on the port side took the blow. For a time the ship was unable to move, and 4000 tons of water poured in through the breach. It was a critical moment, but after a few minutes the ship was able to get under way again for Taranto, still 420 miles away.(6)

Because of considerable confusion over sightings by various Allied aircraft and the reported presence of another Italian battleship in the area, Cunningham decided that he needed to sort out the exact position. He now knew that the *Vittorio Veneto* had been hit and slowed, but the general position was confused. Pridham-Wippell's cruiser force was sent ahead to try to establish visual contact with the retiring Italian battleship. The destroyers *Nubian* and *Mohawk* were tasked with acting as a visual link between the battlefleet and the scouting cruisers.

During the afternoon there was, much to Admiral Cunningham's annoyance, to be a slight delay in the chase. The *Warspite*'s spotter planes had been flown off around midday. One of them had been ordered to fly on to Suda Bay after completing its reconnaissance. The other, piloted by Petty Officer Rice, had no such orders and had 'stooged around' waiting for further orders. Finally, at around 17.00 hours, with fuel for only another fifteen minutes' flying and with Suda Bay now one hour's flying time away, the Swordfish turned up overhead. The C-in-C was reportedly furious at the lack of clear orders to the aircrew and the resulting confusion, and wanted the aircraft to ditch in the sea, to avoid having to slow down the *Warspite*, leaving the crew to be picked up by one of the destroyers. He was persuaded that the Swordfish might be wanted later for further reconnaissance and agreed to a speedy, if unorthodox, attempt at a sea pick-up.

The Swordfish, K8863, was ordered to alight ahead of the *Warspite*. Fortunately the sea was calm, and P.O. Rice made a good landing ahead of the oncoming battleship, turned onto a parallel course and taxied at about 10 knots with the *Warspite*, starboard crane extended outwards with hook dangling, coming up astern at some 18 knots. The aircraft's crew had never practised this unorthodox method of recovery and were a good deal disturbed by the onrushing bow wave of the battleship. P.O. Rice judged it to a nicety, turned the aircraft to starboard as the bow wave came up so that it hit the floats squarely on their stern without damage or undue disturbance to the plane. Directed, or 'conned' by Lieutenant-Commander Bolt, P.O. Rice manoeuvred the plane under the path of the approaching hook, and P.O. Pacey hooked on at the first attempt. The float-plane, thus 'picked up on the run' was hoisted inboard.

Petty Officer Rice enlarges upon events immediately prior to the pick-up:

> ... we were carrying four 250lb armour-piercing and eight 40lb anti-personnel bombs. He [Lieutenant-Commander Bolt] suggested to me that we jettison them before alighting on the sea. I went to a position astern of the fleet and did this. On hitting the

> water all the bombs went off. I forget what was said between us in the Gosport-tube* but the remark from him was 'The bombs exploded' 'I know, I dropped them live.' 'Why?' 'Because I wanted to see if they worked.' I can't print his reply. This also caused a little consternation in the destroyer screen as they thought we had spotted a submarine, and I think it was HMS *Hotspur* which rushed round to investigate. P.O. Pacey called her up with the Aldis lamp and informed her what had happened.(8)

Once safely on the *Warspite*, the Observer went to make his peace with the Admiral and his staff, and the Pilot and T.A.G. went off to the Petty Officer's mess:

> Once inboard a quick cup of tea was all one could hope for, if one could persuade the P.O.'s messman to 'wet it'. There were no aircrew meals or rations in those days.(8)

The decision to retrieve the Swordfish, at the expense of one mile in *Warspite*'s position relative to the other battleships, was a fortuitous one. At 17.45, with the plane refuelled and the crew briefed and somewhat arbitrarily refreshed, it was catapulted off once again. The Swordfish's new mission was to try to clarify the enemy's strength and position for the Commander-in-Chief.

> We were catapulted again at 17.45 in the same aircraft, putting four flare floats on the port light series rack as there was a possibility that we would have to alight at night on the open sea with no organised flare path. The task given us as soon as we were refuelled and catapulted, was to clear up the situation caused by conflicting reports about the position, course, speed, composition and disposition of the enemy fleet. It was known that *Vittorio Veneto*'s speed had been reduced, but it was not clear whether another force reported consisted of battleships or 8-inch gun cruisers. The enemy fleet was sighted at 18.20. ...
>
> We carried out our reconnaissance duties and passed out reports by W/T, in Morse, direct to Alexandria W/T station at a distance of some 400 miles. We had carried out a great deal of practice with this station during dawn and dusk anti-submarine patrols from Alexandria and it was very satisfying that P.O. Airman M. Pacey, my Telegraphist/Air Gunner, was able to clear

* Connecting voice tube between the pilot and observer.

> some dozen Operational Immediate messages in a matter of minutes. These signals, repeated by Alexandria W/T to Malta and Gibraltar, were received immediately in Whitehall W/T and the Admiralty had them nearly as soon as the Commander-in-Chief in *Warspite*. I think Maurice Pacey deserved great credit as an airborne W/T operator. I also learned later, reading Admiral Iachino's report from the *Vittorio Veneto*, that he [also] received all our signals. It was also gratifying to note from this report that we were only one knot out in estimating his speed.(8)

By 18.30 Cunningham was able to establish that only one Italian battleship, the *Vittorio Veneto*, was at sea, forty-five miles ahead and travelling at approximately 15 knots. All the other reported large ships were confirmed as 8in cruisers. With nightfall at around 19.30, Cunningham made plans for a night action. He set up a striking force of eight destroyers under Captain Philip Mack on the *Jervis*, whose task was to launch torpedo attacks under cover of darkness if and when the Italian ships were positively located by the British cruisers. A further strike force of torpedo bombers was launched at dusk from the *Formidable*, and, at about the same time, Pridham-Wippell reported that the cruisers had found the Italian force some nine miles to his north-west. The Italians had anticipated further air attacks at around nightfall and their Admiral had repeatedly requested air support for his retiring force and damaged flagship, but it was not forthcoming:

> Iachino had often repeated, but in vain, his request for Italian and German protection. X CAT* whose intervention was requested by Supermarina with increasing urgency, especially after the *Vittorio Veneto* had been torpedoed, replied at 17.50 that it could not go out on such a mission because there was danger that its planes might accidentally attack the Italian ships, since the position of the British ships was not known.(6)

Without the air support, Admiral Iachino decided to concentrate his force into a defensive formation of five columns with the damaged battleship in the middle, surrounded by cruiser and destroyer screens. Two destroyers were ahead and two astern of the battle-

---

* German air command in the Mediterranean.

ship, which had columns of cruisers on either side; *Trieste*, *Trento* and *Bolzano* to port, and *Zara*, *Fiume* and *Pola* to starboard. There were two further outlying columns of screening destroyers, one on either side. The cruisers *Abruzzi* and *Garibaldi*, plus two destroyers, were ordered to return to their home port of Brindisi.

As the sun was setting, the strike force of six Albacores and two Swordfish from *Formidable* found them. They were joined by two Swordfish from Crete. At nightfall the torpedo planes moved in to attack:

> At sunset we saw the dusk attack by 826 and 829 Squadrons plus two Swordfish from Malea, Crete. The Italian Fleet had formed itself into a compact mass which made it a difficult target. I saw the attack develop from a position about five miles astern of the Italian Fleet and regretted very much that we had to jettison our four 250lb bombs before our previous recovery by the ship. The attack was most spectacular, the Italians pouring out vast quantities of coloured tracer from their close range weapons.[8]

Seen from the Italian viewpoint:

> At 18.23 nine of these planes were sighted. Always out of range, they cruised round undisturbed and studied the situation for almost an hour, while the Italian ships were powerless to do anything to drive them away. At 18.51 the sun went down, and at 19.20, with the coming of darkness, the enemy planes began to come in closer. It was a tense moment as the Italian formation enveloped itself in a smoke screen and the cruisers turned on their searchlights to blind the attacking pilots. At 19.25 the outlying Italian destroyers saw the enemy planes coming in to attack, and all ships began to throw up a heavy curtain of fire. The attack lasted for twenty minutes and caused many moments of extreme suspense. The ships manoeuvred expertly amid the smoke and darkness, though they were in a close and unusual formation. The enemy torpedo plane pilots were surprised and intimidated by the violent defence put up by the Italians, and the fliers launched their torpedoes at random. When the firing stopped, it seemed as though none of the ships had been damaged at all. Shortly after, however, it was learned that the *Pola*, at the very end of the attack, had been hit by a torpedo and left dead in the water.[6]

The *Pola*, deprived of all power, pulled out of the line and stopped; the remaining Italian ships, oblivious to her plight, pressed on at 19 knots.

Back in the air, *Warspite*'s spotting floatplane was at last relieved by an Albacore from *Formidable* at 19.50 and left station to find her way home in the darkness:

> We took departure for Suda Bay at 2000 feet. After about half an hour I enquired when we might expect a land fall, and where, as I was getting interested by this time as it was rather dark. Up came Sir, '21.13 Akra Spatha, Ht. 1214 feet'. So I enquire further 'Where is Akra Spatha, Sir?' 'It is the north west tip of Crete'. At about five past nine, I observed a large black mass ahead to starboard which I reported to the observer who informed me it was the mountain range on the north west tip of Crete, highest point 2454 feet. At 21.13 we passed over Akra Spatha. I suggested to Lieut.-Commander Bolt that we ask Maleme, which was about ten miles south, if we could land on the grass there. He then told me we might damage the floats doing this! A small understatement on his part, I thought! So he suggested, as we had flare floats we go and alight in Suda Bay. I had landed and taken off from there a couple of times in daylight so I knew the harbour. We set course for Akra Malchas lighthouse [and] on arriving I turned south for Suda Bay. Lieut. Commander Bolt gave me a wind of 250 degrees, 10 knots. I then turned into the Bay on this heading at 1000 feet and dropped the flares at 100 yard intervals outside the boom. Reports from the back seat 'Flares gone, first one burning brightly.' 'Don't muck about, they only burn for five minutes.' 'High ground to port 2000 feet.' Steep turn to port onto 070 degrees, all flares burning, turn again to port about one mile from first flare, losing height. Flare path right ahead. Better than Air Traffic put out and much quicker. Line-up and sit down by number two flare, time 2125. After about two minutes all the flares went out, and it was dark!
>
> Next question from me 'What do we do now?' From the Navigator 'We are now waterborne,. Steer 310 degrees for the boom gate.' Pacey climbed up onto the centre section (of the wing) using the Aldis lamp as a headlight and we taxied at about 20 knots on this heading for a distance of about 5 miles which seemed to me to take a long time. Every time I throttled back the Aldis lamp went dim, as our battery was getting low. At about

2200 we identified ourselves to the patrol vessel on the boom. He enquired by light 'What type of vessel?' To which we replied 'Floatplane.' His amazement was illustrated by the switching on of an enormous searchlight which confirmed our statement. He opened up the boom-gate and we taxied into harbour and met a motor boat from HMS *York* which guided us to a mooring for the night, then took us to HMS *Carlisle*. Total time airborne 8 hours 20 minutes, including 2 hours night-time.

Furthermore, as there was a shortage of spares we had surrendered our instrument panel to the carrier squadron and the aircraft was fitted only with a primitive turn and bank indicator, P.10 compass and the old type altimeter fitted with one needle giving about one inch of movement for every thousand feet. We returned to Alexandria on 30 March via Mersa Matruh.(8)*

Returning to the sea battle, the torpedo hit on the *Pola* changed both the course of the battle and that of some of the Italian cruisers. Made aware of *Pola*'s plight, dead in the water, Admiral Iachino ordered the rest of his Force Z to which *Pola* belonged, the 8in cruisers *Zara* and *Fiume* plus the destroyers *Alfiere*, *Carducci*, *Oriani* and *Gioberti*, to go to the aid of their stricken sister-ship. The Italian Admiral decided on this course of action following an intelligence report from his Supermarina headquarters that radio bearings taken at 17.45 hours indicated a British formation about 75 miles from his flagship. He wrongly assumed that it was merely a force of British destroyers on night patrol; he was still unaware of the nearby presence of the British battlefleet. Admiral Iachino on his damaged battleship determined that, while the rescue of the *Pola* was being attempted, his first priority was to get the *Vittorio Veneto* back to her Taranto base. This he successfully did. According to Bragadin:

> The comportment of all the Italian ships during the afternoon phase of the enemy air attacks was of the very best, and the *Vittorio* was hit only because of the sacrifice of a courageous British pilot. Equally as good was the effective but difficult protective formation adopted on the spur of the moment by Admiral Iachino and executed in the fog and darkness. The *Vittorio Veneto*

* For the operation the Observer was awarded a bar to his D.S.C. and the Pilot and T.A.G. were mentioned in Dispatches.

> achieved wonders through the skill and organisation of her personnel. She travelled 420 miles, manoeuvring under air attacks with only half her engines working and with her stern all but awash, yet managing to ring up 20 knots.[(6)]

Meanwhile Admiral Iachino's 1st Cruiser Division, Force Z under Admiral Catteneo, and Admiral Cunningham's battlefleet and scouting cruisers were rapidly coming together. Both Commanders-in-Chief were still unclear as to their opponents' strength and disposition. On *Orion*, leading the British scouting cruiser squadron ahead of the battlefleet, a radar contact at 20.15 hours showed a stationary ship some six miles away. *Orion* and her fellow ships moved forward cautiously at 15 knots until, at 20.33, with the vessel still unseen in the darkness and only some three or four miles away, it was decided that it must be a battleship because of its size on the radar screen. *Ajax* also reported the position of the stationary ship back to the *Warspite*.

Having 'fixed' the position of the ship, presumed to be a battleship, Pridham-Wippell moved away to continue his search in the darkness for the rest of the Italian force, leaving the ship to be dealt with by destroyer torpedo attack or Cunningham's oncoming battlefleet. On *Warspite*, at 20.37 hours, Cunningham decided to force the issue and sent two flotillas of destroyers, five under Captain Nicholson on *Ilex*, and four under Captain Mack on *Jervis* into the attack:

> Destroyer flotillas attack enemy battlefleet with torpedoes. Enemy on course 295 degrees, speed 13 knots. Estimated bearing and distance of centre of enemy battlefleet from C-in-C 286 degrees; 33 miles at 20.30.[(9)]

Admiral Cunningham was taking a big risk:

> My morale was reasonably high when I returned to the bridge, and I ordered the destroyer striking force off to find and attack the enemy. We settled down to a steady pursuit with some doubts in our minds as to how the four destroyers remaining with the battlefleet would deal with the enemy destroyer attacks if the Italians decided to make them. At this stage the enemy fleet was estimated to be thirty-three miles ahead making good about fifteen knots.[(1)]

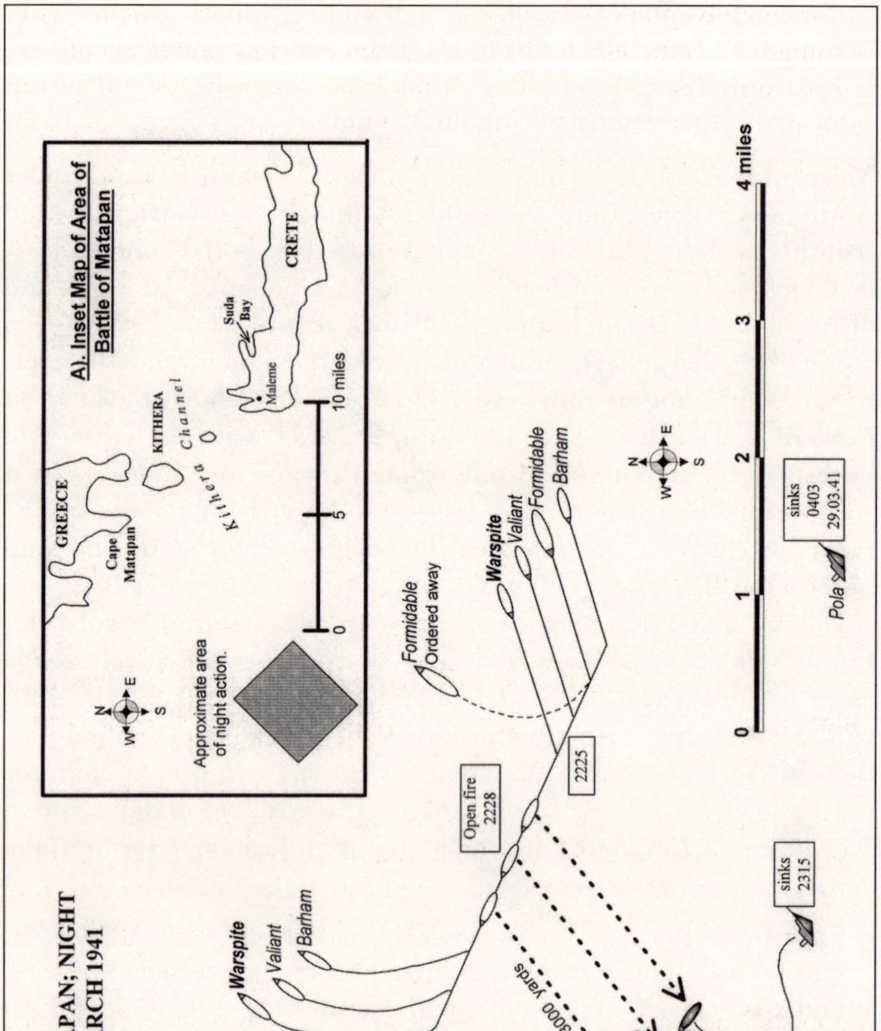
BATTLE OF MATAPAN; NIGHT ACTION, 28 MARCH 1941
A). Inset Map of Area of Battle of Matapan
GREECE
Cape Matapan
KITHERA
Kithera Channel
Maleme
Suda Bay
CRETE
0
5
10 miles
Approximate area of night action.
N
E
S
W
B). Schematic Diagram of Night Action.
Warspite
Valiant
Barham
Formidable
Formidable Ordered away
Warspite
Valiant
Formidable
Barham
Open fire 2228
2225
Cease Fire 2235
3000 yards
Fiume
Zara
Alfieri
sinks 2315
sinks 0240 29.03.41
sinks 2315
Pola
sinks 0403 29.03.41
N
E
S
W
0
1
2
3
4 miles

Unfortunately the estimations were not correct. Lieutenant-Commander Bolt, when observing from *Warspite*'s spotter plane, had, because the sleeker Italian ships made less bow wave than the equivalent British ships, underestimated the Italians' speed. Iachino's battleship was some fifty-seven miles away, not thirty-three. To compound the situation, in the darkness and the fog of war, there was considerable confusion over the interpretation of the readings of the then still-primitive radar sets, which were fitted to only some of the British ships. Because of these problems of identification, and of the radar interpretation of the positions of both the Italian battle formations and the scouting British cruisers, the destroyers held back. *Warspite*, the Commander-in-Chief's flagship, was not fitted with radar at this time, and Cunningham had to rely on *Valiant* for the battlefleet's own radar detection facility. Despite this handicap, Cunningham was infinitely better-served than his opponent Iachino, since none of the Italian ships had radar.

Then at 22.10 hours *Valiant* reported that her radar had picked up a large ship six miles away on her port bow. It was estimated to be over 600 feet long and thought to be the stopped ship earlier reported by Pridham-Wippell.

> Our hopes ran high. This might be the *Vittorio Veneto*. The course of the battlefleet was altered 40 degrees to port together (in order) to close. We were already at action stations with our main armament ready. Our guns were trained on the correct bearing.(1)

A few minutes later, on *Warspite*'s bridge, Commander Edelson, searching ahead through his binoculars, reported two large cruisers with a smaller one ahead crossing the bows of the battlefleet from starboard to port. Commander Power, another member of Cunningham's staff, with the ex-submariner's keen skill in the quick identification of enemy surface ships, immediately identified the two larger ships as being *Zara* class 8in cruisers. It was the remainder of Admiral Iachino's 1st Cruiser Division, Force Z, come to the assistance of the stricken *Pola*. The British battlefleet was turned into line ahead on virtually a reciprocal bearing to sail past the Italian ships, still unaware of the battlefleet's presence:

> I shall never forget the next few minutes. In the dead silence, a silence that could almost be felt, one heard only the voices of the gun control personnel putting the guns on to the new target. One heard the orders repeated in the director tower behind and above the bridge. Looking forward, one saw the turrets swing and steady when the 15-inch guns pointed at the enemy cruisers. Never in the whole of my life have I experienced a more thrilling moment than when I heard a calm voice from the director tower – 'Director layer sees the target' – sure sign that the guns were ready and that his finger was itching on the trigger. The enemy was at a range of no more than 3800 yards – point blank.(1)

The next few minutes were to be complete bedlam and utter carnage:

> It must have been the Fleet Gunnery Officer, Commander Geoffrey Barnard, who gave the final order to open fire. One heard the 'ting-ting-ting' of the firing gongs. Then came the great orange flash and the violent shutter as the six big guns bearing were fired simultaneously. At the very same instant the destroyer *Greyhound* ... switched her searchlights on to one of the enemy cruisers, showing her momentarily up as a silvery-blue shape in the darkness. Our searchlights shone out with the first salvo, and provided full illumination for what was a ghastly sight. Full in the beam I saw our six great projectiles flying through the air. Five of the six hit a few feet below the level of the cruiser's upper deck and burst with splashes of brilliant flame. The Italians were quite unprepared. Their guns were trained fore and aft. They were helplessly shattered before they could put up any resistance. In the midst of all this there was one diversion. Captain Douglas Fisher, the captain of the *Warspite*, was a gunnery officer of note. When he saw the first salvo hit he was heard to say in a voice of wondering surprise 'Good Lord! We've hit her'.
>
> The *Valiant*, astern of us, had opened fire at the same time. She also had found her target, and when the *Warspite* shifted to the other cruiser I watched *Valiant* pounding her ship to bits. Her rapidity of fire astonished me. Never would I have believed it possible with these heavy guns. The *Formidable* had hauled out of line to starboard, but astern of the *Valiant* the *Barham* was also heavily engaged.
>
> The plight of the Italian cruisers was indescribable. One saw whole turrets and masses of other heavy debris whirling through

the air and splashing into the sea, and in a short time the ships themselves were nothing but glowing torches and on fire from stem to stern. The whole action lasted no more than a few minutes.(1)

For younger men such as Roy Emmington, working on the 15in guns of *Warspite*, the experience was equally unforgettable:

I was in X turret's control cabinet. That was a night to remember because at night actions the 15-inch turrets fired broadsides.* Salvoes shook the insides out of you so we were wondering what broadsides would do. We didn't have long to wonder; we got the orders to load both guns and we heard the breach workers shout 'Ready', and a few seconds after they fired. The feeling in a 15-inch turret firing broadsides would be hard to explain, especially the feelings of a seventeen year old boy. A number of broadsides were fired that night. ... It took us hours on the boys' messdeck to unwind that night.(10)

Perhaps it was as well for the young sailors that they did not witness the instantaneous carnage created by their guns, although one young seaman, Wilfred Hatch, saw the aftermath:

My action station was sightsetter, left 15-inch gun, A turret. We had moved into number one degree readiness and action was imminent as we were approaching the Italian Fleet, and the order came and we started firing. I managed to get a glimpse of a ship ablaze.(5)

Any stress and trauma suffered by the younger crew members of the *Warspite* and her sister ships were as nothing compared to the shock and terror suffered by their counterparts on the Italian ships. They were taken completely by surprise when the *Warspite*, *Barham* and *Valiant* opened fire:

... Cattaneo's ships, completely unaware of the danger, had half their crews away from the battle stations in order to be ready to assist the *Pola*. On the *Fiume* they were actually getting the towing cables ready. ... At 22.28 the British destroyer *Greyhound*, the enemy vessel nearest the Italian ships, threw its searchlight on the

* Salvoes involved firing the two guns in each turret alternately; with broadsides both guns were fired simultaneously.

> Italian group and the other British ships quickly followed suit. Immediately the three British battleships opened fire with their 381mm guns on the cruisers almost at point blank range and joined the destroyers in turning their medium calibre guns on the Italian destroyers. The surprise could not have been more complete. The *Zara* and *Fiume* were almost instantly immobilised, shattered and set on fire. The British battleships quickly fired several salvos [*sic*] and then, at 22.31, turned to the right to avoid the torpedoes of the Italian destroyers, which had now gone on the attack. There followed an indescribable mix-up of Italian ships and British destroyers, during which several British ships were almost hit by the fire from other units of their own side.(6)

It was indeed a confused melee, with *Warspite* making her own contribution to the confusion. She had fired first at the *Fiume*, then shifted target to the *Zara*. In an action lasting only a few minutes she fired forty rounds of 15in armour piercing shells and forty-four rounds of 6in high-explosive shells. With the speed of decision making and the almost-instantaneous reaction times of a night action, it was miraculous that some ships were not sunk by so-called 'friendly fire'. At one point, Cunningham recalled:

> To my horror I saw one of our destroyers, the *Havock*, straddled by our gunfire, and in my mind wrote her off as lost.(1)

After the battle, when the scattered destroyers all reassembled off Cape Matapan at 04.00 hours on the 29th, the C-in-C was relieved to see *Havock*, unscathed, among them. Other ships, including the aircraft carrier *Formidable*, had also nearly met disaster:

> The *Formidable* also had an escape. When action was joined she hauled out to starboard at full speed, a night battle being no place for a carrier. When she was about five miles away she was caught in the beam of the *Warspite*'s searchlight sweeping on the disengaged side in case further enemy ships were present. We heard the 6-inch control officer of the starboard battery get his guns on her, and were only just in time to stop him from opening fire.(1)

The destroyer *Griffin*, in company with *Greyhound*, was caught in the beam of the latter's searchlight and was sent on her way by a straddling salvo of 6in from *Warspite*, and a brusque 'Get out of the way you b.f.'(9) signal from Cunningham on her bridge.

The end of the shattered Italian ships was, as reported by Bragadin, accompanied by acts of collective courage and supreme personal gallantry. In his summary of the ships' end:

> On the *Fiume*, listing badly and prey to a violent fire, the commander was forced to order the crew to abandon ship, and he went down with it at 23.15. On the *Zara* the flames were raging so high that the order was given to its crew also to abandon ship, for it was impossible to control the fire or man the guns. However, since the ship was sinking slowly, a group of volunteers, led by the second in command, went below to the ship's magazine to blow it up. Admiral Cattaneo and the ship's commander also remained on board. When the *Zara* exploded at 23.40, it carried these officers and many of the crew to the bottom. On the destroyer *Alfieri*, despite the many casualties and the damage caused by the first hits, the survivors tried to get the engines going, and, when they saw a British destroyer pass, they fired on it as best they could. One torpedo tube had remained miraculously undamaged in the middle of the debris, and its crew was still imperturbably waiting at their battle stations. An ensign, therefore, succeeded in launching three torpedoes at the British destroyer, but they all went wide because of the heavy list of the stricken ship. A short time later the *Alfieri* came under the fire of another British destroyer. By this time she was listing more and more, and the commander ordered the ship abandoned. Perfectly calm, he himself refused to get into the lifeboat. Instead he lit a cigarette and turned his attention to the wounded. Soon afterwards he disappeared with the ship.
>
> On the *Carducci*, victim of a fire completely out of control, the commander took measures to scuttle the ship; then he also remained on board until it sank. The *Oriani* had received a hit which put one of its engines out of action, but nevertheless it succeeded in manoeuvring with the other one ... and was able to reach the waters off Calabria. The *Gioberti*, the only ship undamaged amid all this destruction because it was the last in the formation went courageously to the attack. Swept by enemy shells and with the enemy guns zeroed in, the gallant ship had to pull away under a smoke screen, breaking off the attack.(6)

Admiral Cunningham confirms the Italian destroyers' gallant attempt to attack the British battlefleet:

> Our searchlights were still on, and just after 22.30 three Italian destroyers which had apparently been following the cruisers, were seen coming in on the port bow. They turned, and one was seen to fire torpedoes, so the battlefleet was turned 90 degrees together to starboard to avoid them. Our destroyers were engaging, and the whole party was inextricably mixed up.(1)

While this mayhem was taking place the *Pola* lay helpless nearby, spectator to the annihilation of comrades and sister ships, but powerless to help either them or herself. *Pola* was without power, completely dead in the water, unable to train her 8in guns or feed ammunition to her secondary armament. Expecting their own end at any moment her captain ordered her seacocks opened and her crew to abandon ship. She was eventually found at 00.20 by the British destroyer *Havock* which, out of torpedoes, withdrew without attacking. The *Pola* was by now slowly sinking, but the order to abandon ship had only been half-heartedly carried out, with some men deciding to take their chance and stay on board in the hope of rescue, in preference to casting adrift in the cold and dark sea. Many were becoming unnerved by the fate of their comrades and the prolonged uncertainty of their own prospects. At about 03.00 several British destroyers came up to the half-abandoned, half-sunk ship, the sea almost lapping her decks, alone and silent. On board, traumatised by their ordeal, the morale and discipline of many of the men had broken down. As viewed from the *Hotspur*:

> This was getting too fantastic. They made no effort to fight, but just lay there. The *Jervis* put a searchlight on her and saw a large number of men still on board, all crowded aft. She slid in alongside and put a brow out to the *Pola*'s quarterdeck – for this was the *Pola*. On board the *Pola* discipline had been the first to dive over the side. The men had broken into the officers' wine store and were wandering about in droves, partly drunk.(7)

The *Jervis* was able to take off the 258 survivors, out of a ship's complement of 1000, before pulling away at 03.40. With no torpedoes left the *Havock* had already asked permission to blow off *Pola*'s stern with depth charges, but was ordered to 'get clear'. *Jervis* fired one torpedo in the *Pola* followed by two from the *Nubian*. Meanwhile the rest of the destroyers were picking up men from the water:

> The sailors were in pathetic little groups on the rafts. The whole thing gave one the same feeling as when, out shooting, you find you have done a left and a right with a couple of thrushes by mistake.[7]

The *Pola*, given the torpedo *coup de grace*, blew up and sank at 04.03; it was the final act of destruction in the battle of Cape Matapan.

The Navy continued to rescue what survivors it could prior to regrouping:

> All the destroyers we could spare were detached to save what life was possible. In all, counting the men from the *Pola*, British ships rescued 900, although some died later. In the midst of this work of mercy, however, the attentions of some German Ju88's pointed the fact it was unwise to dally in an area where we were exposed to heavy air attack. So we were compelled to proceed to the eastward, leaving some hundreds of Italians unrescued. We did the best we could for them by signalling their exact position to the Italian Admiralty. They sent out the hospital ship *Gradisca*, which eventually saved another 160.[1]

It had been an overwhelming British victory, achieved with the loss of one aircraft and its crew of three. The Italian losses had been far heavier:

> Although the *Vittorio Veneto* had escaped, we had sunk the three 10,000 ton, 8-inch cruisers *Zara*, *Pola* and *Fiume*, together with the 1,500 ton destroyers *Alfieri* and *Carducci*. The Italian loss in personnel was about 2,400 officers and men, most of them caused by our devastating bombardment at close range. The *Fiume* received two 15-inch broadsides from the *Warspite* and one from the *Valiant*; the *Zara* four from the *Warspite*, five from the *Valiant* and five from the *Barham*. The effect of these six or eight gun salvoes of shell, each weighing nearly a ton, cannot be described.[1]

The battlefleet returned, with their prisoners, unscathed to Alexandria.

Elsewhere in the Mediterranean theatre, by early April, the situation was deteriorating. The Germans had taken a more direct role and attacked Greece and Yugoslavia, and were the senior Axis partner in a major onslaught in Libya, where the British and Commonwealth forces, weakened by having to send troops and equipment to support Greece, were being forced into a hurried retreat. In an attempt to slow down the Axis advance by disrupting their supplies, the Navy was ordered to attack their main supply port of Tripoli. The initial plan was to carry out a combined harbour bombardment and blocking operation, sacrificing the *Barham* as the main blocking ship, to be deliberately sunk in the harbour entrance. Cunningham strongly objected to losing one of his three battleships in this way, given the continuing potential threat of the Italian battlefleet and the ongoing requirements to protect eastern Mediterranean convoys to and from Malta and Greece. The blocking element was dropped from the plan and a heavier bombardment by the whole battlefleet became the agreed alternative.

The battlefleet – *Warspite*, *Barham*, *Valiant*, the carrier *Formidable*, the cruiser *Phoebe*, the anti-aircraft cruiser *Calcutta* and escorting destroyers – left Alexandria at 07.00 on 18 April, and, reinforced at sea by the cruiser *Gloucester*, were at their bombarding positions just before dawn at 0445 on 21 April. The plan called for bombing by Wellington aircraft from Malta prior to the bombardment, with the intention of starting harbour fires as aiming points for the naval gunners. At 05.02 the bombardment began at ranges of between 11,000 and 14,000 yards.

> Then with a roar the *Warspite* opened up, and within a minute the whole fleet had followed suit. Three battleships, two cruisers and seven destroyers were all pitching salvo after salvo into the docks and other prearranged targets. It must have caused a big surprise ashore, and although the whole vista out to sea must have been rippling with flashes, it took a good twenty minutes for the enemy to hoist in the idea, and open fire back at us.(7)

When it came the return fire was ineffective, and the bombarding ships reversed course at 05.24 and continued the onslaught of the harbour installations, now lit up by flares dropped from aircraft of HMS *Formidable*. The bombardment ceased at 05.45. In just over forty minutes some 530 tons of shell were poured into the target. *Warspite*'s contribution was one hundred and thirty-five 15in and one hundred and six 6in shells. However, the effect of the shelling, it was later found, was only minimal. One ship only was sunk in the harbour, and little permanent damage done to the installations or the port's operational efficiency.

The bombarding force arrived back in Alexandria unscathed, somewhat to the surprise of those who had taken part:

> I must say I fully expected a heavy air attack by way of revenge. We were close to aerodromes at dawn, and everyone knew that the Germans were massing their dive bombers in this part of the world, but once again we got away with it.(7)

They were very fortunate. The Luftwaffe was by now making Mediterranean naval operations, to assist the Army with offshore bombardments and protect the supply convoys, increasingly both hazardous and costly in terms of ships and men. In contrast to the German air force's efforts, the Royal Air Force was comparatively ineffectual. Short of trained aircrew and modern aircraft, the R.A.F. was hard-pressed to provide adequate protection for Malta or to help much with the disruption of Axis supply routes. Constantly harried by Churchill and the War Cabinet to help the Army, now in dire straits in both Egypt and Greece, Cunningham felt that:

> The Navy alone could not save Egypt, or even play its full part, until the air situation was squarely faced. It was doubtful if the weakened Army could hold its position on the Egyptian frontier. In my opinion we should lose Egypt in the course of a few months unless every nerve were strained to increase our air forces, and if this were not done, we should lose a great proportion of the fleet in the endeavour to save the situation.(1)

He was to be proved right within a month.

On 6 April the Germans had launched their long-awaited attack upon Yugoslavia and Greece. They made rapid progress and, on 21 April, about the time *Warspite* was preparing to bombard Tripoli, the decision was taken by the War Cabinet back in London to evacuate the British Army from Greece. This was accomplished, with some difficulty for the Navy, by the end of the month, evacuating some 40,000 British and Commonwealth troops, out of an original force of 55,000, to the nearby island of Crete. There was to be little respite.

The Germans began an airborne assault upon the island on 19 May. The Navy, without air cover, took the brunt of the Luftwaffe attacks in its efforts to prevent German seaborne landings on the island, and to keep it supplied through its bases and ports on the northern coast. Suda Bay, facing and near to the now German-controlled airfields on the Greek mainland, was subjected to almost constant air attack, such as to be almost unusable in daylight. At sea the ships were without fighter protection and forced to fend off air attacks with their guns, and to rely on their speed and manoeuvrability to avoid the bombing and strafing.

Cunningham, in order to keep ships constantly on station off Crete, had split his forces into a number of squadrons: Force A comprised, under Admiral Pridham-Wippell in the *Queen Elizabeth*, the *Barham* and five destroyers; Force A1, initially intended to be kept in reserve, consisted of the *Warspite*, flying the flag of Rear-Admiral H.B. Rawlings, the *Valiant*, the cruiser *Ajax* and eight destroyers. There were also three squadrons of assorted cruisers and destroyers, employed on sweeps to find and destroy enemy seaborne supplies. These various formations had to be rotated to allow for refuelling and reammunitioning, particularly of anti-aircraft ammunition, at their base in Alexandria. Forces A and A1 had to be rotated in order to keep a constant watch for the Italian battlefleet, putting to sea in support of their German partners.

At dawn on Wednesday 21 May, Cunningham had his fleet deployed in the following formations and locations:[11]

- Admiral Rawlings with Force A1: *Warspite*, *Valiant*, and the four escorting destroyers *Napier*, *Decoy*, *Griffin* and *Hotspur*, were sixty miles west of the Antikithera Strait, steering south east to rendezvous with Admiral Glennie's Force D;
- Force D, comprising Glennie's flagship the cruiser *Dido*, together with the cruisers *Orion* and *Ajax* and the destroyers *Isis*, *Kimberley*, *Imperial* and *Janus*, was returning from an uneventful night's sweep of the Maleme/Canea and Kissamo Bay waters;
- Rear-Admiral King was with his Force C, flying his flag in the cruiser *Naiad* and accompanied by the cruiser *Perth* and the destroyers *Kandahar*, *Nubian*, *Kingston* and *Juno*. Force C had clashed, without damage to either side, with Italian torpedo boats in the Kano Strait, and had been joined by the anti-aircraft cruiser *Calcutta* at 06.00;
- Force E, the 14th Destroyer Squadron, was under Captain Mack on the *Jervis*, in company with *Nizam* and *Ilex*. The three

destroyers had bombarded Scarpanto airfield under cover of darkness and was proceeding to join up with Force C;

- Force B, consisting of the cruisers *Gloucester* and *Fiji*, had passed uneventfully through the Kano Strait and swept up to Cape Matapan during the night and were now heading to join Rear-Admiral Rawlings and the battle squadron. Both these cruisers were brand new ships; *Gloucester* had been launched in 1939 and *Fiji* in 1940; and
- the anti-aircraft cruiser *Carlisle* had sailed from Alexandria with orders to join Admiral King's Force C.

Throughout the day the British ships, completely lacking in air cover, were subjected to air attacks by the VIII Fliegerkorps. The destroyer *Juno* was struck by three bombs and sank in two minutes. As planned, Force A1 remained patrolling in the area south west of Kithera and was joined by the *Gloucester* and *Fiji* and Force D. The C-in-C, remaining on this occasion in Alexandria the better to control the complex and evolving operations in the eastern Mediterranean, had now assembled a formidable force to defend Crete against any Italian-led seaborne invasion. He had collected together the two battleships *Warspite* and *Valiant*, the five cruisers *Gloucester*, *Fiji*, *Ajax*, *Orion* and *Dido*, and eight destroyers, *Isis*, *Imperial*, *Kimberley*, *Janus*, *Napier*, *Decoy*, *Griffin* and *Hotspur*. Cunningham's intention was to challenge the Italian battlefleet, or alternatively to deter it from leaving harbour. At nightfall the British force of cruisers and destroyers was again broken up into separate hunting groups, to seek out and destroy any attempts to land supplies or troops on Crete.

Cunningham was not to know that the Italian battlefleet was not planning to come out and assist their German ally in the invasion of Crete. Shortage of fuel oil and lack of suitable air cover were the reasons later put forward for their remaining in harbour:

> In the summer of 1941, when only 103,000 tons of fuel oil had arrived from Germany, the Italian reserve was completely used up. From that moment on the Italian Navy was forced to conduct operations only as the arrival of fuel oil permitted them. During those periods in which deliveries were postponed or suspended, Fleet activity was completely paralysed. ... The Italian Supreme

> Command, following the experience of Matapan, ordered provisionally that the battleships would not carry out any further missions 'beyond the range of fighter protection'. This order of 31 March 1941 further circumscribed the operational freedom of the Italian capital ships, and if it had been interpreted narrowly, would have practically paralysed them except if the British had approached close to the Italian coast.(6)

In contrast to the indolence of the Italian Battlefleet, elements of their light forces were very active, acquitting themselves with considerable honour when escorting convoys trying to land supplies on Crete. Thus in an action on the night of 21/22 May, Admiral Glennie's Force D came across the small Italian ship *Lupo*, 676 tons and armed with four torpedo tubes and three 3.9in guns, escorting a mixed group of twenty-five commandeered Greek caiques, or small coastal vessels, carrying troops, guns and ammunition to Crete. It was a bloody action. The *Lupo*, captained by Commander Francesco Mimbelli, laid a smoke screen to give his charges a chance of escape, and bravely attacked the vastly superior British cruisers and destroyers. Fortune favoured the brave; although hit by eighteen 6in shells, the *Lupo* survived and was able to make good its escape. For the rest of the convoy it was death and destruction, with no quarter, in the bitter struggle for Crete in the desperate days of 1941:

> The spectacle was fairly gruesome with the sea spotted with the shadows of caiques, and lit in flashes at each gun salvo, the caiques pitifully loaded with helpless soldiers, and the destroyers darting here and there, snapping and tearing like a team of wolves who had broken into a flock of sheep. Every gun was blazing, pom-poms and machine-guns riddling the caiques and their poor occupants. Germans were leaping into the sea fully equipped, and between the roars of the guns could be heard the unearthly yell of the doomed men and the last cry of the drowning. The cruisers were ramming all they could catch, and the *Ajax* came out with half a caique on her bows, which threw up a huge bow wave. It was appalling slaughter.(7)

The next day, 22 May, was to be a day of disaster for the Royal Navy and one of triumph for the Luftwaffe. The British Fleet was totally without air protection against the expected onslaught. By mid-May the number of serviceable R.A.F. fighters still flying from airfields in Crete had been reduced to seven, and these had been withdrawn from Crete on 19 May. Neither was the fleet able to rely on this occasion on aircraft from the *Formidable*:

> Shore based air cover was virtually non-existent, and our carrier, the *Formidable* ... could not take part in the operations until May 25th. She had been reduced to no more than four serviceable aircraft because of losses and wear and tear during the bombardment of Tripoli and the more recent Tiger convoy. There were no reserves of naval aircraft or flying personnel.(1)

In contrast, Air General Freiherr von Richthofen, commanding the VII Fliegerkorps, had under his command 228 bombers, 205 dive bombers, 233 fighters and 50 reconnaissance aircraft; a total of 716 front-line aircraft. It was under these conditions that the Navy prepared to take on the Luftwaffe.

Against the expected onslaught Cunningham now had disposed the battle squadron, *Warspite* and *Valiant*, off Crete some 45 miles south west of the Kithera Channel. Force B, the cruisers *Gloucester* and *Fiji*, sailed to join up with the battlefleet at 08.30 hours, having already endured, at 06.30, ninety minutes of bombing which damaged both cruisers. The 5th Destroyer Flotilla, under Captain Lord Louis Mountbatten* in *Kelly*, with the *Kashmir*, *Kipling*, *Kelvin* and *Jackal*, had sailed from Malta and was expected at 10.00. The 14th Destroyer Flotilla, under Captain Mack, after refuelling, was now heading back to the Kaso Strait; and the 10th Destroyer Flotilla, under Captain Waller in the *Stuart*, together with the veteran Australian destroyers *Vendetta* and *Voyager*, had left Alexandria to join Admiral Rawlings' force. Both *Vendetta* and *Voyager* were nearly as old as *Warspite* and *Valiant*, having been launched in 1917 and 1918 respectively. Force D, having been subjected to heavy air attacks during the morning of the previous day, when *Ajax* was damaged by near-misses, followed by its night action against the convoy, was now short of ammunition. *Dido* had expended 70 per cent of her anti-aircraft ammunition, *Orion* 62 per cent and *Ajax* 58 per cent. Cunningham, considering that Glennie's ships would not be able to defend themselves if they ran completely

---

* Later Admiral of the Fleet The Earl Mountbatten of Burma, Viceroy of India. Assasinated by the Provisional I.R.A. in a bomb explosion on 27 August 1979.

out of ammunition, ordered them home to Alexandria to replenish their stocks. After briefly joining up with Admiral Rawlings' force at 07.00, Force D received Cunningham's orders and left for Alexandria at 10.45.

Force C, meanwhile, had come across a very large and strung-out convoy of some thirty caiques and small cargo vessels, escorted by the Italian destroyer *Sagittario*, at 08.30. Evading a torpedo attack from the *Sagittario*, Admiral King's ships set about destroying the enemy convoy, which had dispersed under cover of *Sagittario*'s smoke screen, and a running battle ensued. Throughout the action the British ships were subjected to extremely heavy and continuous air attacks. So ferocious were the attacks that King, with his ships badly scattered and in danger of being picked off one by one, the cruisers limited in their scope for manoeuvring action by the *Carlisle*'s top speed of 21 knots, and all running low on ammunition, decided to break off the chase. It was a decision for which he was later, and probably unfairly, criticised by both his Prime Minister and his C-in-C.

> His situation was extremely difficult; but the decision to retire, I think, was a faulty one. It is probable that the safest place was in amongst the enemy convoy, and retirement could not better the most unpleasant position in which he found himself. ... However, it is easy to criticise others when one is not on the spot. Admiral King and his squadron had had a gruelling time. He had been in action with torpedo boats two nights before. Without any air cover whatsoever he had been bombed continuously for more than four hours the previous day and had lost the *Juno*. His ship's companies had been on alert for more than forty eight hours ... It was a cruel situation; but I have always held that if the enemy is in sight on the sea, air attacks or other considerations must be disregarded and the risks accepted.(1)

Even further away from the spot, Winston Churchill, according to his Private Secretary's diary, was as determined as Cunningham, and even more scornful of the risks:

> The navy are having a heavy task off Crete and have lost a lot of ships. ... I expressed grief to the P.M. who replied 'What do you think we build the ships for?' He deprecates the navy's way of treating ships as if they were too precious ever to risk.(2)

The men on the spot, off Crete that day, were to show the world, as well as their Prime Minister and C-in-C, that they were not afraid to take risks and lose ships.

After breaking off the chase of the convoy, Rear-Admiral King's ships were bombed continuously for three and a half hours. His flagship, *Naiad*, had two turrets put out of action, compartments flooded and her speed reduced to 16 knots. The *Carlisle* was hit and her captain killed. All four cruisers and their attendant destroyers were low on anti-aircraft ammunition and in a parlous state. It was unlikely that they could survive, as they strove to join up with Rear-Admiral Rawlings' patrolling battlefleet in the Kithera Strait; there the latter were, in Rawling's words: 'Serving a useful purpose in attracting enemy aircraft.'(1)

On hearing, just before 12.30, that *Naiad* had been badly hit and that King's force was in urgent need of help, Rawlings increased speed to 23 knots and took *Warspite*, *Valiant*, his two cruisers and attendant destroyers to the aid of Force C. He did this although some of his own force were also dangerously low in high angle anti-aircraft ammunition. *Warspite* had 66 per cent remaining, *Valiant* 80 per cent, *Fiji* 30 per cent and *Gloucester* only 18 per cent. In the words of one of his fellow officers:

> It was a most courageous decision to make. He normally commanded one of the cruiser squadrons, and he had been given command of this battle squadron in order to allow the C-in-C to remain in Alex, where he could conduct all the multifarious operations that were going on, and be in immediate touch with the Army and R.A.F. Headquarters. To take therefore, the first battlefleet one has ever commanded into such dangerous waters, in order to give help to a cruiser squadron in dire difficulties, was a most daring moral decision to make. It was not as if his fifteen-inch guns were wanted. They were as useless as torpedoes that morning. It was rather the offering of more targets, and therefore the diluting of danger. It was like taking in a couple of carthorses to help draw off an attack on four polo ponies by a swarm of infuriated hornets. And, secondly it was because he had more ammunition than the retiring squadron, and once the fleet was together there was much more mutual protection and economy of shellfire.(7)

The two British forces were only a few miles apart when *Warspite* received her full share of the Luftwaffe's attention:

> At 13.32 in position 150 degrees Kapsali Bay Light 8 miles (36 degrees N, 23 degrees E approximately) approaching formations of aircraft sighted on either beam were about to be engaged when three ME 109s appeared through smoke bursts 2000 yards ahead at an altitude of 800 feet, making a shallow dive attack on the ship. Full port wheel was ordered and fire was opened from B2 machine gun. The 4-inch HA guns and pom-poms did not fire.
>
> Before avoiding action became effective each aircraft had released one bomb at a range of 500 yards and altitude 500 feet. The first bomb, estimated to be 250kg, S.A.P. type, fused delay action, struck the Forecastle Deck on the starboard side of 111 station.
>
> The second and third bombs fell 50 yards and 100 yards clear of the ship, exploding underwater, but did no damage.
>
> The bomb which struck the ship perforated the Forecastle Deck ... 6 feet from the deck edge starboard, passed through 112 bulkhead ... struck the baseplate of S.4 6-inch gun, was deflected inboard and burst about twelve feet from the ship's side and two feet above the Upper Deck at 124 station.
>
> The angle of descent of the bomb was approximately 45 degrees and distance from point of impact to point of burst was 29 feet. Detonation was complete and splinter effect severe.(12)

The three fighter-bombers which so successfully attacked the *Warspite* were led by Lieutenant Wolfdieter Huy. His two companions were Flight Sergeant Furth and Sergeant Eduard Isken. Lieutenant Huy recalled:

> I remember the attack quite precisely still. On that day I flew four sorties, and returning from the third sortie in the area of Crete we saw from about 6,500 feet two British flotillas, one of them more or less west of Crete steering north east, the other about thirty seven miles north east of it steering south west. In the larger of the two flotillas which was steering north eastwards there was, as far as I can remember, a battleship which I took to be *Barham* and at least two cruisers. In the second flotilla there were one or two cruisers and some destroyers.
>
> Since we had no bombs left, I reported the two flotillas by radio to our ground station and hastened my flight back to

> Malaoi. After the landing, refuelling and re-arming my three undamaged aircraft was begun straight away so that we were able to take off again about an hour after landing. We very quickly found the two flotillas again in the good visibility. From our height of around 10,000 feet we could see very well that the two flotillas were considerably nearer to each other. I sought out the largest ship and attacked in tight formation. The attack took place on the opposite heading to the flotilla, i.e. from forwards in a steep dive at about 12.30p.m.* At about 1,000 feet, on my orders, the bombs were released simultaneously, and must all have fallen more or less in the same hole [*sic*]. As we flew away we saw that black smoke was developing on *Warspite*, and that the ship had lost way. We must, therefore, have hit it. We flew straight back to Malaoi to get more bombs. Nothing more came of it however, since the aircraft needed a thorough service after this fourth sortie. I can still remember that before our dive there were a few flak clouds at our altitude, but I cannot remember any signs of gunfire during the dive.(13)

The bomb that struck the *Warspite* weighed 250kg. Arguably, once again she had been lucky. It could have been so much worse had the Luftwaffe been operating according to its more normal practices; the bomb could have been twice as big:

> For our bombing missions during the Greece and Crete campaign we used solely bombs of 250kg weight with time fuses which had a four second delay. The M.E. 109E which we were flying at that time could carry one bomb of 500kg, or 250kg, or four fragmentation bombs of 50kg each. Since we were only attacking shipping targets, we naturally flew with the largest possible bombs. However, since we had no bomb loading equipment, we had to load bombs by hand and we could not manage bombs larger than 250kg. You could not get more than four people at a time underneath the fuselage of the 109!(14)

However, the 250kg bomb did quite enough damage; all four starboard 6in guns were put out of action and the starboard forward 4in anti-aircraft twin mounting was blown completely overboard. The final toll of casualties was eight killed, eleven died of wounds,

* There was one hour difference in the British and German local times.

twenty-four missing and sixty-nine wounded. This one small bomb had done more damage, and caused more casualties in an instant, than all the hours of pounding and thirteen hits from heavy shells that *Warspite* had received at Jutland almost exactly twenty-five years before.

The uninjured crew members did what they could to help their stricken comrades:

> I saw to the starboard side two cruisers' bows as I entered the turret ... and then came the bump. I left the turret and went to the damaged area which was just aft of the base of the bridge superstructure. There was a hole in the deck where a pair of 4-inch [guns] were, which must have been blown over the side. I was joined by two other boys, one named Wilson, full of life; we threw over the side all the loose ammunition, I then went to the deck below, 6-inch battery, to help. I saw a Royal Marine lying near the gun and went to his side and said 'I will give you a hand'. As I knelt down to help him up I saw he was dead. The blast had blown him against a gusset which helped support the bulkhead. I then returned to my messdeck where a number of stretchers were laid out with the injured.(5)

The ship's Executive Officer, Commander Sir Charles Madden*, responsible for the ship's operational efficiency, found a state of devastation and scenes of horror below decks:

> The ship was at action stations and I was stationed in the Upper Conning Tower, listening through the voice pipe to what went on the bridge. I heard the report 'Hit starboard side amidships' and left the U.C.T. to investigate. As I reached the back of the bridge I saw dense smoke coming from the starboard 4-inch battery. On reaching the upper deck level it was apparent that one 4-inch mounting had gone overboard completely, and that the other was at an angle. There was a huge hole in the deck between the two mountings from which smoke and flame were pouring out.
>
> I then went down to the port 6-inch battery to see if fire parties were ready, and to try to get at the seat of the fire through the armoured door that connected the port and starboard 6-inch

---

* Baronet, later Admiral Sir Charles Madden. His father was Admiral Jellicoe's Chief of Staff at the Battle of Jutland, commanded the Atlantic Fleet in the inter-war years and became First Sea Lord.

battery decks. I found the fire party lined up ready by this door, asked two ratings to enter with me, and told the fire parties to open the door and follow us in. We had great difficulty in opening this door and had to use a sledgehammer. Finally it gave, to display a gruesome scene. The starboard battery was full of flames and smoke, in among which the cries of burned and wounded men could be heard. These were very unnerving and I remember thinking how accurate were the descriptions in C.S. Forester's books of the carnage on the gun-decks in Nelson's day. The flames seemed pretty fierce and I was doubtful if we would make headway against them. However my two volunteers came either side of me with their hoses and we walked into the battery.

To my surprise the flames, which I suppose were dying down, seemed to subside before us, and soon we had the fire parties following us and were putting out the flames as we advanced.

I was soon joined by more fire parties coming from the after end of the starboard battery and I felt confident that I could get the fires out, but was hampered by the continued cries of the burned men, which distracted the fire parties, who wanted to leave their hoses to assist their comrades. I therefore concentrated on administering morphia.

About this time the smoke cleared in the hole in the deckhead, and I could converse with those on the deck above. I sent for all officers with morphia, and soon had several on the job, which became the main task as soon as the flames were out. As it was dark and wounded men were thrown in all directions amidst piles of ironwork and rubbish this was not easy.

The hole in the upper deck was now clear of smoke, and through it we could see the deep blue sky and the next wave of attacking aircraft coming at us. The 4-inch battery being out of action made it seem unpleasantly quiet, until the pom-poms started up, which caused a lot of broken ironwork to fall about. I can remember the pom-pom bursts filling up the area of sky we could see and the aircraft still coming on, and some of the fire parties dropping their hoses to shake their fists at them.

I now had plenty of officers to take charge in the battery and we were moving the wounded out, so I went down to the mess-decks under the battery. The port side was cleared for casualties, which were being laid out in rows. A surprising number of men had trickled down to look after their friends, and I had some trouble in reducing their number, as they were all being kind and helpful.

I then went to the starboard mess-decks, where a fresh and unexpected scene of carnage greeted me. The armoured deck overhead, that of the starboard 6-inch battery, had been pierced by the explosion, the force of which had descended into a mess-deck where communications ratings off watch were resting. These, contrary to instructions, and because of the heat, were lightly clad, and there were heavy casualties from burns. The great amount of water we had pumped into the battery above to put out the fires had poured into the mess-deck, which was in parts knee deep in water, thus adding to the confusion of scattered mess tables, lockers and bodies.

When all was under control I went to the bridge to report. The calm, blue afternoon seemed unreal after the dark and smelly carnage below. I then busied myself with removing the dead. I made as I thought sensible arrangements for laying them out in one of the after flats, but had not counted on the strong feelings of the men, who insisted that they should all be taken to the chapel – a tortuous journey through the armoured 'dips'. Sorting the dead and identifying them occupied most of the dog watches, and they were then sewn up in hammocks for burial. The stout Corporal of Marines who served so cheerfully in the Wardroom bar, volunteered for, and personally led this operation throughout the next two days until we returned to harbour.(15)

After the bombing of *Warspite*, and under incessant attack, the now-combined squadrons of King and Rawlings withdrew southwards. Rear-Admiral King, as the senior officer, assumed command of the whole fleet. It was not long before there were other casualties among the ships and men. The destroyer *Greyhound*, detached to attack and sink a caique heading for Crete, was severely hit and disabled. Admiral King sent back the cruisers *Gloucester* and *Fiji*, plus the destroyers *Kingston* and *Kandahar*, to assist her. They were all overwhelmed by air attacks, and the *Gloucester*, *Fiji* and *Greyhound* were lost. *Valiant* was hit aft by two bombs and damaged. The next day, 23 May, the *Kelly* and *Kashmir* were both sunk and the *Kipling* damaged while picking up survivors from her two sister ships. To cap a tragic two days, the fleet heard, on returning to Alexandria, that the battlecruiser HMS *Hood*, pride of the Navy, had been sunk by the *Bismarck* thousands of miles away in the North Atlantic. There were only three survivors of her crew of over 1400 men. The

Bismarck's own sinking a little later, by heavy units and aircraft of the Home Fleet, was little consolation.

The *Warspite* and the remnants of the battlefleet arrived back in Alexandria in the early hours of 24 May. They had lost two cruisers and three destroyers, and all the surviving ships had taken a battering. The first task on docking was to offload the wounded. One of *Warspite*'s more seriously wounded was Chief Petty Officer D. Reardon. His lasting memories of the *Warspite*, as he was carried ashore on a stretcher, were:

> Second Battle of Narvik, bombardments in the Western Desert, Malta convoys, Greek convoys, bombardments of Valona and Tripoli, the Battle of Matapan, and now that of Crete. The team worked well, but now I was leaving them. Those who come after will carry on where we left off. My last look at Her is from a stretcher as we are being gently carried ashore. Famous Old Lady! We who served in you will always have a weak spot for you.(15)

The next day, in a calculated act of defiance, and as an encouragement to the crews of his battered fleet, Admiral Cunningham moved his flag back on board the *Warspite* and addressed the men. A memorial service was held for those killed in action or lost at sea. For the remaining crew of *Warspite* there was to be no immediate respite, no ready release from the trauma of losing so many comrades, the work of dealing with the dead had still to go on for another week. Commander Madden, with a working party from *Warspite*:

> ... spent the mornings digging out dead sailors and soldiers from one of the badly damaged cruisers, and the afternoons conducting funerals. We started to do this in full ceremonial manner, but had to change the pall bearers into boiler suits as blood leaked out of the hastily made coffins.(16)

Warspite was too badly damaged for local repairs and too far from home to risk the U-boat-infested and Luftwaffe-dominated waters of the Mediterranean and Bay of Biscay to return to Britain for more permanent repair. It was therefore decided to send her, via the Suez Canal, Red Sea, Indian and Pacific Oceans, to the western coast of the still nominally-neutral United States of America for repairs. It took a month to effect the necessary temporary repairs and make her sufficiently seaworthy to attempt the long journey. When these repairs were virtually finished, *Warspite* suffered from another air attack on Alexandria harbour. During the night of 23/24 June a large bomb fell alongside her already-weakened starboard side, and exploded abreast of 'A' turret. There was some flooding of the bulges and splinter damage, a motor boat lying alongside was destroyed and the crew on board thrown about, but otherwise *Warspite* escaped unscathed. Two days later, on 25 June 1941, *Warspite* left Alexandria and the Mediterranean for America.

She left behind a fleet whose difficulties were far from over. On Crete the military position was rapidly collapsing, and the decision to evacuate the island had been taken on 27 May. The task of carrying this out again fell on the Navy and led to further heavy losses in ships and men:

> The Mediterranean Fleet had paid a heavy price in the battle for Crete – the *Gloucester*, *Fiji* and *Calcutta* sunk, with the destroyers *Juno*, *Greyhound*, *Kashmir*, *Kelly*, *Hereward* and *Imperial*. The *Warspite*, *Barham*, *Formidable*, *Orion*, *Dido*, *Kelvin* and *Nubian* were damaged beyond repair on the spot, and would be out of action for some months; while the *Perth*, *Naiad*, *Carlisle*, *Napier*, *Kipling* and *Decoy* would be under repair for some weeks, and the *Havock*, *Kingston* and *Nizam* for a fortnight. Of the grand men of the fleet who had shared in our triumphs and adversities for so long well over two thousand were dead.[1]

The loss of Crete was still not the end of the Mediterranean Fleet's, or the Navy's, adversities in 1941. On the afternoon of 25 November *Warspite*'s sister-ship *Barham* was sunk by three torpedoes from *U 331*, with the loss of over 860 men; and on 19 December both the *Queen Elizabeth* and *Valiant*, the last of the Mediterranean Fleet's battleships, were so badly damaged as to be all-but-sunk in the shallow waters of their moorings by underwater charges placed by Italian frogmen. Away from the Mediterranean, the Navy's final disaster of 1941 was the sinking of the battleship *Prince of Wales* and the battlecruiser *Repulse* by Japanese aircraft off Singapore on 10 December. The year 1941 was to mark, effectively, the end of the battleship's era as the supreme ruler of the seas.

CHAPTER 6

American Hospitality and the Far Eastern Fleet

On leaving Alexandria on 25 June 1941, *Warspite* proceeded via Port Said into the Red Sea and on into the Indian Ocean, reaching Ceylon on 7 July. She arrived at Singapore on 12 July, Manila in the Philippines on 16 July, and Honolulu in the Pacific in early August. The ship had a few days' break in Honolulu, where the crew had their first taste of the welcome and hospitality that they were later to receive in America, with large numbers of visitors coming to see the bomb-damaged ship. *Warspite* left Honolulu on 4 August and arrived in Esquimalt, British Columbia, Canada on 10 August, where a draft of 284 men left for posting to other ships. She finally arrived at Puget Sound Navy Yard, abutting the town of Bremerton, near Seattle, U.S.A., on the next day. Roger J. Paquette, working on a nearby American warship, recalls that:

> August 11, 1941, I was working graveyard shift, midnight to eight a.m., on the battleship *Arizona* in Puget Sound Navy Yard. We had heard rumours of our first visitor from the war. We were on the quarterdeck that morning and we watched HMS *Warspite* slowly come into Port Orchard Bay to the Navy Yard in Sinclair Inlet. It was 8a.m. and we heard their call to colours. We were impressed by the marines on deck formally marching with their beautiful hesitation steps, a much classier ceremony than the *Arizona*'s with its squawky public address system.(1)

The arrival of the bomb-damaged ship aroused tremendous local interest, although the event was not widely known or publicised, and the repair programme for *Warspite* was only officially known in the dockyard as 'Request 126'. For some weeks strict censorship was maintained, largely at the request of the British. Her presence was not officially acknowledged until 19 September, by American Navy Secretary Frank Knox, who explained, when disclosing that by then more than a dozen British ships were under repair in United States dockyards:

> A reasonable degree of information will be made public, but no information will be disclosed which might be of value to the enemy.(2)

There is little doubt whose side 'neutral' America was favouring.

After her removal to Dry-dock No. 4, the work of clearing out the shattered insides of *Warspite* began. Below decks she was in a frightful state, with buckled decks, distorted beams and torn plating impeding the work of the recovery and repair teams. The immediate effect of the bomb had been to damage the forecastle deck over an area some ninety feet long and thirty feet wide. The upper deck had been driven downwards, to a depth of two feet at its maximum point, over an area of one hundred and thirty feet long by thirty feet wide, and had been holed by some eight feet by six feet at the point of the bomb-burst. The ship's side at this point was destroyed for a length of some fifty feet. On the top deck, the secondary and anti-aircraft guns which had not been blown away by the bomb explosion were badly damaged or their alignment distorted. All in all it was a rude introduction for the shipyard workers to the types of war damage and scenes of destruction with which they would become all too familiar in the months ahead. Sam Caretti, then ten years old, recalls:

> ... my father telling me how shocking it was to the workers when they finally had the ship in dry-dock and began opening compartments where doors between compartments had been closed and dogged [*sic*] shut to maintain water-tight integrity.(3)

Rumours abounded: '... word in town was she was badly damaged and portions were sealed off and had remains in them.'(4)

Keith Schick, then a maintenance electrician in the dockyard, also remembers the rumours:

> I remember the day they put the *Warspite* in dry dock. The big speculation around the yard was, what would they find in the flooded compartments? Rumour had it that there were dead seamen to be removed. The rumour died, and no more was heard

about it. If dead were removed it was done quietly, nobody seemed to know anything about it.(5)*

During the clearance of the debris from between decks in readiness for repairs and replacement of the damage, a number of oddments – rivets, shell-cases and the like – were found by the dock workers. They are kept to this day as cherished souvenirs of *Warspite*'s stay in Bremerton. Among the debris one more significant item was found, and unwittingly retained, by a lead welder working on the ship:

> My father was working in and near the wardroom cutting out and repairing bulkheads. As a bulkhead was removed a lot of debris was found between walls. This had to be shovelled out and disposed of in garbage bins. While shovelling out garbage he found an item that looked like a beermug. It was covered in dirt, oil and other garbage. He took it home to clean it up and see what it was. When he got home he put it in a box and it was not until the *Warspite* had left that he cleaned it up and discovered it was a presentation mug.(7)†

While the ship was put into the hands of the dockyard workers, the crew were being taken to the hearts of the local community. The bearing and standards of discipline of *Warspite*'s crew, particularly the Marines, made a lasting impression on Clyde C. Caldart, a shipfitter apprentice:

> Ship's company included a Royal Marine contingent. They were most impressive with their crisp precision, even when marching to waltz time up and down the dock alongside. They performed in several locations around the general area, including British Columbia. The entire ship's company was well received during their stay. Discipline for minor offences included running up and down the dock-pier at attention, rifle held high above them.(8)

---

* One sailor from *Warspite*, Petty Officer A.W. Penn, is buried in Ivy Green Cemetery, Bremerton, but his date of death is given by the Commonwealth War Graves Commission as 20 December 1941.(6)

† The son of the welder sought the author's help in returning the tankard to its rightful owners, believing that 'it belongs to a war museum and not a private collection'. The silver tankard, which bears the inscription 'The Wardroom Officers, HMS *Warspite*, September 1926', has now been returned, after nearly sixty years, to the Trophy Centre, HMS *Nelson*, Portsmouth, to await the commissioning of the next HMS *Warspite*. It had been written off as lost due to enemy action.

On the other hand, dockworkers sometimes found the standards of the British sailors hard to bear:

> While at Bremerton the crew were assigned to guard duty on the shipyard gates, relieving the U.S. Marines for other duty. The *Warspite* crew having been through battle were much stricter and conducted many more searches of the civilian workforce. After several weeks the civilian workforce demanded the *Warspite* guards be removed or there would be a revolt. After a review of the problems at the gates the *Warspite* crew were removed from guard duty. This gave them a lot less to do and a lot more free time while the ship was being repaired.(7)

Perhaps there was method in their madness! By now the *Warspite*'s crew had been reduced to about 600 in number, sufficient to maintain the ship while in the dockyard and assist with repairs. One man who remained was the Captain, D.B. Fisher, who greatly impressed Harry McIntyre, then a sixteen-year-old Western Union messenger, when he carried out a delivery to the ship's Captain:

> The captain, an elderly man of perhaps fifty [*sic*], took the extended message, looked at it briefly and handed it to an orderly for decoding. I turned to go when the Captain asked me to sit down. I was surprised but sat in the offered chair. He leaned back in his chair with is hands behind his head, smiled and said, 'Do you know anything about the Olympic mountains?' I told him that I had been a Boy Scout and had been through them three times. This impressed him (and me) and he shot a stream of questions about them at me for about fifteen minutes. ... He asked how to get there and I flippantly said 'Oh, just take a car'. His reply was something like 'I certainly don't have access to an automobile'. Somehow I had the impression that he had never had access to an automobile. It was like I was giving him a glimpse into a world that he had never experienced; neither the world of autos or mountains. He was like a little boy filled with wonder. ... As I left my escort said, 'My God, I never saw the old man talk to anyone like that'.(8)

The rest of the ship's crew, with time on their hands and, at least for the present, released from the pressures of war, relished their newfound freedoms and the hospitality offered them. For the first few days after their arrival they gorged themselves on fresh foods and new tastes, as a reaction to the dull monotony of sea-going wartime diet. Fresh milk and fresh vegetables were apparently popular among the *Warspite* seamen during their first few days in the Puget Sound Area. Bremerton residents reported that the men swarmed the markets in that city jubilantly buying lettuce. For some sailors, there was opportunity to try more exotic foods:

> In our neighbourhood was a popular tavern ... the Blue Moon. My mother and father met an English sailor there one evening in November 1941. His name was Carl. My parents were going to downtown Bremerton for a Chinese dinner and invited Carl along. He told them that he had never had Chinese food before. My mother says that he truly enjoyed the evening. She remembered the local paper asking the community to invite servicemen to their homes for the holidays and they invited Carl to join the family for Thanksgiving Dinner at our home.(4)

The amount of genuine interest from the local community in the British sailors and concern for their welfare was at times overwhelming. Lieutenant-Commander P.D. Hoare, then the *Warspite*'s Liaison Officer, recalls:

> Invitations poured in for any number from two to two hundred members of ship's company for afternoon tea in private houses to large dances. It was very difficult not to give offence by sending refusals to the very well-meant invitations, but fairly soon after arrival those who wished had already found friends among the very kind local community, who welcomed them into almost a second home.(9)

The hospitality was not completely one way; the officers and men reciprocated as best they could, although for one little boy the sailors were a little too enthusiastic:

> As a boy of six I got to meet the officers of the *Warspite* and had dinner aboard her with my parents. The officers spent Christmas Eve at our house and had one wild time. They broke my electric train set, got well oiled along with my Dad, uncle and a few friends, and it was a fine time for all.(10)*

* Robert Lamb, the then-little boy, still has the invitation to the dinner on *Warspite*, with the ship's woodpecker crest, and the letter of apology from the officers for breaking his train set.

Many such memories still remain of *Warspite*'s few months in Bremerton:

> I was about thirteen years old when it was here. Our neighbours ... had read in the paper that people were asked to invite the sailors to their homes for dinner. They invited two young sailors. ... After dinner they took them around the neighbours to meet us all. While they were visiting with my family they each signed my autograph book. Their names were Leading Stoker K.A. Cole and the other was A.R. Burdett, Stoker. ... My family and I have always wondered what happened to them, they were such nice people.(11)

Such meetings of the crew and the residents led to life-long friendships, such as that between John R. Fallis and Wilfred 'Bill' Hatch, then a young sailor on *Warspite*, who has contributed his own memories elsewhere in the book. Others led to marriages, some of which did not survive the pressures and long separations that were to come. For other Bremerton residents there are bittersweet memories. Those of Loretta Stone concern her first born son, now sadly deceased:

> My first born was delivered ... on November 16, 1941. When the nurse brought the baby in to present him, she explained his plentiful black hair had been styled by her boyfriend and her before she brought the baby in. His hair was styled in the 'Barber Shop Quartet' style and it was quite a sight! Her friend was one of the crew members from the *Warspite* and she had introduced him to the nursery full of babies when he came to visit her. ... He would probably be in his late 70s now and may remember.(12)

For a then sixteen-year-old girl living in Bremerton, bittersweet memories of two short meetings with an equally young sailor still remain:

> I had a girlfriend classmate named Margie Foster. Seems Mr Foster was a liquor salesman, and he had gone to a bar in Bremerton by the main gate of the Navy Yard and met up with these two charming and polite HMS *Warspite* boys. He was impressed by them and their stories, and decided to invite them along with Margie and come out to our place to invite me along for an evening of chaperoned fun with them. My dad and Mr

> Foster hit it off, and he was also impressed with the fine British boys, when Mr Foster asked his permission to let me join them.
>
> To put it mildly, I was more than surprised when Dad accepted, as he was very strict, and even at sixteen I had not yet dated. ... The 'Limey' that I sort of paired off with was Ralph A. Cobb, whose nickname was Tony. I believe he was eighteen at the time having been in the Navy since he was fourteen.
>
> Well, off we went to a dance place near Bremerton, which in the winter was an ice skating rink. We mostly watched other young people 'jitterbug', our generation's kind of dance, but we had fun giving it a short try anyway. We had a jolly time, it was very enjoyable and interesting, learning things from one another's country, as well as their experiences on the *Warspite*. ... We later went to the 'Wigwam', a bar nearby. Mr Foster ordered beers all round, and I was shocked that we were all served 'liquor'. ... My parents would have come unglued to know I had a beer before me. So I just sipped a bit, warily, but to be a sport.
>
> The evening ended when Mr Foster took me home, and the boys back to the Navy Yard. I was very excited about the evening, as well as having a bit of a teenage crush on this nice young sailor. My parents enjoyed hearing of the experience, however I didn't tell them till I was older about being served beer! Ha.[13]

That was not the end of the affair:

> ... two days later, Tony called my home for permission to come out and pick me up, as we had been invited for supper and visiting at Margie's boathouse, along with her mother and stepfather. Well I was amazed again that I was allowed to go, but I did, and again had a wonderful time, and there was young chemistry between Tony and I. When we cabbed home, Tony gave me a sweet quick kiss in the cab, and of course, at sixteen, this was quite a moment for me. [13]

When the *Warspite* left, Virginia and Tony corresponded for two or three years, but never met again.

It would be distorting the truth to pretend that the men from the *Warspite* were always so courteous and gentlemanly. There were the inevitable seaport bar-room brawls:

> Two belligerent British sailors who were jailed Tuesday night after they and two companions (American civilian dockworkers)

> fought four policemen and several civilians at a Queen Anne bar parlour, were turned over to an officer from the *Warspite* for punishment today. ... Their companions were fined $25 each and sentenced to ten days in jail. The sentences were suspended.
>
> 'We'd killed about five pints of whisky and a certain amount of beer' one of the civilian dockworkers testified. Then somebody called the British sailors 'Dirty Limeys'. The next thing I knew the fight was on. We didn't know we were fighting cops until we sobered up the next morning.'[14]

Not all the *Warspite*'s crew occupied their time socialising, courteous or courtroom-style; sport was the outlet for their energies, with keen participation and varying success, in football and boxing activities:

> Not quite as agile on a wet slippery field as on fast going, the sailors of HMS *Warspite* suffered a soccer surprise yesterday. They were beaten for the first time this season by the burly lads who won the soccer league title for Black Diamonds last winter. The Diamonds played an inspired game, took a 3-0 lead in the first half, and went on to a 5-3 victory. ... Even in the rain, the game drew a goodly crowd to Lower Woodfield Park.[15]

In the ring, sailors from the *Warspite* took part in supporting bouts of local matches:

> Promoter Nat Druxman today announced the completion of his five-bout boxing card for next Tuesday evening at the Civic Auditorium. ... Sailors from HMS *Warspite* box in two four round preliminaries. Wally Downs faces Al Reado, Everett Negro welterweight in a rematch, they drew last time, and Irish Jack Wilson takes on Al Kuchu, stoop-shouldered Everett heavyweight.[16]

The officers of the *Warspite* were in demand as guest speakers. On 22 October, Commander Sir Charles Madden, Bt, Executive Officer of the ship, spoke at the annual meeting of the Greek War Relief Association on the British battleship's part in the battles for Greece and Crete. The next month, Lieutenant-Commander W.F.B. Lane, D.S.C., Senior Engineering Officer of the *Warspite*, addressed the November meeting of the Western Section of the American Society of Mechanical Engineers in Bremerton Eagles' Hall.

Meanwhile, the work of repair had been steadily progressing. Large quantities of spares and stores had to be assembled, much of it brought out from Britain, including new 15in guns. To spread the risk against loss by enemy action during their passage across the Atlantic, these were brought out in separate merchant ships. In a signal on 30 September from the Admiralty to the British Advisory Repair Mission, which had been set up in the U.S.A., it was advised that:

> Exchange of five 15-inch guns approved with ... delay [of] one week. Delivery in three vessels by end of Oct. Existing breech mechanism to be used.(17)

One week later the Admiralty instructed the senior officer responsible for the assembly of the convoy taking the guns:

> Three ships due to sail in [convoy] ON24 are carrying 15-inch guns and ammunition. Give safe place in convoy.(17)

'Safe places', in a Second World War convoy crossing the Atlantic, is a relative term; but the guns, each weighing some 100 tons, arrived safely and were transported by rail across America to Puget Sound Navy Yard.

During *Warspite*'s stay at Bremerton, the opportunity was taken to refit and upgrade her radar, transmitting and gunnery control facilities, and for an enhancement of her anti-aircraft capability. Fifteen 20mm Oerlikon guns were positioned around her upper works, replacing the Vickers 0.5in machine guns. In carrying out the repairs and renovations, the American shipyard workers had to come to terms with some rather antiquated and unexpected British equipment; Palmer O. Hanson found that:

> We at Puget Sound Navy Yard had of course not seen battle damaged ships, which we were to see plenty of a little later. Besides the battle damage, we got a liberal education in life at sea on a British man-o-war. My job was some extensive rewiring in the superstructure where I saw some curious differences in shipboard lifestyle from what we were used to. We had never seen bath tubs, for example, as we did in 'Senior Officers' Country' on *Warspite*. Electrical cabling was covered with a lead sheath, differing of course from our basket-woven steel. This gave us trouble when installing new cable supports, by our spot-welding process tending to melt off the lead sheathing.(18)

Warspite's bathroom facilities and the ship's internal communication system also drew the attention of John Lee Jordan:

> The Captain's bathroom had a regular bathtub, ours had showers. ... Communications in *Warspite* were by voice tubes rather than electronic means as on American ships.[19]

As the repairs neared completion, *Warspite* received some 500 replacements in December – officers, specialists and seamen – for those released four months previously. *Warspite* began preparations for departure in early 1942. She was originally scheduled for return to the Mediterranean, and a planning order of late October 1941 had her scheduled to leave the U.S.A. on 10 January 1942 for Suez, via Singapore and Trincomalee, with arrival at Suez on 4 March. The Japanese attack on Pearl Harbor and the entry of the United States into the war changed all that. *Warspite*'s departure, route and destination were all changed. Changed too were the lives of the people of Bremerton, as the town, with a pre-war population of 12,000, swelled with the influx of dockworkers to over 80,000 by the end of the war.

The Japanese attack on Pearl Harbor was a great shock to the inhabitants of Bremerton, and there was initially a great fear of the threat of follow-up bombing raids upon the town and Navy Yard. At this time, immediately after the 7 December 1941 attack, the presence of the now newly-serviceable *Warspite* was a comfort for some. Moulton Phillips remembers: '... how lucky we were supposed to be because the HMS *Warspite* was here and they had the only anti-aircraft guns around.'[8] While Jim Braman found reassurance '... in realising the best anti-aircraft weapons were aboard HMS *Warspite* and had sailors who knew how to use them.'[8]

Early in 1942 *Warspite* was indeed ready to go back to war. She left Bremerton and Puget Sound on 7 January and, after working up off Vancouver Island, Canada, left for Sydney, Australia, on 22 January, escorted for part of her journey by two destroyers of the Royal Canadian Navy. Her journey was not without incident, according to Leading Cook R.B. Buckle:

> Not long after leaving Bremerton, an artificer was lost overboard. He was leaning on the guard-rail near the catapult when it gave way. We hove to and lowered the whaler and the men pulled

> round for about ten minutes while the searchlight played on the water. We had no escort at this time and Jap subs were known to be in the area. The man was never found and his belongings were auctioned off on the forecastle the next morning as Dead Man's Effects.[(20)*]

Warspite arrived in Sydney on 20 February, where her crew again enjoyed warm hospitality, before sailing on for Trincomalee, Ceylon, where she arrived on 22 March. Five days later Captain Fisher was relieved for a well-earned rest by Captain F.E.P. Hatton, and a few days later another of her former captains, now Admiral Sir James Somerville, hoisted his flag in *Warspite* as Commander-in-Chief, Eastern Fleet. Once again *Warspite*, now twenty-eight years old, was a flagship. It was the third fleet, after the Mediterranean and Home Fleets, where she had held that honour.

It was not a happy or promising time for the C-in-C or for the men of the *Warspite* and the other ships of the Eastern Fleet. The heavy losses of 1941 in the Mediterranean and Atlantic, followed by the sinking by the Japanese of the *Prince of Wales* and *Repulse* off south-eastern Malaya three months previously, had made the build-up of an adequate naval force to oppose the Japanese in the Far East an impossibility at that time. Furthermore, the loss of the supposedly impregnable naval base at Singapore, in mid-February 1942, had robbed the Fleet of its dockyard, facilities, stores and ammunition. Ships of the American Pacific Fleet which had survived the attack on Pearl Harbor had been temporarily withdrawn to bases on the west coast of America. The Japanese were for the moment effectively masters of all they surveyed in the Pacific and Indian Oceans and in the South China Sea.

The Japanese had at their disposal, to roam where they wished, a fleet of eleven fast modern battleships, six fleet aircraft carriers, four smaller aircraft carriers, thirty-six cruisers and over one hundred destroyers. They also had a significant submarine fleet. Among the battleships was the *Yamato*, later to be joined by her sister-ship the *Musashi*, both monsters of 71,600 tons, 860 feet long, armed with nine 18.1in guns, twelve 6in and twelve 5in guns, and capable of a speed of 27 knots.

---

* The proceeds would be sent on to the dead man's dependants.

To oppose any further westward thrusts of the Japanese across the Indian Ocean towards India, Ceylon, and beyond to the oilfields of Persia and Iraq, Admiral Somerville had a scratch fleet comprising five battleships, three aircraft carriers, two 8in cruisers, five 6in cruisers and a heterogeneous collection of sixteen destroyers. What appeared on paper to be formidable was in practice frail. The five battleships consisted of *Warspite* and the four 'R' class ships – *Resolution*, *Royal Sovereign*, *Ramillies* and *Revenge*. Like the *Warspite* they were built and had served in the First World War a quarter of a century before; they were of low endurance and totally unsuited for long-distance sailing in the tropics. The squadron speed of the four ships was only some 18 knots, and they had only three or four days' endurance at these speeds, not at all suitable for the vast oceans and the great distances between bases in the Far Eastern theatre. Additionally, they were unable to distil sufficient fresh water at such speeds to replace boiler losses, and the shortage of fresh water for cooking, washing and laundry purposes was a constant trial for their crews in the badly-ventilated ships. All five battleships had been designed for a different war in a different part of the world; the Indian Ocean was not the North Sea. Somerville's aircraft carriers, the *Indomitable* and *Formidable*, carried a mixed bag of largely obsolescent aircraft, no match for the infinitely more numerous and modern Japanese carrier-borne planes. Perhaps more seriously, neither ship had worked up to wartime operational efficiency with the fleet, having been used in recent months on independent duties, largely ferrying aircraft. The *Hermes*, Admiral Somerville's third carrier, was small, old and slow; built in 1923, she only carried twelve aircraft and was totally unsuited for action with the fleet. To compound the new C-in-C's problems, his fleet was scattered between bases at Trincomalee in the north of Ceylon, Colombo in the south of that island, and Addu Atoll, a hastily-contrived base in an anchorage some 600 miles to the south west of Ceylon, on the southernmost of the Maldive Islands.

Admiral Somerville and his Second-in-Command, Vice-Admiral Willis, decided upon a strategy to deal with the unfolding situation. It was thought by the War Cabinet and Admiralty that the Japanese could conceivably continue their conquests westwards by a pincer attack upon the Indian sub-continent: an advance in the north through Burma coupled with a seaborne attack upon the south of India. Ceylon, with its airfields and deep-water harbours, was seen as an essential staging post for any southern thrust. In order to help protect Ceylon, Somerville wanted to keep his fleet 'in being' as a whole force, and to avoid piecemeal actions against the Japanese with their vastly superior air capability. To do this he needed to keep his ships at sea as much as possible, to distract the enemy with threats and feigned attacks, and to avoid his ships being caught and attacked, helpless, in their bases. With his inferior force, all he could do was to contain Japanese naval ambitions in the Indian Ocean.

Somerville went aboard his flagship on 30 March 1942 and found the crew of the *Warspite*, in a gale and pouring rain, loading great quantities of army rifles, which were being removed from the possibility of falling into Japanese hands. It was a depressing and morale-lowering task. However, on meeting with the Captain, F.E.P. Hutton, and the Executive Officer, Commander Sir Charles Madden, Bt, both old friends, he felt that they had the ship's company 'very much on their toes'(21), and the C-in-C had a rousing reception when he addressed the ship's company. His morale-raising good humour was soon to show itself. When the fleet rendezvoused on 31 March some eight miles south of Dondra Head, the southernmost point of Ceylon, he signalled Rear-Admiral Willis, bringing in the four 'R' class battleships:

> So this is the Eastern Fleet. Never mind, many a good tune is played on an old fiddle.(21)

The crews of *Warspite* and the other ships would need all Admiral Somerville's leadership and morale-raising skills over the next fortnight which would prove to be disastrous for the Eastern Fleet.

The C-in-C decided to split his fleet into two divisions; Force A and Force B. Force A, the 'fast' division, was made up of his flagship the *Warspite*, the two carriers *Indomitable* and *Formidable*, the 8in cruisers *Cornwall* and *Dorsetshire*, the 6in cruisers *Enterprise* and *Emerald*, and six destroyers. Force B, the 'slow' division, under Vice-Admiral Willis, consisted of battleships *Ramillies*, *Resolution*, *Revenge* and *Royal Sovereign*, the carrier *Hermes*, the Dutch cruiser *Jacob van Heemskerck*, the old 6in cruisers *Caledon* and *Dragon*, both built in 1917-18, and eight destroyers. Apart from *Warspite*, few of the ships were in first-class condition, and most, especially the destroyers, were in need of docking and repairs.

During the night of 31 March the two forces cautiously probed for the Japanese, who, it was anticipated, would launch an air attack against Ceylon in early April. Six land-based Catalina aircraft, all that were available in the area, searched the waters to the south-east of Ceylon from where the seaborne attack was expected. Force A was positioned between the direction of the anticipated attack and Force B, which was in a supporting role. No enemy forces were found, and after three days the battleships were running low on fuel and water. Admiral Somerville decided to return the fleet to Addu Atoll, 600 miles away, rather than risk refuelling at the nearer, but inadequately-protected Colombo base. He made the decision because he feared replays of the British attack on Taranto and the Japanese attack on Pearl Harbor, while his ships were helplessly refuelling. Not all the ships returned to Addu Atoll. The aircraft carrier *Hermes* and her consort, the old destroyer *Vampire*, were sent back to Trincomalee, to continue preparations for a planned attack upon the Vichy French-controlled island of Madagascar; and the two 8in cruisers *Cornwall* and *Dorsetshire* returned to Colombo, the *Cornwall* to take over escort of an expected Australian troop convoy and the *Dorsetshire* to resume her interrupted refit.

At about the time that Admiral Somerville was forced to abandon his search his opponent, Admiral Nagumo, was off the southern tip of Sumatra, heading for Ceylon, with his fast modern fleet of four battleships, five fleet carriers, three cruisers and eight destroyers. On the morning of 4 April, as the British ships were refuelling at Addu Atoll, and with a captains' conference taking place on board *Warspite*, a lone R.A.F. Catalina sighted the Japanese force some 360 miles S.S.E. of Dondra Head, steering north-west towards Ceylon. Somerville's fleet was caught out of position and out of fuel. Although frantic efforts were made to refuel, Force A was not able to sail until midnight, and Force B six hours later. There was insufficient time to intercept the Japanese fleet before it delivered its air onslaught upon Colombo, but Somerville hoped that bombers of the R.A.F., based on Ceylon, might possibly damage and slow down some of the Japanese ships so that they could be brought to battle. Force A, followed by Force B, sailed at their respective best speeds towards the enemy force. *Cornwall* and *Devonshire* were ordered back to Addu Atoll to join up with Force A, and *Hermes* was told to leave harbour and sail to the north-east, hopefully out of harm's way.

Colombo was attacked by over seventy Japanese planes at 08.00 on Easter Sunday, 5 April, but, because of Somerville's anticipation of the danger, they found the harbour virtually empty. Had the fleet returned there instead of to Addu Atoll it would probably have been wiped out, or at best suffered heavy losses in ships and men. As it was, the Japanese only found and sank the destroyer *Tenedos*, immobilised because of a refit, and the *Hector*, reconverting from an armed merchant cruiser to her former civilian role.

At 13.40 hours, over fifty Japanese planes found the *Cornwall* and *Dorsetshire*, when only some ninety miles from Force A coming up to meet them. Force B was a further 100 miles away. The two British cruisers were smothered with bombs and sunk within a few minutes of each other. There was little that Somerville could do. HMS *Enterprise* was sent ahead to rescue survivors and managed to pick up 1112 officers and men from the two cruisers, but over 400 sailors were lost. To add to the C-in-C's frustration, the force of nine R.A.F. Blenheims, all that were available on the island, sent to find, attack and disable the Japanese force, was unable to locate them. The Japanese planes were more successful: on 9 April the *Hermes*, the destroyer *Vampire*, the corvette *Hollyhock* and two accompanying oilers were found and sunk by some fifty carrier-borne aircraft.

Somerville and his sailors were helpless in the face of such overwhelming superiority of ships and aircraft. Although it was not appreciated at the time, the Easter period of 1942 marked the high tide of Japanese aggression towards India and the limits of her expansion west. In mid April, Admiral Nagumo and his fleet headed back to Singapore, to prepare for the drive southwards towards Australia. Then Japanese seapower began to suffer reverses at the hands of the reviving might of the American Navy. An American bombing raid on 18 April on Tokyo, by carrier-borne aircraft, heralded the start of this revival. This was followed by the Battle of the Coral Sea on 7 May. Although this was an indecisive, drawn encounter, with the Japanese and Americans each losing one aircraft carrier, worse was to follow for the Japanese. On 4 June, at the

Battle of Midway, the Japanese lost four carriers, one cruiser and 332 aircraft, against American losses of one carrier and 137 aircraft. Thereafter, Japanese threats in the Indian Ocean and along the traffic routes off East Africa would come from their submarines. However, at the time, the Eastern Fleet did not know what the immediate future held; they did not know that it was to be the Eastern Fleet's darkest hour before a brighter dawn. They could only remain watchful, for opportunities to deter and distract Japanese ambitions to expand their influence even further westwards. The Admiral did his best to keep up morale and to show that, whatever the dangers and however dark the outlook, he was till his rumbustuous self. To try to lighten the gloom, he and the *Warspite*'s Executive Officer, developed something of a regular double act, with Sir Charles the butt of the Admiral's contrived grievances. Thus after paddling about in several inches of water in a teeming tropical downpour, the Admiral sent for the Commander:

> 'Good morning, Charles. What is this place called?'
> 'It's the Admiral's shelter, Sir.'
> 'Is it indeed? Well, I call it a ****** waterfall. Do something about it.'[21]

On a later occasion, after the ship's company had been stood down from Action Stations and had gone to breakfast, a note arrived from the Admiral:

> Dear Charles, I am well aware that as a Baronet you are indifferent to the sufferings of mere Admirals, but would you mind having my lavatory unblocked?[21]

As Somerville was well aware, such exchanges became embellished in the telling on the messdecks and helped to keep up the men's spirits.

Any evolving relief for the Eastern Fleet was tempered by continuing problems in the Mediterranean. The Axis partners, Germany and Italy, were now threatening Egypt and the Nile Delta; and, with their control of the air, making the passage of supplies through the Mediterranean to the British Middle East forces virtually impossible. It was therefore imperative that the passages for troops and supplies, from India across the Indian Ocean, and from the United Kingdom round the Cape, up the coast of East Africa, and then through the Red Sea and the Suez Canal, were kept open. To safeguard these passages Somerville sent Force B, with its almost useless 'R' class battleships, to Mombassa in East Africa, to help protect the Cape convoys; while Force A, with the *Warspite*, went to Bombay to deter any Japanese attacks against shipping movements between India and the Red Sea and Persian Gulf. As the C-in-C succinctly put his strategy at the time:

> I shall have to lie low in one sense but be pretty active in another – keep the old tarts out of the picture and roar about with the others.(21)

By mid-May *Warspite* was back at Kilindini, the fleet anchorage at Mombasa, for dockyard attention. From here the C-in-C flew to Nairobi for a conference. The trip was made over the bush, at low altitude in a light aircraft, and prompted the Admiral to send a signal to their Lordships at the Admiralty:

> During my passage to Nairobi I was able to observe the majority of animals usually found in Noah's Ark and noted that in their efforts to keep their eyes on the aircraft while proceeding at full speed, the wildebeest frequently carries out the evolution of A ... over T. ...(21)

As the Japanese threat to India and the Persian Gulf receded, and as it became obvious that British First World War battleships had no place in American-led, wide ranging, carrier-borne operations across the vast expanses of the Indian and Pacific Oceans, there was the question of how best to use the ageing ships of the Eastern Fleet. In the Middle East, the situation in the summer of 1942 was critical. Malta was on the verge of collapse and Rommel and his Afrika Corps were at Alamain and the gates of Egypt. The Nile delta was in danger of being overrun and the vital Suez Canal sea passage lost. Winston Churchill, belligerent as ever, suggested to the Admiralty that *Warspite* and Somerville's carriers should go back to the Mediterranean, via the canal, and help fight a convoy through to beleaguered Malta, tempting the Italian Fleet into battle on the way. The plan came to nothing, and the Eastern Fleet was gradually stripped of its more useful ships. *Indomitable* left in July to help guard a convoy from Gibraltar to Malta, and the following month

Formidable left to take part in the North African landings. In the late summer of 1942, the conclusion of successful action against Vichy French control of Madagascar, and the take-over of its airfields and naval bases, helped to reduce the Japanese threat to convoys coming round the Cape and through the Madagascar Channel. It was only a matter of time before *Warspite*, now mainly idling her time at anchor, was called home.

In harbour, some of *Warspite*'s crew had a regular and somewhat hazardous nightly chore:

> ... we did spend many nights in our picket boat, dropping small depth charges along the boom nets that were spread across the harbour. This was to deal with any one-man submarines that might be lurking. even though the depth charges were small, having dropped one, it was 'Full Speed Ahead' to get out of the way of the blast. Thank goodness we never had to drop a big one (as were our orders if we ever saw a submarine) because we'd probably have blown our stern off.[22]

In October *Warspite* was dry-docked at Mombasa for essential maintenance. Then, early in February 1943, she briefly helped in covering the passage of a convoy of five of the world's largest liners, *Queen Mary*, *Aquitania*, *Île de France*, *Nieuw Amsterdam* and *Queen of Bermuda*, carrying the 9th Australian Division back home.

Late in the same month *Warspite* was ordered home. At Durban, en route, she changed Captains, with Captain H.A. Packer* relieving Captain Hutton. The new Captain was very much an old *Warspite* hand. He had been a Sub-Lieutenant on her between 1915 and 1917, taking part in the Battle of Jutland, and again served on her as a Gunnery Officer in 1926, at the time of the General Strike. The new Captain was delighted to be back in command of his old ship. He was pleased with his crew, and, in particular, with one new crew member. In a letter to his wife in mid-April he wrote:

> I am delighted with my new ship – or rather old ship. I have fine officers as far as I can see and a happy ship's company. ... I also have in my ship's company Able Dog Pluto. Born during the siege of Tobruk he came to this ship via a destroyer in which he was in

* Later Admiral Sir Herbert Packer.

many engagements. I will interview him, photograph him, and let you know more about him.(23)

The ship left Durban for home on 16 April and helped to provide part of the escort for a U.K.-bound troop convoy. *Warspite* was soon to remind her new captain of her old tricks, when her steering broke down on the way home. Repaired at sea, she docked on 10 May at Princes Dock, Greenock, on the Clyde, the very dock that she had briefly guarded during the General Strike of 1926. It was over three years since she had last been home.

CHAPTER 7

Salerno and the Invasion of Normandy

After attention to her steering gear and other maintenance work, *Warspite* spent the first two weeks of June 1943 on exercises and shore bombardment practice off Scapa Flow. She was to take part in Operation 'Husky', the invasion of Sicily, following the expulsion of all Axis forces from North Africa. On 15 June *Warspite* carried out final exercises off Scapa Flow with the reconstituted and reinforced Force H, and two days later sailed with that force to Gibraltar. She was in company with the battleships *Nelson*, *Rodney* and *Valiant*, the aircraft carrier *Indomitable* and twelve destroyers, and was later joined by the aircraft carrier *Formidable*. The force arrived at Gibraltar on 23 June. That same day Rear-Admiral Bissett hoisted his flag as Rear-Admiral Second-in-Command, Force H, in *Warspite*. Admiral Willis, the Commander-in-Chief of Force H, was operating it as three divisions from Gibraltar, ports in North Africa, and Alexandria. *Warspite*, together with *Valiant* and *Formidable*, were allocated to Alexandria, where they arrived on 5 July. They were scheduled to help cover the Sicily landings on 10 July, supporting the army by bombarding inland targets and dealing with any attempted interference by capital ships of the Italian Navy. The ship's morale was high and Able Dog Pluto was making a great impression upon the Captain:

> Pluto the dog is very impressive. ... He is always the first on the scene when the Cable Party is piped to muster before anchoring. Straight away when the Cable Party bugle sounds he dashes up forward, through the guard rails into the very eyes of the ship and stands there, strong and vigilant, until he is satisfied that the anchor has been cleared away and all is ready for letting go. Then he trots back and joins up with the common sailors until the anchor goes and the cable roars out. Then he trots aft sedately to

> the Quarterdeck to supervise the marines lowering the after-gangway. Just about then, preceded by Corney, I arrive on the Quarterdeck on my way to my day-cabin. Pluto doesn't fawn, lick one's hand or jump about; on an even keel he approaches me with great dignity, cocks his head on one side with one ear up and one down, gives me a knowing look, winks his port eye, hesitates for a polite second, and off he goes to his next activity. He's a great dog – a dog of the world who doesn't work but superintends like hell and criticises not a little.(1)

The landings on Sicily duly commenced on 10 July. For the first few days *Warspite*'s guns were not needed, and she and her companion ships patrolled off Cape Passaro at the south-eastern corner of Sicily to ward off any threat from the Italian Fleet. She returned briefly to Valetta to refuel on 12 July, which allowed her Maltese ratings, some of whom had not seen their families for four years, a few hours ashore. In the early hours of 15 July, the aircraft carrier *Indomitable* was hit by an aerial torpedo and was escorted back to Malta by *Warspite*. Two days later, *Warspite* and *Valiant* were ordered to bombard Catania between the hours of 18.30 and 19.00 as part of a synchronised attack with the held-up Eighth Army. For once it was not the *Warspite* that had a mishap on leaving harbour; the *Valiant* became entangled in the torpedo defences and had to be left behind. *Warspite*, now made late by the incident, left at 13.30 hours with her destroyers and had to put on maximum speed, working up to some 23.5 knots, in order to make the scheduled time. In a letter to his son, Captain Packer told how the ship:

> Quickly worked up to eight revs over our maximum. Suddenly our steering gear jammed and we went around in a savage circle and lost ten precious minutes getting our steering connected. At 18.43 we were passing thro' [*sic*] the Open Fire Position at sixteen knots and opened fire. A great mass of dust and smoke rose from the town right on target. We had exactly twenty minutes to do our dirty work.
>
> Then everything happened at once. In those twenty minutes two submarines appeared and were quickly depth charged by our destroyers. Three FW190s* got a load of Oerlikon, pom-pom, 4-inch and 6-inch but got away. They were moving at about

* Single-engined German fighter planes.

> 400 m.p.h. and machine gunning like fury but with indifferent accuracy. The shore batteries opened up and the destroyers took them on as our big guns were pouring in the stuff. So it was a fine twenty minutes for the old *Warspite*.(1)

Warspite was escorted by seven destroyers; *Faulkner*, *Fury*, *Eclipse*, *Inglefield*, *Raider*, *Petard* and the Greek destroyer *Queen Olga*. As seen from the *Petard*, the bombardment of Catania had been clinically executed:

> At 18.40 *Warspite* was in position 180 degrees Cape Molini light, 10.45 miles, steering north 15 knots closing the target, the northern half of Catania clear of the port area and railway station. The area was a triangle 1,000 × 800 yards centred on the military barracks, with other military quarters on the N.E. and N.W. corners. The battleship opened fire at 18.44, position 141 degrees Sciara Biscari light 13,000 yards, salvos fired at minute intervals. After A and B turrets fired eight ... salvoes, *Warspite* altered course at 18.50 to 020 degrees to allow X and Y turrets to fire six ... salvoes from each turret. The bombarding finished at 19.03.(2)

The effects of the bombardment had been devastating; as observed by Yeoman Chapman from the *Petard*:

> It was a terrific occurrence. The town is something like Portsmouth and we were so close that we could see large buildings collapsing as the huge projectiles tore their way through them. Large hotels went up in dust, theatres were laid in complete ruin ... but the slaughter of innocent people must have been awful.(2)

On *Warspite*'s return to harbour Admiral Cunningham, the C-in-C, signalled:

> Operation well executed. When the Old Lady lifts her skirts she can run.(3)

HMS *Petard*'s reward from *Warspite* was less than friendly. At the end of July she collided with the battleship and was badly damaged. The captain of the *Petard*, approaching *Warspite* from astern, was attempting to place his port bow close to *Warspite*'s starboard quarter to allow the transfer, by line, of a bag containing dispatches from the forecastle of *Petard* to the quarterdeck of *Warspite*. The latter, with a large turn of helm, suddenly swung and rammed her armoured stern into *Petard*'s light plated bows, which were badly holed leading to extensive flooding of the destroyer's forequarters. It was not the last embrace that *Petard* was to receive from *Warspite*.

By now events in the Mediterranean were all going the Allies' way, with the Italians in particular becoming increasingly despondent and in political turmoil, culminating in the deposition of Mussolini on 26 July 1943. Early August was a relatively quiet period for *Warspite* and her crew. The entertainer Noel Coward, an old friend of Captain Packer, visited the ship on 13 August, and two days later the C-in-C, Admiral Cunningham, came aboard to inspect and address the officers and men of his favourite flagship. All this socialising and entertaining was perhaps too much for Able Dog Pluto who, about this time, and as described in a letter from the Captain to his wife, drew unseemly attention to himself; or perhaps he was settling an old score:

> Just as the stately Marine Guard marched off for colours this morning Pluto laid an enormous egg on the Quarterdeck right in their path. This mined the Sergeant in the lead and he skimmed down the deck like Donald Duck on skates. With a crash, as his rifle clattered to the ground, he fetched up on his enormous tail still moving South-South-West at 25 knots. It was unseemly and I believe, strictly between you and me, that Pluto and the Sergeant of Marine did not get on well. Anyhow the only thing smoothed out by this incident is the Quarterdeck. I swear I saw Pluto watching from behind a turret.[(1)]

Other ships had their own pets and pet problems. Captain Packer noted one exchange of signals between the medical staff of *Warspite* and HMS *Gavotte*, an accompanying minesweeper:

> 'Pet monkey dying from eating red lead. Request any help or instructions please. 13.00. 31/8/43.'
>
> 'Reply your 13.00. Give half teaspoon Epsom Salts in cup of water followed by common salt until monkey is sick. Small doses of brandy diluted in water may be given. P.M.O. *Warspite*. 14.20. 31/8/43.'
>
> 'From *Gavotte*. V.M.T. for your assistance. Regret the poor little fellow passed away. 14.50. 31/8/43.'[(1)]

By late August the Allies had the upper hand in Sicily and were threatening the Italian mainland with invasion. On 2 September

Warspite bombarded gun positions in the town of Reggio. It was a devastating onslaught, delivered with great accuracy at almost point-blank range, such that the excitement proved rather too much for the observer of *Warspite*'s spotter plane relaying the fall of the shot:

> We had a very young South African from Rondebosch called Webb spotting for us from an aeroplane and when we got onto the target, instead of ordinary formal spotting reports, he started getting enthusiastic and saying 'OK, OK, give them all you've got. You're plastering them. Repeat, repeat. Give them the works.'(1)

On 7 September, *Warspite* sailed with the rest of Force H for bombardment duties in Salerno Bay as part of an audacious Allied plan to land there and take Naples. During the night of 8 September Force H was heavily attacked from the air in bright moonlight and *Warspite* barely escaped an aerial torpedo attack:

> I had one moment as bad as any in this war. I heard above the sound of our pom-poms, Oerlikons, 4-inch and 6-inch guns an aircraft roaring in. It skimmed down the safe edge of our barrage about 40 degrees off the port bow. ... I saw this Ju88 drop his torpedo and I saw it splash, and down the voice pipe to the Quartermaster I roared 'Port 35'... it seemed a thousand years before I saw the electric repeat from the rudder-head showing that the rudder was 35 degrees to port. ... I can honestly say that I was holding on to things waiting for the bump and so was everyone else on the bridge. I steadied up with my course parallel to the track of the torpedo and it literally missed the stern by feet. The parallel track was so close that I had to climb up on the side of the bridge and look over the edge to see it.(1)

On 8 September the surrender of Italy was announced, and *Warspite* and *Valiant* were deputed by Admiral Cunningham to rendezvous with the surrendered heavy units of the Italian Fleet on the 10 September and escort them into Malta. The battleships *Roma*, *Vittorio Veneto* and *Italia* (formerly named *Littorio*), six Italian cruisers and a force of Italian destroyers sailed from La Spezia. En-route they were attacked by their former German allies and the *Roma* was hit, blew up and sunk in twenty minutes with heavy loss of life, struck by a new German weapon, the FX1400 radio-controlled bomb. The remainder of the ships were met by *Warspite* and the other British ships and, with guns trained on them, were escorted into Malta. As they came into sight Admiral Cunningham recalled:

> It was a most moving and thrilling sight. To see my wildest hopes of years back brought to fruition, and my former flagship the *Warspite*, which had struck the first blow against the Italians three years before, leading her erstwhile opponents into captivity, filled me with deepest emotion and lives with me still. I can never forget it. I made a signal congratulating the *Warspite* on her proud and rightful position at the head of the line.(3)

Over the next few days other Italian warships surrendered and, on 11 September, with the main bulk of the Italian Fleet in captivity and others on their way to surrender, Admiral Cunningham formally signalled to the Admiralty in London:

> Be pleased to inform Their Lordships that the Italian battlefleet now lies under the guns of the fortress of Malta.(3)

On 13 September *Warspite*, at sea, accepted the surrender of the *Giulio Cesare*, her adversary and the recipient of one of her 15-inch shells in the action off Calabria three years before.

With the elimination of the Italian Navy, and the attack on the Italian mainland apparently under control and proceeding satisfactorily, the ships of Force H were withdrawn. *Warspite* and *Valiant* were to stand down and make way for the newer British battleships now becoming available for service. The crew of *Warspite* were anticipating a return to the United Kingdom, to prepare the ship for action in the rumoured invasion of Europe. Paymaster Commander Duckworth's diary(4) records that on 12 September the Rear-Admiral in command of Force H transferred his flag from *Warspite* to the new British battleship *Howe* in order to escort, in company with *Howe*'s sister-ship *King George V*, the surrendered Italian Fleet to Alexandria, away from the threat of German radio-controlled bombs. Two days later, at 1800 on 14 September, *Warspite* was again at sea, together with the *Valiant* and *Illustrious*, proceeding to Algiers and, the crew hoped, starting on the passage home. *Warspite*'s affairs, however, rarely went to plan.

On land, back at Salerno, things were not going well. The Germans, now without the help or hindrance of their former ally, were mounting a stout defence. Early on 14 September they were threatening to drive down the Sele Valley to the sea, forcing a wedge between the American and British sectors, with four Panzer divisions supported by artillery and Tiger tanks. The American and British troops were desperately in need of reinforcements to try to break out of their narrow bridgehead, which had left a four-mile wide gap between the two Allied landings, which had only secured a foothold some five miles deep. The troops on the beaches were being battered by artillery and mortar fire, and heavy losses from Luftwaffe attacks were being suffered by the ships trying to bring in reinforcements and supplies. The Allies were in danger of being thrown, neck and crop, back into the sea. An urgent call was made by Admiral Hewitt, the American commander of the Salerno landings, to Admiral Cunningham for heavy gun support against the encroaching tanks and the artillery which was dominating the beaches.

Admiral Cunningham's response, besides sending three cruisers loaded with fresh troops, was to recall *Warspite* and *Valiant* for further bombarding action. Thus at 19.00 on 14 September, barely one hour after leaving Malta for Algiers and home, the two battleships reversed course and returned to Malta. They left again, with the destroyer escort of *Jervis*, *Ilex*, *Pathfinder*, *Penn* and *Petard*, at 20.40, and sailed at top speed through the Straits of Messina for Salerno, arriving at their bombarding stations at 11.00 the next day. Inshore, destroyers and cruisers were already engaging the encroaching tanks and dug-in artillery at close range. After threading their way through the crowded shipping, the two battleships took up position further offshore. *Valiant* was further to the north, supporting the American sector, with *Warspite* taking up position opposite Sele Valley and opening up with her 15in and 6in guns at 17.00 hours. Both ships had sent observation officers ashore to establish communication links, spot the fall of shot, and adjust fire instructions to meet the needs of the troops ashore.

> *Warspite*'s forward observation officers quickly established communication with the battleship whose great bulk, a mere 2,000 yards out from the shore, loomed through breaks in the dense smokescreen laid by the destroyers to protect her from the enemy artillery.[2]

The combined firepower of the offshore warships broke up the German attempts to concentrate their armour, and gradually silenced their artillery positions so as to relieve the pressure on the bridgehead and allow the landings to progress. It was not accomplished without cost; there were heavy losses among the bombarding ships from the new German FX1400 radio-controlled bomb, and damage from so-called 'friendly fire'. The destroyers, closer inshore and under attack from German fighters and bombers, radio-controlled bombs and artillery fire, were particularly susceptible to being unintentionally hit on their blind side by gunfire from bombarding ships lying further out. HMS *Petard*, one of *Warspite*'s escorts, was so hit at Salerno by a 6in shell, incorrectly fused or faulty, from either *Warspite* or *Valiant*, which entered the port side of the seamen's upper forward messdeck where it exploded, killing two and wounding six men of an ammunition supply party.

At nightfall the two battleships retired out to sea, returning the next morning to resume their onslaught. The morning went well, but it was soon to be *Warspite*'s turn to be hit, devastatingly, by the new German bomb:

> Just after 1pm fire was opened on enemy traffic concentrations and ammunition dumps. ... It must have been heartening to the hard-pressed soldiers to see the great ships steaming up and down only half a mile offshore, their guns belching flame, to hear the 15-inch shells screaming overhead, and then see the heavy explosions in the enemy lines. ... .At 2.30pm only a few minutes after the fighter bombers had disappeared, the ship's lookouts sighted what were first thought to be three high level bombers at about 6000 feet. They were actually wireless controlled bombs, whose controlling aircraft was far away overhead at about 20,000 feet. The three bombs when directly overhead looked like three very white mushrooms as they turned vertically down and dived for the ship at great speed. From the time of sighting to the time of the bomb's arrival was only some seven to ten seconds...in the congested area avoiding action was not possible – and would in any case have been ineffective.(1)

One of the three 3000lb bombs, with their 600lb warheads, was a near miss amidships, abreast of the starboard bulge. The second was a near miss also, on the starboard side. The third one struck

Warspite astern of the hanger, penetrating through six decks to No. 4 boiler-room where it exploded. The boiler-room was completely destroyed, and four of the remaining five boiler-rooms were flooded. Nine men were killed and fourteen wounded. On the bridge, immediately after the explosion:

> I was not thrown off my feet but for a fraction of a second had a kind of black-out like when you take a hard toss at football or off a horse. But I could see and think perfectly clearly all the time. Black smoke and dirt from the funnel and a hell of a noise. Thought the whole mast was coming down as it rocked, bent and whipped. For a moment I thought we were probably sunk and was quite prepared for the ship to break in two. No-one lost their heads or shouted or anything on the bridge. They were all first class and the anti-aircraft guns which had opened fire kept firing. That was good.(1)

For those below deck the sudden impact of the bomb was an unnerving experience.

> It seemed as if an express train travelling at high speed had hit the ship; one tremendous explosion which seemed to jar every nerve in one's body. ... The ship seemed as if it had been picked up by some devilish hand then dropped. Dust was everywhere and most of the crew rushed to the upper deck. A second explosion occurred, followed by more intense shuddering, which must have been the bomb exploding in the region of the boiler rooms. Twelve members of the engine room and boiler room were killed and about thirty-forty people injured [*sic*]. The stoker's messdeck was cleared and turned into a temporary sick bay for the wounded. Most of the injuries were shrapnel wounds and very bad burns.(5)

Not all the burns were confined to the men in the boiler-rooms. C.P.O. Sewter reported that:

> When the bomb hit us at Salerno the lagging around the boilers came up the boiler room exhaust and covered the port 'pom-pom' gun's crew with red-hot asbestos like a heavy snow storm. I believe all members of the gun's crew died eventually within twelve hours except one who was correctly dressed in anti-flash gear who escaped injury. The pom-pom's crew were taken to the quarterdeck mess where one-by-one they succumbed to their very serious burns.(6)

For a short time after the bomb strike *Warspite* continued under power and control:

> I found the ship would steer, the engines were going ahead. A fire was reported in the hangar. 'Put it out' I said. Then to Guns 'If we can steam and shoot we'll carry out our final bombardment ...' I kept going at six knots. Then the ship would not steer. We were in the swept channel and we steered in a circle. I stopped engines. We were heading straight for the mines. A minesweeper sent us violent signals to get out of it. I couldn't for the helm was hard over, and finally the starboard engine room died out too. So there we were, once again, going round in circles with our way carrying us and quite helpless.(1)

With some 5000 tons of Mediterranean sea inside her increasing her draught by four feet, a list to starboard and no power, *Warspite* was helpless and effectively dead in the water. The American tugs *Hopi* and *Moreno* took her under tow by late afternoon; and, at a speed of 4 knots and with an escort of four destroyers, the 300-mile haul of *Warspite* through the Straits of Messina and back to Malta began.

By dawn on 17 September the situation had further deteriorated. *Warspite*'s draught and list had both increased, the flooding was getting worse and the men were exhausted. They had been working feverishly, without respite, to keep the ship afloat and get her home; shoring-up and pumping out, with 200 men at a time bailing out compartments with buckets, trying to keep the flooding under control. There was no fresh water, nothing to eat except hard tack biscuits and corned beef, and nothing to drink but a limited quantity of lemonade. There was only emergency stand-by lighting and no forced ventilation, so that conditions below decks in the late Mediterranean summer heat were appallingly hot and fetid:

> Fearful continuous heat and perspiration in action clothing. My legs rubbed raw with sweat. ...(4)

In mid-morning the British tugs *Nimble* and *Oriana* joined in the tow and speed was increased to 6 knots; and in the early evening the United States tug *Narragansett* and the British salvage ship *Salvella* also joined in, to help the Old Lady through the more turbulent waters of the Straits of Messina. British cruisers were also called to her aid, but the next few hours were to be a nightmare for the ship and her crew. At dawn on 18 September, Captain Packer reported that:

We had a hell of a night. ... When we struck the tide-rips and whirlpools the ship became unmanageable. From midnight until 5am we were completely out of control and going through the Straits broadside on with all tow parted except one. However just as the tide turned off Reggio to take us back up the straits again, I got a tug alongside each side aft and straitened her up sufficiently for the tugs forward to go ahead and get some way on the ship. Since getting through Messina all has gone well and now at 9pm we are off Cape Pasero and should reach Malta tomorrow morning. ... The sailors were splendid, as they always are when things go wrong. I see them naked on the deck washing each other from buckets of salt water dipped over the side.(1)

The next morning, on Sunday, *Warspite*'s tired sailors, at least all those who had reasonably clean clothing, were lined up on deck and, with her band playing*, and the sirens of other ships welcoming her, the Old Lady entered Grand Harbour, Malta:

Arrived safely in tow of our tugs at 09.00 and berthed in our old billet. In a few hours we are outwardly back to normal – you could search the ship decks for an hour without discerning the hole drilled through us from top to bottom which has flooded our boiler rooms and put us completely out of the war for six to nine months. All done in a split second.(4)

Any outward appearance of normality was deceptive; *Warspite* was now effectively non-operational, and, as such, needed to reduce her crew, albeit temporarily, to match her reduced circumstances. Accordingly a draft of 381 men left the ship on 26 September for duty on other ships, redeployment, or, for some of the longer serving, home leave. Captain Packer also left on 12 October, for a staff appointment on the C-in-C's headquarters staff in Algiers, and the ship's Executive Officer, Commander the Hon. D. Edwardes, assumed temporary command of *Warspite*. Paymaster Commander Duckworth's personal diary for 10 October probably accurately reflects the crew's feelings at this time:

Captain Packer is to leave the ship – new administrative job on C-in-C staff at Algiers. Very sorry Captain is going – had him just six months. I hate all this change and uncertainty.(4)

---

* The band played 'Little Old Lady', a popular, perky song of the time, as the ship sailed in.(7)

Patched up, *Warspite* left Malta for dry docking at Gibraltar at 07.00 on Monday 1 November 1943. She sailed using one shaft and boiler-room, and the assistance of three tugs, at a speed of six knots, for Gibraltar, over one thousand miles away. Accompanying her was a screen of four destroyers. The next day the patched-up boiler failed, and *Warspite* had to be towed the rest of the way by, initially, the four ocean-going tugs *Restive*, *Nimble*, *Oriana* and *Jaunty*. The dead-weight battleship, with water still inside her, was now approaching some 38,000 tons displacement and proved to be a hard pull. The *Oriana* broke down on 5 November and had to be relieved off Algiers by the *Zwartzee*.

Warspite arrived at Gibraltar at 08.00 on 8 November, and four days later entered dry dock. Pumping out of the flooded compartments began almost immediately; and revealed a grim reminder of Salerno: 'Two bodies were got out from the boiler room in the afternoon in a frightful state. ...'(4)

It was a necessary but heartbreaking task for the volunteer working party:

> When we entered Dry Dock at Gib. [*sic*] after being towed from Malta, Leading Stoker Smith and some mates volunteered to enter No. 4 Boiler Room which had received a direct hit at Salerno and recover the bodies of their messmates. They found very little of them due to the explosion of super heated steam. The remains were buried at Gibraltar Cemetery.(8)

The crew were not yet done with heartbreak:

> Soon after this our dog Pluto was run over and killed by a lorry in the Dockyard. Lofty, the Torpedoman who looked after him, was nearly beside himself with grief. He carried the body up the gangway and sat down outside the workshop in the Galley Flat with the tears streaming unashamedly down his face and cradled poor Pluto like a baby. Everybody on board was upset and our Captain [David Edwardes] ordered that Pluto be given a sea burial with naval honours. He also attended the ceremony.(8)

When the flooded compartments were finally drained it was found that *Warspite*'s hull had been more severely damaged than first thought:

> Damage [is] a huge hole about twenty feet all round and jagged. Hole on starboard side amidships about thirty feet long – like a

crumpled ping-pong ball on bottom plating. This was from the near miss. I have never seen such a sight.[4]

Admiral Cunningham, on his way back to the United Kingdom, broke his journey at Gibraltar and visited the ship to see the damage for himself. Quite obviously *Warspite* would again be out of commission for some time and, with the Navy now severely short of experienced manpower in the build-up for the planned invasion of mainland Europe, now only some six months away, *Warspite*'s complement was again reduced in number. A draft of a further 206 men was posted away from the ship at Gibraltar, leaving her, by wartime complement standards, with effectively a care-and-maintenance crew of some 780 men.

Warspite was to remain in Gibraltar dockyard for the rest of 1943 while the worst of the damage was hurriedly repaired. Only two of her 15in turrets could be made operational, and a huge concrete caisson, or patch, was put over the hole in her bottom. No. 4 boiler-room could not be repaired with the facilities and resources available at Gibraltar. On 10 January 1944 *Warspite* was back at sea for trials, managing 15 knots, and hopes were high for an early return to the United Kingdom for further repairs and, perhaps, some home leave for her by now thoroughly bored crew. One week later she embarked a mixed cargo of 56 cases of Swiss lenses and instruments, 62 boxes of West African gold bullion and some 280 naval and military personnel, for the journey back to the United Kingdom. Three days later her sailing was cancelled and the mixed cargo disembarked. It was not until 9 March, after four months at Gibraltar, that *Warspite* finally left the Mediterranean, scene of many of her triumphs and disasters, for the last time.

Warspite took with her some 350 soldiers including the Royal Artillery band, and sailed with a fast convoy of twenty-four ships bringing some 67,000 military personnel back to Britain. It was an uneventful passage, and *Warspite* parted company with the convoy off Northern Ireland at 09.00 on 15 March. From there she sailed round the top of Scotland, passing Pentland Firth, and then Scapa Flow at 09.00 on 16 March, anchoring at 23.30 below the bridge of the Firth of Forth. The next day her military passengers were disembarked to Leith, and *Warspite* entered Rosyth dockyard on 18

March. Each watch, in turn, was sent on seventeen days' leave. It was a time of further change; the appointment of a new Captain, the influx of a new crew and a new role for the *Warspite*.

On 19 March Captain M.H.A. Kelsey* took up appointment as the new Captain of *Warspite*, and on 22 March a draft of 450 men joined the ship to bring her complement back up to operational strength. On the *Warspite*, further repairs and modifications were taking place to her boiler-rooms and armament. Her boiler-rooms were further patched-up, although boiler-room No. 4 remained unserviceable, and her 6in guns were removed and the casemates plated over. One of her two unserviceable 15in gun turrets was made good, but 'X' turret was beyond repair in the time available before the planned invasion of the European mainland. *Warspite* was now, to all intents and purposes, a six 15in gun shore-bombardment ship and that was to be her role for the remainder of her days.

The month of mid-April to mid-May was spent exercising and carrying out trials and practice firings off the Firth of Forth in an attempt to get the patched-up ship, and her much-changed and largely inexperienced ship's company, worked up to the *Warspite* standard of old. Battered as she now was, and despite her reduced boiler-room capability and patched bottom, the Old Lady still managed 21 knots during her speed trials. The ship and crew were driven hard in preparation for one last fling in the forthcoming invasion of Europe.

British planners had first begun to think about a return to the Continent towards the end of 1941, only eighteen months after Dunkirk, when the country was standing alone. The envisaged earliest date had been the summer of 1943. The entry of Japan and America into the war, the German invasion of Russia and her successes there and in the Middle East, together with Japanese successes in the Far East, had moved the target date to and fro as the war progressed and priorities changed. Eventually, the invasion plans were finalised and approved by the American and British war leaders at the Quebec Conference in August 1943. The date was set for the summer of the following year. The plan, designated 'Overlord', was put under the overall command of General Eisenhower, later destined to become President of the United

* Later Vice-Admiral M.H.A. Kelsey, C.B., D.S.C.

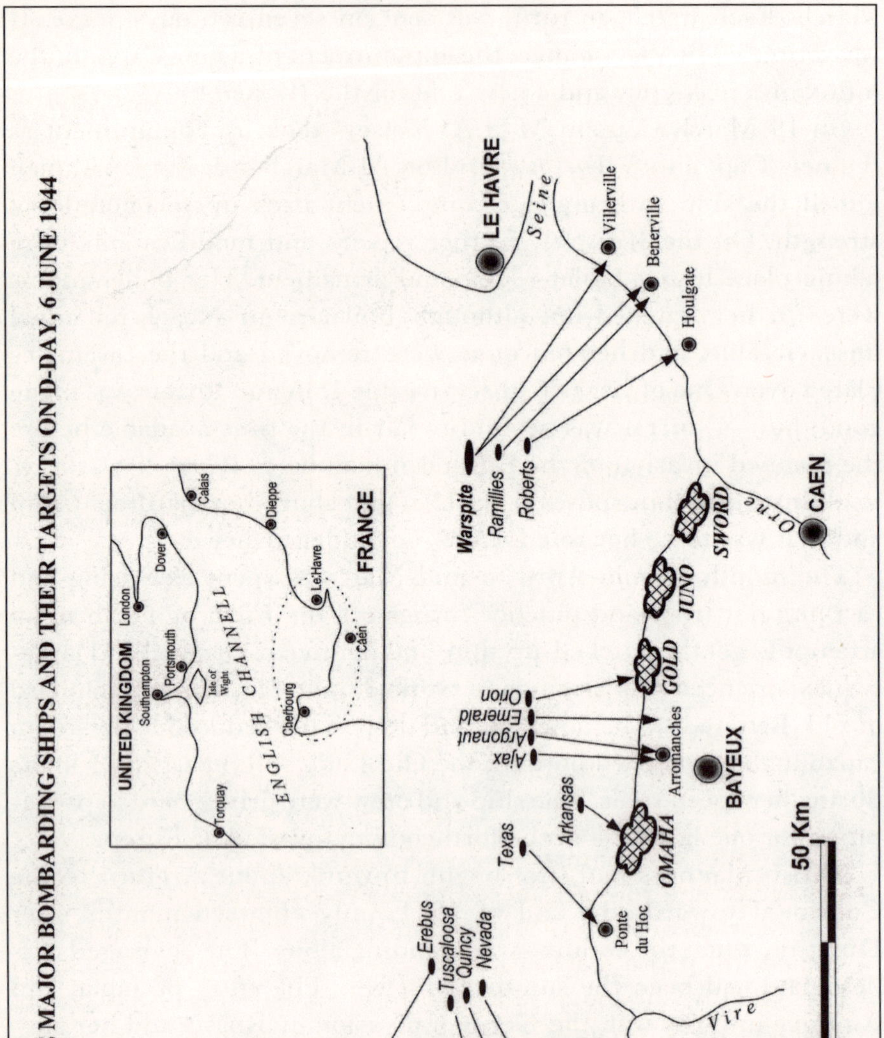
SOME OF THE MAJOR BOMBARDING SHIPS AND THEIR TARGETS ON D-DAY, 6 JUNE 1944
UNITED KINGDOM
London
Dover
Calais
Southampton
Portsmouth
Isle of Wight
Torquay
ENGLISH CHANNELL
Cherbourg
Caen
Le Havre
Dieppe
FRANCE
CHERBOURG
Bayfleur
Ozville
Fontenay
Azville
UTAH
Erebus
Tuscaloosa
Quincy
Nevada
Vire
Ponte du Hoc
Texas
Arkansas
OMAHA
Arromanches
BAYEUX
Ajax
Argonaut
Emerald
Orion
GOLD
JUNO
SWORD
Orne
CAEN
Warspite
Ramillies
Roberts
Houlgate
Beneville
Villerville
Seine
LE HAVRE
N
E
S
W
0
50 Km

States. It called for landings on a fifty-mile stretch of the Normandy coast extending east and west of the Orne and Vile rivers. The vitally important seaborne part of the operation – codenamed 'Neptune' – was put under the command of Vice-Admiral Sir Bertram Ramsey, who had masterminded the withdrawal of the British Expeditionary Force from Dunkirk in the summer of 1940.

Operation 'Neptune', involving the synchronised movement of 4126 ships engaged in landing and supplying two armies, one American, the other British, on a defended enemy coast, was a colossal undertaking. Included in the 'Neptune' force were 1213 warships, ranging from battleships to midget submarines, with 107 heavy units designated as bombarding ships. Among these were some illustrious names: the British Navy supplied the battleships *Nelson*, *Warspite* and *Ramillies*, with *Rodney* in reserve, the US Navy supplied the *Texas*, *Nevada* and *Arkansas*.

The bombarding ships, with designated targets in their sealed orders, assembled in the Clyde and off Belfast in preparation for taking their places in the greatest assembly of ships ever seen. *Warspite* joined them during the evening of 12 May, and sailed from Greenock on the evening of 3 June to her start position in the English Channel:

> ... we sailed in company with *Ramillies* and *Roberts** down the west coast and round Land's End ready for invasion on June 5th. Bad weather delayed the operation for twenty four hours and we turned to steam back towards Plymouth and then back off Portsmouth, at about midnight, for transit down the Solent Channel to Normandy. I remember countless major and minor warships being sighted at last light together, with hundreds of small landing craft pitching in what were very rough seas. I felt very sorry for soldiers having to go through that with their landings yet to come. As we turned south and passed the Nab Tower a dimly lit blue V for Victory sign showed ashore. Soon after that we went to action stations and remained at our stations for many hours in what was a bitterly cold night.(9)

* The British monitors *Roberts* and *Erebus*, bombardment ships each armed with two 15in guns, added further punch to the heavy units of the bombarding force, which was also supplemented by twenty-three 8in and 6in cruisers.

After turning for France, *Warspite* reached her bombarding position at 05.25 on D-Day, 6 June 1944. Selected extracts from her log show her contribution throughout that momentous day in the history of the twentieth century. Her principal designated targets were the German coastal batteries at Benerville and Villerville, and she pounded these throughout the day. Her first onslaught commenced at 05.30, barely five minutes after reaching her position, when, with no spotting aircraft to report on the fall of her shells, she fired three 'blind' salvoes at the Benerville battery.

With the arrival of spotter plane assistance, *Warspite* gave the battery further doses of 15in shells between 05.45 and 05.58. L.C. Glover, flying as a reconnaissance pilot directing the ship's gunfire, recalls that:

> I arrived over the beachhead . . . for the first of five sorties on D-Day. We were flying Spitfire Mk 5 in pairs and speaking by R.T. directly to the gunnery officers aboard the ships. The fireworks display which ensued as every craft opened up, viewed from 10,000 feet in the dawn light, is something I shall never forget. The battleships, ... were lying about twenty miles offshore so the shells had quite a high trajectory and a 15 to 20 second time of flight. On one occasion when firing with HMS *Warspite* ... and flying midway between the ship and the beachhead at between 9,000 and 10,000 feet, I gave the order 'fire' and turned slowly broadside on to the shore to wait for the fall of shot. Suddenly, in the clear blue sky my aircraft experienced a most violent bump which practically shook me out of my wits. At the same moment, I saw two enormous objects moving rapidly away from me towards the shore and immediately realised that I had flown at right angles through the slipstream of *Warspite*'s two ranging 15-inch 'bricks'. Awe-struck, I followed the shells down quite easily with my eyes during the rest of their curved flight and saw one of them actually hit the gun emplacement we were engaging! Not only that, the German gun was blasted out of the rear of the emplacement.
>
> I think my report of the fall of shot to *Warspite* was a little incoherent, but I did manage to assure them that no further 'fire for effect' was needed and after congratulations all round, we switched to another target ... we had one or two inexplicable losses during those weeks which we finally had to attribute to pilots being hit by their 'own' shells.(10)

Sadly this assumption proved to be only too true, as confirmed by another pilot flying later over the invasion beaches:

> Off the Normandy coast, where our troops and the Americans were forcing their way ashore, lay a semi-circle of grey battleships. Some like ... the *Warspite*, were immediately recognisable, and as we flew over them at some 2,000 feet (for it was no longer necessary to skim the waves to outwit enemy radar) we could see their huge guns belching flame and smoke as they fired at targets inland. On a return flight that morning one popular member of our squadron, Flying Officer Barnard, was, by a million to one chance, struck by a 15-inch shell from *Warspite*. He and his Mustang disintegrated.(11)

Shortly after 06.00 *Warspite* was engaged by a small force of German torpedo boats, or possibly destroyers, and narrowly missed being torpedoed. They were driven off and reliable crew lookouts confidently claimed that one of them was sunk. Although *Warspite* was not officially credited with the sinking, it was later confirmed that a German patrol vessel was sunk in the vicinity at that time.

As soon as the torpedo attack had been repulsed, *Warspite* switched target to the Villerville coastal battery, claiming three hits. The bombardments continued throughout the day, alternating between Benerville and Villerville targets, with an interlude in the early afternoon period when concentrations of enemy vehicles and a command headquarters were shelled. Between firings the *Warspite* gunners came out of their turrets for a breather, as noted by John Godwin, then a Lieutenant R.M. in passage to the beachhead:

> ... further out we saw destroyers, battleships and cruisers firing their large guns. We could see the gun crews of the battleship *Warspite* wearing anti-flash gear standing on the turrets to watch the landings and the bombardment.(12)

With darkness and the end of a very long day, *Warspite* finished her bombardment, finally dropping her starboard anchor about four miles offshore at 23.05, ready to resume her firing, as required, the next day. Although her two main targets had been effectively silenced by mid-morning on D-Day, it had been necessary to periodically 'revisit' the two coastal battery installations throughout the day to deter any attempt at repair or replacement. Mobile guns brought to the emplacements to replace the knocked-out guns had been destroyed before they could interfere with the build-up of the landings on the beaches below them. *Warspite* had fired seventy-three 15in rounds at the Villerville battery obtaining nine direct hits.

The next day, 7 June, *Warspite*'s bombardment routine was repeated, except that, having effectively dealt with her designated targets of the previous day, she was now offered a variety of targets as need arose or opportunity presented itself. In the morning these included gun emplacements and batteries further inland, strategic crossroads, and concentrations or build-ups of enemy transport and guns. In the afternoon *Warspite* fired a further eight salvoes into the Benerville position in order to keep that battery out of commission. *Warspite* then returned to Portsmouth to re-ammunition. She had fired over three hundred rounds of 15in shells in two days, one hundred and eighty-one rounds of high explosive and one hundred and thirty-three of armour piercing shells.

Warspite returned to the beachhead on 9 June, this time to the western sector where the American bombarding ships, heavily engaged, were running out of ammunition. Here she fired ninety-six rounds of 15in shell in support of American units fighting their way inland. Two days later she was ordered to take up a bombarding position off Gold Beach to fire on German troops and tanks concentrating in a wood in preparation for an attack on the British positions. Having found the range, Captain Kelsey gave the order, probably unique in battleship gunnery, of: 'Fifty rounds, 15-inch, rapid fire.'(13)

It was devastatingly effective naval gunfire which pleased the troops:

> The accuracy of naval gunfire encouraged the Army to call for its support again and again, and this became more effective when forward observation posts were established ashore. The 15-inch guns of the battleships were particularly popular, and the Army had to be warned that the guns of the *Warspite* and *Ramillies* were wearing out.(14)

The firing also impressed a sailor who had sailed with her in earlier times:

> I saw her again briefly in 1944 when I was in Combined Operations Beach Signals on Gold Beach. ... Saw many results of her 15-inch

> shells as we passed the craters ashore following up the Army ... makes a tidy hole wherever it lands does a 15-inch brick![15]

Warspite's 15in guns were indeed now nearly worn out, and on 12 June she was ordered to Rosyth to have new ones fitted. So great was the need for her gunfire off the Normandy beachhead that *Warspite* was ordered to take the quicker, but infinitely riskier, route through the Straits of Dover and up the east coast of England. Going through the Straits she attracted fire, fortunately ineffective, from the German heavy guns opposite Dover. However, having successfully evaded this danger, *Warspite* succumbed to another early on 13 June when she set off a German mine, in an area thought to have been cleared, some thirty miles off Harwich.

The mine, acoustic or pressure-operated, exploded only a few feet off the port side abreast of 'Y' turret. The explosion caused the steering to jam and *Warspite* to go on another of her gyrations to starboard. When stopped, she quickly took on a 4-degree list to port, having shipped some 700 tons of water. However, the main damage was not to her hull but to her power transmission machinery. She was able to proceed at 7 to 10 knots, arriving at Rosyth late in the evening of 14 June to sympathetic cheers from the lined-up crews of other warships.

Although no-one was killed by the mine, there were some injuries among the crew and one Royal Marine had his pride hurt:

> The whip forward took the armour plated door off its hinges. Our Chief Shipwright saw a Royal Marine who had just left the heads* and was jumping along with his trousers down. 'Chippy' said 'Royal, you will go faster if you pull your trousers up'.[16]

Dockyard examination showed that *Warspite*'s driving shafts were badly distorted and out of line. The normal peacetime procedure for such damage would have been to withdraw the long shafts from the bowels of the ship for rectification ashore in the dockyard machine shops, but the battle for Normandy could not wait for peacetime procedures. Instead wartime 'make-do-and-mend' was employed and the shafts were roughly straitened *in situ*, using blowtorches and hydraulic jacks. *Warspite* was left, in the words of

* Lavatories.

her Captain, with: '... one good shaft, one fairly good one, one very wobbly shaft. The fourth one remained jammed solid.'(13) While these repairs to her shafts were taking place *Warspite* had her six usable 15in guns replaced and left Rosyth on 11 August for sea trials. Although the days of the Old Lady lifting her skirts and running had now passed, she could still manage 15.5 knots, and limped off for practice with her new guns off the west coast of Scotland.

Warspite reported for further bombardment duty off Brest on 25 August, this time in support of the American Army, trying to capture the major port of Brest. She poured two hundred and thirteen rounds of armour-piercing and high explosive shells into a German heavy gun position, and received some accurate return fire from the enemy 11in guns. Fortunately she only received relatively slight splinter damage. During the hectic exchange a Halifax bomber, 'T for Tommy', inadvertently flew over the *Warspite*, and received a very curt flashed 'clear off' from the warship.

Early in September, with the British fighting their way up the Normandy coast still meeting stiff opposition, a German gun battery at Le Havre was proving very troublesome. It was so positioned that it could fire directly onto Sword Beach, still being used to land and supply British troops and equipment. Smoke screens helped to hinder the ranging of the enemy guns, but it was felt that heavy naval gunfire was needed to harass and destroy the threatening battery. Thus on 10 September *Warspite* was off Le Havre bombarding the position at extreme range. It took her some time, with aircraft spotter assistance and the expenditure of over three hundred 15in shells, to silence the enemy guns, but her determined efforts impressed one British Medical Officer. Dr Peter Johnson was operating a Field Dressing Station near Asnelles in the Le Havre area:

> *Warspite* and, I believe, *Rodney* came and anchored ten miles out and took the slates off my house in handfuls as they fired salvo after salvo continuously day and night for four or five days at a time, then a pause, and begin again.(12)

By late summer the Allied landings had fanned out and were freeing occupied Europe. Paris was liberated by American and Free French troops on 25 August, and Brussels fell to British troops on 3 September. As the drive through France and the Low Countries towards Germany met increasingly stiff resistance, so the Allies felt an increasingly urgent need to have at their disposal the facilities of a large port, near to their advancing front, in order to shorten their lines of supply. Such a port was Antwerp, which fell to the Allies in early September. However access to Antwerp was via the Scheldt estuary and river, and the Germans were doggedly hanging on to their fortified positions on islands, especially Walcheren, at the mouth of the estuary. Their strong defensive position was further improved by extensive flooding of the surrounding area, from breaches in the dykes caused by allied bombing of the positions. The defenders had at their disposal four 8.75in and a number of 6in guns, plus some one hundred and fifty lesser-calibre guns including 88mm and four high-velocity 3.7in anti-aircraft guns, deployed for low-angle fire, that had been captured from the British at Dunkirk in 1940.

On 1 November 1944 an attack was launched on Walcheren. The plan called for a bombarding force of some twenty-eight vessels, including *Warspite* and the two monitors *Erebus* and *Roberts*, to bombard the defences, while Marine commandos tried to land and attack via the dykes, and Canadian troops attacked from the landward side. *Warspite* and her two monitors left Portsmouth on 30 October to carry out their mission. They opened fire at 08.20 on 1 November while still some twelve miles out from their target, and continued firing at the batteries throughout the day. It was not a significantly successful shoot. One of the monitors had a turret failure which lasted for ninety minutes at the start of the bombardment, and *Warspite* had trouble with her after 'Y' turret. Bad weather prevented the use of Spitfire spotter aircraft, and rendered the observation and adjustment of the fall of shot very difficult and the results mixed. Nevertheless the batteries were silenced, and the islands taken within a few days, although it took a month for minesweepers to clear a safe passage to Antwerp through the waters of the Scheldt estuary.

Warspite fired three hundred and fifty-three 15in shells on that day, before ceasing fire at 17.23. It was to be her last action, and the last time her great guns would fire, nearly thirty years after they had first fired in anger at Jutland, not so many miles away across the North Sea, in 1916.

CHAPTER 8

Final Days and Home to the West Country

The Admiralty had decided that *Warspite*'s days were done even before her bombardments at Le Havre and Walcheren. It had become obvious that her grievous wounds, culminating in the mining off Harwich, had rendered her unable to take her place in the forefront of any future battles. She was simply worn out. Since D-Day she had fired over fifteen hundred 15in shells; she had had a concrete patch put over the hole in her bottom, and had a badly battered hull; one gun turret, one boiler room and one propeller shaft were either wrecked or unserviceable; and she was nearly thirty years old.

Moreover, the need for and continuing use of battleships was being increasingly challenged in political and naval circles. The war in Europe was obviously drawing to a close; the threat from German heavy surface units had all but evaporated, and with the land action moving into the heart of the Continent there was no foreseeable need for many more naval bombardments. In the longer term, *Warspite* could not be repaired in time to join the new, fast *King George V* class of battleships and the American fleets, now dominated by aircraft carriers, continuing the war against Japan in the Pacific. In any case, experience with *Warspite*'s generation of battleships in the Eastern Fleet two years earlier had confirmed their unsuitability for long-distance, high-speed cruising in tropical waters. Looking even further ahead, technological developments in air and underwater weaponry, not to mention the advent of the atomic bomb, were to throw into doubt the whole future of large capital ships.

Thus on 9 August 1944 the Admiralty decreed that, upon completion of her present bombarding duties, HMS *Warspite* should be transferred to Category C Reserve. This was the lowest category of preparedness; in effect she was to be all but written off. After her last bombardment at Walcheren she moved back to Portsmouth and there, on 1 February 1945, HMS *Warspite* was paid off into Reserve. With a care and maintenance skeleton crew, she moored with other veterans at the Reserve Fleet position off Mother Bank, Spithead, Portsmouth. There she lay throughout the final months of the war and the early months of peace until 31 July 1946, thirty-one years after first entering service with the Royal Navy, when HMS *Warspite* was 'approved to scrap'. She lay at her mooring while being stripped of any reusable items, in preparation for the breaker's yard. *Warspite* was almost forgotten in the new excitement of peace, but not by her old Admiral. Admiral of the Fleet Viscount Cunningham of Stanhope had retired from his last posting as First Sea Lord on 6 June 1946, to his home at Bishop's Waltham, Hampshire. There:

> He had *Warspite*'s bell hanging outside his front door. Nona [his wife] struck it to summon him from the other end of the garden to answer the telephone. One day he stopped on Portsdown Hill to look through binoculars at the ship herself, moored out in the harbour. Still awaiting removal to the shipbreaker's yard, she was stripped of her armament and seemed to ABC to be looking depressingly rusty, and down at heel.(1)

Eventually, on 19 April 1947, *Warspite* left Portsmouth for the last time, under tow on her final journey. Not this time to the beachhead at Normandy but to the breaker's yard at Faslane on the Clyde. She was under the charge of a civilian captain, A.A. Baxter, and had a further seven-man crew of merchant seamen, mainly from the London and Portsmouth areas. Their job was to maintain a round-the-clock watch on the tow hawser attachments and to monitor the general progress of the tow. The veteran ship was to be towed westwards along the south coast, 'round the corner' of Lands End and up the Irish Sea to the Clyde, by the two tugs *Bustler* and *Metinda III*.

The tow started well enough, but late on 21 April a strong south-westerly gale blew up and the two tugs struggled to hold her. Then, shortly before midnight, *Bustler*'s towing hawser parted off the Wolf Rock Light, some nineteen miles south west of the Lizard. At that time the towing party had plenty of sea room and there appeared to be no imminent danger, but nevertheless the duty officer at Portsmouth requested the Lizard and Penlee lifeboats to stand by. By the next morning the gale had abated somewhat and the two lifeboats were stood down. For the remainder of the day, and throughout the following night, the two tugs and their charge rode out the storm. *Metinda III* fought hard to hold the battleship's head into the wind in the heavy seas, but at 12.30 on 23 April the tug was forced to slip her hawser after towing *Warspite* into the shelter of Mount's Bay. One of *Warspite*'s civilian crew, Mr Davies of Portsmouth, related how:

> We then had orders from the tug *Bustler* to let go the ship's anchor, but after a while we found that we were dragging towards the coast at a fair speed. The vessel then grounded after on either a very high bank or a reef.(2)

Warspite had grounded, appropriately for so English a ship on St. George's Day, on Mountamopus Ledge, a reef a mile or so to the south-west of Cudden Point. The Penlee lifeboat was again called out, but the skeleton crew of the *Warspite* declined to abandon their charge and the lifeboat, the *W & S*, withdrew to Newlyn, since the seas were too rough for her to return to her slipway in Mousehole harbour. The hope was that, since it was low water, the coming flood tide might lift the 30,000-ton battleship off the reef and onto the shore. With the flood tide *Warspite* did indeed lift off Mountamopus Ledge but only to embed herself more firmly on the rocks of Prussia Cove. A clifftop onlooker, Mr R. Whitford related what he saw:

> On Wednesday afternoon, it was between 4.30 and 4.45, when she was still stuck on the Mopus rocks where she had been since the early afternoon. As I watched from Cudden Point, the gigantic battleship suddenly heeled over, until she was almost touching the water with the top of her mast. Up she came again and sped, yawing all over the place, towards Prussia Cove at a great pace.(2)

Warspite seemed determined that she was not going willingly to the breaker's yard. She was going home to the rocks of Cornwall, home to the West Country whence she had first sailed over thirty years before.

Warspite was now wedged with her bows to the storm, her forecastle awash and the seas breaking around the 'B' turret position. The Penlee lifeboat had little room to manoeuvre or seek shelter as her crew tried to effect a rescue of the eight men on the ship. The seas around *Warspite* were rising and falling some twenty to thirty feet as great waves broke over her. 'The lifeboat looked just like a cork beside the great grey bulk of the stricken battleship.'(2)

A narrow channel, about forty yards wide, between the *Warspite* and the shore offered the only sheltered access to the battleship; and Coxswain Edwin Madron, on his first rescue mission as the newly-appointed skipper of the lifeboat, managed to bring the *W & S* close under the *Warspite*'s stern before choosing a rescue point at the far end of her quarterdeck. In a moment of slack water, two lines were got aboard the *Warspite* and secured:

> Then began the perilous task of holding the lifeboat close enough for the men to jump into her. The rise and fall of the seas was so great that sometimes the lifeboat's crew were looking down on the battleship's deck and the next moment the boat was in grave danger of being smashed against the bulge near the battleship's waterline. Watching each sea, the coxswain went full speed ahead to meet it, as it broke around 'B' turret, and then, as it passed him, went full speed astern again. For thirty five minutes he was manoeuvring in this way, and as the life-boat swung close enough to the battleship, he would call on the men one by one to jump. Seven of them jumped as soon as they were called, but the eighth took a long time before he could dare it. Through those thirty-five dangerous minutes the two motor mechanics were kneeling perilously under the canopy in front of their controls. They could see nothing, and one error on their part in carrying out the coxswain's stream of orders would have meant disaster for the lifeboat.
>
> In this way all eight men were rescued and the lifeboat brought them into Newlyn Harbour at a quarter to eight that evening.
>
> It had been a difficult and dangerous service, and the coxswain had shown not only great courage in deciding to take the life-boat by that narrow channel, but, once in it, great skill in handling her.(3)

The rescued men were put up overnight in Warren's Restaurant in Greenmarket, Penzance. They were tired but safe, and, as seamen, fully appreciative of the courage and seamanship of their rescuers. As one survivor put it:

> The men of the Penlee lifeboat certainly did a good job of rescue work. They can certainly handle their boat.(2)

The Royal National Lifeboat Institution marked the occasion, and their appreciation, by making awards to all members of the volunteer rescue team:

> To Coxswain Edwin F. Madron*, the silver medal for gallantry, with a copy of the vote inscribed on vellum. To John B. Drew, the motor mechanic, the bronze medal for gallantry, with a copy of the vote inscribed on vellum. To each other member of the crew, Joseph J. Madron, second coxswain, John T. Worth, bowman, J.C. Wallis, assistant motor mechanic, and A. Madron, B. Jeffery and C. Williams, lifeboatmen, the thanks of the Institution inscribed on vellum.
>
> To the Coxswain and each member of the crew a reward of £4 in addition to the ordinary scale rewards for the assembly and two launches of £2 8s.(3)

The wreck of the *Warspite* in Prussia Cove made national news and electrified the local inhabitants, particularly those who remembered her glorious former days. One of these was Nigel Tangye, who had known her in earlier times:

> I was having a bite of lunch at Glendorgal when the telephone rang. 'Have you heard?' a voice said 'The old girl's won the last trick. She broke the tow and drifted ashore. *Warspite* is on the rocks near Prussia Cove!'... I had to go and see. At this time I had a faithful AJS motorcycle, and I jumped on this and sped across the county to see *Warspite* and pay her homage. ... Close to Prussia Cove there was a group of cars at the roadside before a gate that led to a field. ... Across the grass field pilgrims that had preceded me had already worked a path towards the goal of the pilgrimage. ... The field ended abruptly with a hedge a few yards back from the cliff edge. ... I sought a protruding tongue of the cliff at which there were no other people before I walked forward to the edge to see the wreck of this battle-scarred warship.
>
> I had last seen her actually in action from my Spitfire when flying at 40,000 feet. And now, I was but 150 feet above her, an inert mass of metal, but displaying the dignity of the dying who have

* Three members of the Madron family took part in the rescue; tragically, the grandson of Coxswain Edwin Madron, Stephen Madron, was one of eight crew members who died when the Penlee lifeboat *Solomon Browne* was lost on 19 December 1981.

> saved their country. What matter that the spotless paintwork I used to know was now more rust than paint? That her great guns ... had been taken out leaving her like an old lady without her teeth? Nevertheless, it saddened me, and I drove home at a more gentlemanly speed than when I came.(4)

Warspite was now firmly lodged on the rocks and, in the immediate aftermath of the disaster, general opinion was that she was a total wreck. Coxswain Edwin Madron was of the opinion that she would never be moved off the rocks of Prussia Cove. Captain Baxter, skipper on her last fateful voyage, agreed: 'I very much doubt whether they will be able to salvage her.'(2)

Nevertheless, and slowly at first, attempts at salvage were started. The Wolverhampton Metal Company had bought the wreck, largely for the thousand or so tons of non-ferrous metal in her engine and boiler rooms, and set about trying to remove as much of the valuable metal as possible from where she lay. A massive wooden post, some eight feet high and one foot square, was erected on the cliff top opposite where she lay, and from the top of this 'Blondin Post'* was attached a cable for winching men, tools and materials, to and from her deck far below. On calmer days, lighters and small boats removed the cut-up metal sections of her superstructure and innards, and she was gradually lightened.

The salvage was not accomplished without trouble and tragedy. On the afternoon of Wednesday 15 March 1950 eight men, working below sea level in the bows of the ship, were overcome by exhaust fumes from a petrol-driven air compressor. They were gallantly rescued from the bowels of the ship by their workmates, some of whom were among those overcome by the fumes, and winched ashore via the aerial cableway to the cliff top and the waiting ambulances. Sadly one of the men died in the accident. Salvage work continued and eventually, in the early 1950s, with some compartments of her hull made watertight and filled with compressed air, the remains of the lightened *Warspite* were dragged off the rocks and beached in the sheltered shallow waters of Mounts' Bay, Marazion, between the shore and St. Michael's Mount. It was to be her final resting

* The post is still in place on Prussia Cove headland, with the slot in its top which held the pulley wheel in line with where the *Warspite* lay. Behind the post are the rusting links of the anchoring chains still firmly embedded in the cliff top.

place. In her lifetime she had sailed hundreds of thousands of miles, but now she lay only sixty-one miles from Devonport Dockyard, where she had been built over thirty five years before. Here she was to be finally and completely dismantled.

Bits of the Old Lady stayed in Cornwall. On the ramparts of St. Michael's Mount, and in Morrab Gardens, Penzance, are benches made from the teak of her deck. Her nameplate, *WARSPITE*, holds pride of place over the fireplace of the Lamorna Wink public house in Lamorna Cove, and wood panels from her wardroom fit out the bar of the Cutty Sark public house in Marazion. Parts of the ship continued to serve: one of the cranes from her deck was used for a good many years in the stockyards of the Wolverhampton Metal Company. Further afield, her ensign is preserved in the drawer of a sideboard in a side-chancel of St Giles Cathedral, Edinburgh. It was lodged there for safe keeping by her old Admiral, Viscount Cunningham of Hyndhope, on the occasion of his investiture there as a Knight of the Order of the Thistle by King George VI on 27 September 1945.

The wreck of the *Warspite* was to be the focus of attention for some years and attracted many sightseers. One, paying a return visit, was Nigel Tangye. One day he hired a dinghy and rowed out to the wreck. Climbing aboard, he remembered a night of long ago:

> I was on the Quarterdeck of the Flagship! And I saw it as it was one June night in Valetta harbour when the officers were giving a ball to which I had been asked from *Valiant*. ... On that night, that Mediterranean night in June twenty years earlier, wives, sisters and girlfriends were ferried on board to be greeted by their officers looking smooth and clean in white mess kit. They came to dance beneath the awning stretched over the deck, taut as a drumskin so that it shielded the deck from the dew. ... Under two shining 15-inch guns, that were so huge in looks and effect, the Royal Marine Band played 'Moonlight and Roses'. ... The deck, always immaculate, had on this occasion been powdered and polished with French chalk for dancing feet to slide the easier. Shaded lights and flowers were there on the flat mushroom tops of the ventilators and on the sturdy barred mahogany skylight of the Admiral's quarters I remember the sweet sadness of it. ... Goodnight. ... Farewell.(4)

It took until 1956 to finally dismantle the stubborn Old Lady. Sightseers came and went, a few of them paying their special final respects. Commander N.S. Griffiths, who had served on *Warspite* as a Midshipman in the gunhouse of 'A' turret at Jutland, should perhaps have the final words. His thoughts, written at the age of eighty-four, were that:

> *Warspite*, at the end of her famous career, was dispatched to the Knacker's Yard, but many of us thought she committed suicide by breaking the tow and running ashore on the Cornish rocks.(5)

Appendix: List of the Captains of HMS Warspite, *1915 to 1945**

Captain	Assumed Command	Relinquished Command
E.M. Philpotts	08.03.15	18.12.16
C.M. de Bartolemé	18.12.16	03.06.18
H. Lynes, C.B., C.M.G.	03.06.18	17.01.19
E.K. Loring	17.01.19	05.05.20
F. Clifton-Brown, C.B., C.M.G.	05.05.20	04.05.22
R.N. Bax, C.B., A.D.C.	04.05.22	04.04.23
R.M. Burmester, C.B., C.M.G.	04.04.23	02.09.24
(Paid off for refit)		
G.K. Chetwode, C.B., C.B.E.	06.04.26	04.08.27
T.N. James, M.V.O.	04.08.27	07.11.27
H.S. Munroe, D.S.O.	07.11.27	01.12.27
J.F. Somerville, D.S.O.	01.12.27	01.09.28
J.W. Carrington, D.S.O.	01.09.28	09.01.29
A.H. Walker, O.B.E.	09.01.29	08.07.30
C.A. Scott	08.07.30	06.09.30
O.H. Dawson	06.09.30	25.04.31
St. A.B. Wake	25.04.31	27.08.32
L.D.I. MacKinnon	27.08.32	15.12.33
(Paid off for refit)		
F.H.W. Goolden	24.02.37	01.05.37
V.A.C. Crutchley, V.C., D.S.C.	01.05.37	27.04.40
D.B. Fisher, C.B.E.	27.04.40	22.03.42
F.E.P. Hutton	22.03.42	01.03.43

* Ref: Roskill, Captain S.W., *H.M.S. Warspite* (London, 1957).

H.A. Packer	31.03.43	12.10.43
Hon. D. Edwardes (acting Capt.)	12.10.43	18.03.44
M.H.A. Kelsey	18.03.44	29.08.44
C.P. Frend	29.08.44	11.09.44
M.H.A. Kelsey	11.09.44	30.12.44
M.H. Evelegh	30.12.44	09.02.45
G.F. Blaxland	09.02.45	15.03.45
P.H. Calderton	15.03.45	26.07.45

(Paid off into Reserve)

References

Chapter 1

1. Edwards, E., *The Life of Sir Walter Raleigh* Vol II: Letters (London, 1868).
2. Williams, N.L., *Sir Walter Raleigh* (London, 1962).
3. Churchill, W.S., *The World Crisis, 1911-1918* (New York, 1923-9).
4. Chatfield, Admiral of the Fleet A.E.M., *It Might Happen Again* (London, 1947).

Chapter 2

1. Austen Chamberlain Papers. Ref No. 4/3/1771 The University of Birmingham.
2. Chessman, Seaman J., Account, Imperial War Museum.
3. Ashworth, Commander A.H., Private diary, Imperial War Museum.
4. Packer, J., *Deep as the Sea* (London, 1975).
5. Gardner, Commander L., Diary and letters, Imperial War Museum.
6. Roskill, Captain, S.W., *HMS Warspite* (London, 1957).
7. Ellis, Surgeon-Captain G.E.D., Diary; Book II (*Warspite*), Imperial War Museum.
8. Walwyn, Commander H.T., Account, Imperial War Museum.
9. Chatfield, Admiral of the Fleet E., *It Might Happen Again: Autobiography of Admiral of the Fleet Lord Chatfield* (London, 1947).
10. Von Hase, G., Commander, *Kiel and Jutland*, quoted from *The World Crisis, 1911-1918* by Churchill, W.S.
11. Fairthorne, R.B., Lieutenant-Commander. Article in *The Medley*, school magazine of the Grange School, Eastbourne, 1916, and personal account, Imperial War Museum.
12. Poland, Captain R. (RM), Letters. The Liddle Collection, Brotherton Library, University of Leeds.
13. Arthur, M., *The True Glory: The Royal Navy 1914-1939* (London 1996).
14. *The Oratory Parish Magazine*, The Oratory, Birmingham, 1963.
15. Chessman, Seaman J.,. Biographical note, Imperial War Museum.
16. Marder, A.J., *From the Dreadnought to Scapa Flow* (Oxford 1961-5).

17. *The Times*, 2 June 1916.
18. *The Times*, 3 June 1916.
19. *The Times*, 1 June 1916.
20. Burton, Commander H.C., Extracts from Midshipman's Journal 1917 – 1918, Imperial War Museum.
21. Dandy, Boy Sailor F., Conversation with the author, early 1980s.

Chapter 3

1. *The Oratory Parish Magazine*. The Oratory, Birmingham. 1963.
2. Cunningham, Admiral of the Fleet A.B., *A Sailor's Odyssey* (London, 1951).
3. Packer, J., *Deep as the Sea* (London, 1975).
4. Andrewes, Admiral Sir William, Papers, Imperial War Museum.
5. Mosse, Commander J.P., Memoirs, Imperial War Museum.
6. Fox, Commander. H., *Letters from the Sea*. Privately published, Imperial War Museum.
7. Divine, D., *Mutiny at Invergordon* (London, 1970).
8. Coles, A., *Invergordon Scapegoat: The Betrayal of Admiral Tomkinson* (Stroud, 1993).
9. Roskill, Captain S.W., Letter to Mrs Anthea Trenchard, 24 November 1971. Roskill Archives, Churchill College, Cambridge.
10. Roskill, Captain S.W., Letter to Mrs Anthea Trenchard, 13 December 1971. Roskill Archives, Churchill College, Cambridge.
11. Duckworth, Captain A.D., Diaries and papers, Imperial War Museum.
12. Roskill, Captain S.W., 'Near Misses', *Blackwood's Magazine*, Vol 265, No. 1604 (1949).
13. Andrewes, Captain G.J.M., Letter to author. June 2000.
14. Earridge, Stoker F.W., Account: Biographical details. Imperial War Museum.
15. *The Daily Mail*, 27 August 1937.
16. McNeile, Midshipman N.A., Midshipman's Log, Imperial War Museum.
17. *The Times*, 27 August 1937.
18. McIntosh, Lieutenant-Colonel N.D., Curator, The Green Howards Museum. Correspondence with author.
19. Roskill, Captain S.W., *H.M.S. Warspite* (London 1957).
20. *The Daily Mail*, 7 August 1939.

Chapter 4

1. Earridge, Stoker F.W. Account: biographical details. Imperial War Museum.
2. Cunningham, Admiral of the Fleet A.B., *A Sailor's Odyssey* (London, 1951).
3. Roskill, Captain S.W., *HMS Warspite* (London, 1957).

4. MacIntyre, Captain D., *Narvik* (London, 1959).
5. Bekker, C., *Hitler's Naval War* (London, 1974).
6. Brennecke, J., *The Hunters and the Hunted* (London, 1958).
7. Doenitz, Grand Admiral K., *Memoirs: Ten Years and Twenty Days* (London, 1959).
8. Whitworth, Admiral W., Whitworth Correspondence. June 1950. Roskill Archives, Churchill College, Cambridge.
9. Coulter, Surgeon-Captain J.L.S., *The Royal Naval Medical Service Vol II:* Operations (HMSO, 1956).
10. Coward, Commander B.R., *Battleship at War* (London, 1978).
11. Hoare, Commander P.D., Account. Imperial War Museum.
12. Lush, R.W., Telegraphist on HMS *Icarus*. Letter to author, June 1986.
13. Rice, Lieutenant-Commander F.C., Letter to author, August 1986.
14. Sheerbrooke, Captain R., Letter to Captain. Roskill, Jan 1950. Roskill Archives, Churchill College, Cambridge.
15. Parker, Chief Petty Officer F., Account. Imperial War Museum.
16. Dewey, M., *Diaries; Letters; Writings*. Eds Grimstone, A.V., Lyons, M.C. and Lyon, U. Pembroke College, Cambridge, 1992.
17. Chalmers, Rear-Admiral W.S., *The Biography of Admiral Sir Bertram Home Ramsey* (London, 1959).
18. Hatch, Seaman W.T., Letter to author, June 1999.
19. Stitt, Commander G., *Under Cunningham's Command 1940-1943* (London, 1944).
20. Bragadin, Commander M.A., *The Italian Navy in World War II* (Annapolis, 1957).

Chapter 5

1. Cunningham, Admiral of the Fleet A.B., *A Sailor's Odyssey* (London, 1951).
2. Colville, J., *The Fringes of Power: Downing Street Diaries 1939 – 1955* (London, 1985).
3. Kesselring, A., *The Memoirs of Field Marshal Kesselring* (Navato, Ca., 1989).
4. Hoare, Commander P.D., Memoirs. Imperial War Museum.
5. Hatch, Seaman W.T., Letter to author, June 1999.
6. Bragadin, M.A., *The Italian Navy in World War II* (Annapolis, 1957).
7. Hodgkinson, Lieutenant-Commander H., *Before the Tide Turned* (London, 1944).
8. Rice, Lieutenant-Commander F.C.,. Letter and report to author, July 2000.
9. Winton, J., *Cunningham* (London, 1998).
10. Coward, Commander B.R., *Battleship at War* London, 1978).
11. Thomas, D.A., *Crete 1941: The Battle at Sea* (London, 1972).

12. H.M.S. *Warspite*. Battle of Crete; Bomb Damage Report, Ministry of Defence Historical Section.
13. Huy, Lieutenant W., German Luftwaffe. Letter to author, May 1988.
14. Huy, Lieutenant W., German Luftwaffe. Letter to author, July 1988.
15. Roskill, S.W., *H.M.S. Warspite* (London, 1957).
16. Tarrant, V.E., *Battleship Warspite* (London, 1990).

Chapter 6

1. Paquette, R.J., Letter to the author, April 1999.
2. Attributed to the *Seattle Times*, 20 September 1941.
3. Caretti, S., e-mail to the author, May 1999.
4. Erickson, S., e-mail to the author, May 1999.
5. Schick, A.K., Letter to the author, May 1999.
6. Commonwealth War Graves Commission. Letter, 23 April 1999.
7. Katzenburger, G.R., Letters to the author, May and August 1999.
8. Wetzel, F., *Victory Gardens and Barrage Balloons: a Collective Memoir* (Bremerton, 1995).
9. Hoare, Commander P.D., Memoirs. Imperial War Museum.
10. Lamb, R., e-mail to the author, March 1999.
11. Riddle, L., e-mail to the author, April 1999.
12. Stone, L.V., Letter to the author, March 1999.
13. Scammell, V., Letters to the author, April and May 1999.
14. Attributed to the *Seattle Times*, 13 November 1941.
15. Attributed to the *Seattle Times*, 29 September 1941.
16. Attributed to the *Seattle Times*, 31 October 1941.
17. Naval Staff Duties (Historical Section), Ministry of Defence, London. Letters to the author, July 1990.
18. Hanson, P.O., Letter to author, June 1999.
19. Jordan, J.L., Letter to author, May 1999.
20. Buckle, R.B., Letter to Captain. Roskill, Oct 1969. Roskill Collection, Churchill College, Cambridge.
21. Macintyre, Captain D., *Fighting Admiral: The Life of Admiral of the Fleet Sir James Somerville* (London, 1961).
22. Finnigan, P., *Knock On Any Door – The Door Opens* (Edinburgh, 1999).
23. Packer, J., *Deep as the Sea* (London, 1975).

Chapter 7

1. Packer, J., *Deep as the Sea* (London, 1975).
2. Connell, G.G., *Fighting Destroyer: The Story of* HMS *Petard* (London, 1976).
3. Cunningham, Admiral of the Fleet A.B., *A Sailor's Odyssey* (London, 1951).
4. Duckworth, Captain A.D., Diaries and papers. Imperial War Museum.

5. Coward, B.R., Commander, *Battleship at War* (London, 1978).
6. Sewter, J.W., C.P.O. Letter to Capt. S.W. Roskill, Aug 1980. Roskill Archives, Churchill College, Cambridge.
7. Finnigan, P., *Knock Any Door – The Door Opens* (Edinburgh, 1999).
8. Buckle, R.B., Leading Cook. Letter to Captain. S.W. Roskill, Oct. 1969. Roskill Archives, Churchill College, Cambridge.
9. Hutton, Captain. M.H., 'Anchors Aweigh', *Journal of* HMS *Warspite Association* (Spring 2000).
10. *D-Day*. Nautical Presentations Ltd. (London, 1974).
11. Colville, J., *The Fringes of Power: Downing Street Diaries 1939* – 1945 (London, 1985).
12. Warner, P., *The D-Day Landings* (London, 1980).
13. Roskill, Captain S.W., HMS *Warspite* (London, 1957).
14. Chalmers, Rear-Admiral W.S., *Full Circle: The Biography of Admiral Sir Bertram Home Ramsey* (London, 1959).
15. Matthews, R. Letter to author. April 1986.
16. Sewter, Chief Petty Officer J.W., Letter to Captain. S.W. Roskill. July 1980. Roskill Archives, Churchill College, Cambridge.

Chapter 8

1. Winton, J., *Cunningham* (London, 1998).
2. *The Cornishman*, 24 April 1947.
3. Journal, Royal National Lifeboat Institution, 1947.
4. Tangye, N., *The Inconstant Sea* (London, 1976).
5. Griffiths, Commander N.S., Account, Imperial War Museum.

Index

Page references in *italics* indicate maps. All ships are British Royal Navy unless otherwise indicated.

Abbreviations
AB = Able Seaman; Cdr = Commander; CPO = Chief Petty Officer; F/M = Field Marshal; F/O = Flying Officer; Fr = France; GB = British merchant ship; Ger = Germany; HMS/M = His Majesty's Submarine; It = Italy; Jpn = Japan; Lt = Lieutenant; Lt-Cdr = Lieutenant-Commander; Neth = Netherlands; Nor = Norway; P/O = Petty Officer; R/A = Rear-Admiral; USA = United States of America; V/A = Vice-Admiral